LEADERSHIP SOLUTIONS

JB JOSSEY-BASS™

LEADERSHIP SOLUTIONS
The Pathway to Bridge the Leadership Gap

DR. DAVID S. WEISS
DR. VINCE MOLINARO
DR. LIANE DAVEY

BICENTENNIAL
BICENTENNIAL
1807
WILEY
2007
BICENTENNIAL
BICENTENNIAL

John Wiley & Sons Canada, Ltd.

National Library of Canada Cataloguing in Publication Data

Weiss, David S. (David Solomon), 1953-

    Leadership solutions : the pathway to bridge the leadership gap / David Weiss, Vince Molinaro, Liane Davey.

Includes bibliographical references and index.
ISBN 978-0-470-84092-4

    1. Leadership. 2. Management. I. Molinaro, Vince, 1962- II. Davey, Liane Margaret, 1972- III. Title.

HD57.7.W5253 2007   658.4'092   C2007-902559-5

Production Credits
Cover design: Ian Koo
Interior text design: Natalia Burobina
Wiley Bicentennial Logo: Richard J. Pacifico
Printer: Friesens

John Wiley & Sons Canada, Ltd.
6045 Freemont Blvd.
Mississauga, Ontario
L5R 4J3

Printed in Canada

1 2 3 4 5 FP 11 10 09 08 07

Table of Contents

List of Figures

Preface

Leadership Solutions challenges the traditional views and approaches of building leadership capacity with a new integrated perspective that recognizes leadership as a source of competitive advantage. To this end, *Leadership Solutions* presents the case for a new pathway for responding to the leadership gap. Based on our extensive work and research in this field, we provide the practical strategies and techniques necessary for business executives and HR leaders to bridge the gap.

Many organizations continue to struggle to build the leadership capacity that they need to thrive in today's and tomorrow's ever-changing global business environment. These organizations are contending with a myriad of leadership challenges including:

- Dealing with the realities of changing demographics in the workplace
- Managing the shifting values and expectations among employees
- Responding to the need for different leadership capabilities
- Accelerating the development of future leaders.

The current or anticipated gap in leadership talent is a very serious global competitive concern in almost all private and public business sectors. As a result, many of today's CEOs and HR professionals continue to have a tremendous thirst for information, techniques, and strategies for building strong leadership capacity and overcoming the leadership gap.

The book, *The Leadership Gap* (Wiley, 2005), by Weiss and Molinaro and the work of other thought leaders, helped many organizations focus on building leadership capacity as one of their top business issues. These organizations have invested tremendous resources to implement strategies to close their leadership gaps. Some have even found the way to build their leadership capacity, and they have leveraged this enviable position as a source of competitive advantage.

However, the continued leadership gap challenge demonstrates the need for more work in this area. Research conducted by the authors suggests that a major problem in bridging the leadership gap is that precise metrics that pinpoint the leadership gap deficiency are elusive. In the absence of data, organizations proceed to spend considerable dollars on fragmented interventions without basing the leadership solutions on a solid assessment of the areas of need.

The authors foresaw this problem in *The Leadership Gap* (Chapter 14) and introduced a preliminary leadership gap audit process to diagnose areas of leadership deficiencies. However, the audit ideas in *The Leadership Gap* were at an early stage of development. The readership of that book wanted to know more about how the leadership gap can be analyzed with greater precision and how to generate leadership solutions that are tailored to their specific organization. Since then, the authors have immersed themselves in the question of how to accurately diagnose the leadership gap. The result is the Leadership Gap Analysis™, which pinpoints organizational, individual and cultural leadership gaps.

Leadership Solutions outlines how organizations must resist the temptation to implement interventions without a thorough analysis. Rather, they must first understand the nature of their organization's leadership deficit through a comprehensive diagnostic process. Armed with this knowledge, they can then take targeted action in the areas that will yield the greatest impact in the most cost-effective manner.

Some of the specific characteristics of *Leadership Solutions* that distinguish it from other works are:

- It describes the top seven risks to organizations if they do not have the leadership requirements for the future and the three failure paths.
- It explains the importance of leadership capacity as a critical organizational capability and how leveraging leadership capacity can emerge as a source of sustainable competitive advantage.

- It describes the three "dimensions" of leadership capacity to help organizations think more comprehensively about leadership capacity. The three dimensions are: (1) the individual leader dimension, (2) the organizational practices dimension and (3) the leadership culture dimension.
- It presents holistic leadership, and it introduces the five capabilities of holistic leaders as the key behaviors for holistic leaders.
- It describes the Four-Step Leadership Solutions Pathway that enables organizations to discover the leadership solutions that meet specific organizational requirements. The pathway includes the Leadership Gap Analysis™ measurement that helps organizations target the specific areas of the leadership gap that should be addressed first.
- It presents a series of vivid stories that show how the challenge of leadership capacity can be overcome. It also provides executives and HR leaders with real and practical case examples that relate the experiences of organizations and individual leaders in multiple sectors.
- It reinforces the need for executives to take accountability to diagnose, build and sustain the leadership capacity in their organization. It also provides practical tools and strategies that organizations can implement to close their leadership gaps.

A DESCRIPTION OF THE BOOK

This section presents a brief overview of the two parts of the book and a description of each chapter.

Part One: Leadership

Part One of *Leadership Solutions* focuses on "leadership." It describes the persistent challenge of the leadership gap and explains why building leadership capacity in the three dimensions of individual leaders, organizational practices and leadership culture are essential to overcoming the gap.

Chapter 1: The Leadership Gap Persists

This chapter explores the challenges that organizations face in building strong leadership capacity and outlines the major reasons for the persistence of the leadership gap. It presents the results of our research that show how many executives are forecasting they will have an unacceptably low level of leadership talent available to meet their future needs. It then explores the top "failure paths" for organizations in all sectors to avoid as they attempt to close their leadership gaps. It also describes the implications of these failure paths and how it will prevent organizations from truly implementing a sustainable solution to close their leadership gaps.

Chapter 2: Leadership Capacity
This chapter introduces the anchor concept of the book—leadership capacity, which is forecasted to be the primary business and organizational challenge facing executives for the next decade. In essence, it has become the new organizational capability. In response to this challenge, organizations need to have a good grasp of the leadership capacity required and the nature of their leadership gap. This chapter describes what leadership capacity is and its importance to achieving sustainable competitive advantage for an organization.

Chapter 3: The Three Dimensions of Leadership Capacity
This chapter describes the three dimensions of leadership capacity. Using a case study, it explores the impact of each dimension on the ability of individual leaders and organizations to build leadership capacity. The three dimensions are: (1) the individual leader dimension, (2) the organizational practices dimension and (3) the leadership culture dimension. It also explores the role that organizational practices and leadership culture play in supporting the development of holistic leadership.

Chapter 4: The Individual Leader Dimension: The Holistic View of Leadership
The purpose of this chapter is to begin the process of exploring the individual leader dimension of leadership capacity. It focuses on holistic leadership—what it is and why it is important. We consider the problems that arise when functional management becomes functional leadership and provide a tale of two leaders that demonstrates the difference between functional management and holistic leadership. We then explain the six elements of holistic leadership to provide a thorough grasp of what holistic leadership is and why it is central to building leadership capacity.

Chapter 5: The Individual Leader Dimension: The Five Capabilities of Holistic Leaders
In this chapter we continue the discussion of the individual leader dimension by describing the five capabilities of holistic leadership and why they are important for leaders and their organizations. We conclude the chapter with the 30-Cell Grid of Holistic Leadership Behaviors, which details the expected behaviors of holistic leaders.

Chapter 6: The Organizational Practices Dimension
This chapter introduces the organizational practices dimension of leadership capacity. The organizational practices dimension includes all official practices, programs and policies and their impact on leadership capacity. The chapter describes two main categories of organizational practices: (1) those that are specifically intended to build leadership capacity, such as succession management, leadership development, embedding leadership in the organization and ensuring executive accountability, and (2) those that indirectly enhance or restrict the ability of an organization to close its leadership gap. This last category includes organizational practices that are not specifically designed to build leadership capacity. We view these organizational practices as the hidden jewel that needs to be nurtured and leveraged to build leadership capacity.

Chapter 7: The Leadership Culture Dimension
This chapter describes the leadership culture dimension of leadership capacity. Leadership culture includes the organization's values, traditions, mythology and expectations of behavior about leadership. Although organizational practices provide explicit guidance in each of these areas, the leadership culture dimension is focused on the implicit rules that guide leadership behavior. We then define three types of leadership cultures: (1) the weakly embedded leadership culture, (2) the strongly embedded functional leadership culture and (3) the strongly embedded holistic leadership culture. The chapter then emphasizes that all three dimensions of leadership capacity need to be aligned to accelerate increased leadership capacity.

Part Two: Solutions

Part Two of *Leadership Solutions* focuses on "solutions" to the leadership gap and describes in detail how to use the Leadership Solutions Pathway to build leadership capacity.

Chapter 8: The Pathway Forward

This chapter introduces the Leadership Solutions Pathway, a process organizations can follow to determine their leadership requirements, measure their current leadership capacity strengths and gaps, take targeted action and then sustain the gains that are made. This pathway puts organizations in the best position to implement precise actions to transform their leadership capacity. It also prepares them to sustain and evolve the positive changes within a constantly changing internal and external environment.

Chapter 9: Step 1: Determine Leadership Requirements

The chapter examines in detail the first step of the Leadership Solutions Pathway: Determine Leadership Requirements. The chapter includes (1) an exploration of how the business environment shapes an organization's leadership capacity requirements, (2) the five key actions an organization can use to determine leadership requirements and (3) a detailed case example that illustrates how an organization implemented the five key actions and their associated results.

Chapter 10: Step 2: Measure the Gap

The purpose of this chapter is to describe how organizations can measure their leadership capacity. This chapter begins with a discussion of the importance of leadership metrics and shortcomings of some of the current approaches to measuring leadership. It then describes the four actions in this step, which are how to (1) audit organizational practices, (2) conduct a survey of leadership culture, (3) assess behaviors of individual leaders and (4) analyze patterns of results. We use a case study to show how this step is implemented in action.

Chapter 11: Step 3: Act to Build Capacity

This chapter examines the third step of the Leadership Solutions Pathway. It describes how organizations can develop a plan for action that will build the leadership capacity they need to shape their future. It then describes the four actions in this step: (1) *target* the priority leadership capacity gap, (2) *integrate* the leadership capacity solutions, (3) *accelerate* implementation by leveraging the three dimensions and (4) *evolve* the solution as conditions change. The four actions are applied to a case example throughout the chapter.

Chapter 12: Step 4: Do Your Part
This chapter describes what is expected of the individual leader so that they do their part of the leadership solution, whether or not they are supported by an organization and its practices. It provides an "individual leader road map" that integrates coaching, assessment, learning and an on-the-job experience into a coherent, integrated solution for the individual leader.

Chapter 13: Shape Your Future
The concluding chapter emphasizes the imperative to shape you own future. It also shows how this book responded to the seven business risks identified in Chapter 1. Finally, it identifies the implications of effective Leadership Solutions for executives, boards of directors, HR professionals and our society.

Who Will Benefit from This Book

Readers hungry for information, ideas and techniques to build their organization's and their own leadership capacity will find *Leadership Solutions* very helpful both conceptually and practically. It delivers its messages in a compelling, practical, story-rich and very readable manner. It will be of particular interest to many professionals including the following:

- Executives and senior leaders in the private and public sectors seeking to understand leadership capacity and how to measure it, as well as their accountability in ensuring they have the leadership capabilities to meet their organization's requirements
- Board of directors, responsible for recruiting senior executive leaders and assessing and managing the leadership contribution to more precisely bridge their identified leadership gap

- Policy makers and strategists seeking ideas and inspiration for developing policy and programs to build strong leadership capacity within organizations and within society
- Human Resources, talent management, leadership development and organizational development professionals, internal and external to an organization, who are interested in understanding how to target limited funds to build leadership capacity
- Members of international and professional associations and conference organizations concerned with leadership capacity issues
- Academics and students in MBA, Industrial and Organizational Psychology, and Human Resources Development programs interested in a well-researched and practical text to teach their students about the changing role of leadership and to shape their understanding of how to diagnose and build leadership capacity
- Management consultants seeking ideas and guidelines to provide advice to organizations about how to assess and build leadership capacity for competitive advantage

How to Read This Book

Most readers will benefit from reading the book cover to cover. However, others will find they can dip into the book for specific ideas and information, and it will add value. Here are some alternative ways this book can be read:

- Some readers—those responsible for the development of leaders—may want to use the book as a study guide. A suggested approach would be to ask leaders to read one chapter at a time and then meet to discuss what they learned and how they can apply it to their work setting.
- Some readers may want to focus specifically on one of the three dimensions of leadership capacity. Here is a guide for these readers:
  - *Individual Leader Dimension:* If the readers are primarily interested in leading-edge ideas for individual leaders, they may want to read Chapters 4, 5, and 12. Chapter 4 focuses on the holistic view of leadership and Chapter 5 introduces the five capabilities of holistic leaders. Chapter 12 describes the individual leader's solution to build their own leadership capacity.

- *Organizational Practices Dimension:* Still other readers may want to explore the topic of organizational practices and how it contributes to leadership capacity (Chapter 6 and Chapters 8–11).
- *Leadership Culture Dimension:* Other readers may want to focus on how the organization can create a leadership culture and what it needs to do to build leadership capacity (Chapters 7–11).

- Some readers may want to read *Leadership Solutions* as a compendium of the authors' prior book, *The Leadership Gap* (Wiley 2005). *The Leadership Gap* explains in detail the holistic leadership framework and the four critical success factors for organizations to build leadership capacity. The summary points of *The Leadership Gap* are presented in *Leadership Solutions* as part of Chapter 4 (on holistic leadership) and Chapter 6 (the four critical success factors).
- Each chapter has case examples to translate the concepts into meaningful action. Some readers may want to focus on the many leadership stories (in italics). We also would encourage readers to develop their own stories so that they can apply the learning to their own experience. Others may want to skip the stories and focus on reading about the ideas, techniques and templates.
- Some may be interested in the book as a resource guide. The Appendix section in the end of this book provides the complete Leadership Gap Analysis™, including the Audit of Organizational Practices, the Survey of Leadership Culture and the individual leaders 360° survey.
- Finally, readers may want to study a topic of their own interest. A detailed index has been prepared for referencing specific topics.

Leadership Solutions is a road map for executives and HR leaders who are considering how to build leadership capacity for competitive advantage. It will help guide executives and HR professionals in the diagnosis and transformation of leadership to drive results. And most important, it will provide executives and HR professionals with the leadership solutions they are seeking.

Author Biographies

 **Dr. David Weiss** is President & CEO of Weiss International Ltd. David leads innovative consulting projects that generate effective strategy, leadership and HR solutions for Boards and executives throughout North America and Europe. David also is an Affiliate Professor of the Rotman School of Management of the University of Toronto, a "Senior Research Fellow" of Queen's University and a Faculty Member of the Technion Institute of Management.

David specializes in facilitating senior executive strategic planning and team development processes; engaging in executive coaching processes; designing and implementing leadership development solutions for organizations; facilitating HR departments to deliver greater strategic value; and achieving win-win resolutions to organizational conflicts and interpersonal disputes. He brings a unique combination of talents to facilitation assignments that are purposeful, dynamic and results-oriented, and at the same time reflective, inspirational and fun.

David received his Doctorate from the University of Toronto and has three Masters Degrees in Philosophy, Psychology and Education. He also has received lifetime honors as an Honorary Member of *The Global Directory of Who's Who*, and he is one of four professionals in Canada honored as a lifetime Fellow Canadian Human Resources Professional (FCHRP). He also is a Past President of the Section of Industrial Organizational

Psychology of the Ontario Psychological Association and an Editorial Board Member of the *Canadian Learning Journal*.

David is an inspirational keynote speaker and frequently appears at national and international conferences to share his latest insights. He has published over 30 professional articles and three best selling books, including *Beyond the Walls of Conflict: Mutual Gains Bargaining for Unions and Management*, (McGraw Hill, 1996), *High Performance HR: Leveraging Human Resources for Competitive Advantage* (John Wiley & Sons, 2000) and *The Leadership Gap: Building Leadership Capacity for Competitive Advantage* (co-authored with Dr. Vince Molinaro, John Wiley & Sons, 2005). *Leadership Solutions* is his fourth book. David can be contacted at david.weiss@ weissinternational.ca or visit his web site at www.weissinternational.ca.

Dr. Vince Molinaro, is Principal and National Practice Lead—Organizational Solutions with Knightsbridge Human Capital Solutions. He is responsible for leading the organizational consulting arm of Knightsbridge, which specializes in providing strategic facilitation, team effectiveness, leadership capacity and talent management solutions to clients.

Vince has dedicated his career to helping leaders and their organizations build strong leadership capacity for competitive advantage. An insightful practitioner, Vince is uniquely able to turn innovative ideas into practical solutions—he is known for taking the complex and making it simple and actionable. He has designed and implemented award-winning programs that have transformed leadership cultures for his clients.

Through his extensive consulting and leadership experience, pioneering research and writing, Vince has established himself as a strategic advisor to senior executives. He is called upon by the media for his innovative opinions on leadership, creating high-performance organizations and executive team development. An engaging speaker, Vince has conducted numerous keynote presentations within corporations, international conferences and business schools.

Vince received his Doctorate from the University of Toronto and has degrees from Brock University and McMaster University.

Vince has also published extensively in journals and business magazines. His book *The Leadership Gap* (co-authored with Dr. David Weiss, John Wiley & Sons, 2005) is a best seller. Vince can be contacted at vmolinaro@knightsbridge.ca or visit his website at www.knightsbridge.ca.

 ***Dr. Liane Davey***, is Principal and Central Region Practice Lead—Organizational Solutions with Knightsbridge Human Capital Solutions.

While known for her extraordinary ability to support team change and growth that results in impressive performance improvement, to characterize her work as "team effectiveness" would be to trivialize its impact. Liane uses keen business insight, powerful questions and innovative facilitation techniques to craft and communicate laser-like insights that enable a team to create, implement and realize the benefits of quantum leap change.

Liane is at her best when faced with a business challenge that can best be solved by a team energized to perform and fully aligned with the right goals. She understands how organizational culture and interpersonal paradigms can truly make or break performance and has a unique ability to help her clients create breakthroughs that drive business results. She believes passionately that sustainable change comes only as a result of genuine understanding and appreciation of the truth and is courageous enough to present the truth in a meaningful way, starting at the very top of her client organizations, to begin the process of cultural and behavioral shift.

Liane received her Master's and Doctorate in Industrial/Organizational Psychology from the University of Waterloo and a Bachelor of Social Science from the University of Western Ontario. She has been widely published in trade and academic journals; *Leadership Solutions* (Jossey-Bass) is her first book.

Acknowledgments

The completion of *Leadership Solutions* has been a deeply collaborative effort. First, this book was possible because of the tremendous support we have received over the years from our clients. We are especially indebted to the many leaders that we have come to work with and know over the years. Thank you for providing us the privilege of working in your organizations. It is because of you that we have been able to refine our ideas, validate our practices and discover what truly works in building leadership capacity for sustained competitive advantage.

Second, we want to thank our colleagues at Knightsbridge Human Capital Management. We have been fortunate to work together in an environment filled with passionate, smart and creative professionals. We thank you for your support, friendship and camaraderie and for the firm's strong leadership culture. A special thank-you goes to David Shaw, the President and CEO of Knightsbridge, for his encouragement and support of this book.

Third, we would also like to thank our publisher, editors and internal support staff, who contributed greatly to this project. A special thank you is extended to Karen Milner and the John Wiley & Sons team for their confidence and support of this project. Thank you also to Mary Jo Beebe for once again lending your editorial guidance throughout this project. Your ideas and suggestions were always on the mark, and helped push our thinking and writing to greater levels of excellence. We also want to express our sincere thanks to Michele Allan for her exceptional support in the creation of graphics, editing and layout of the final manuscript and to Susan Beckley for ongoing support throughout this project.

We also extend our deep appreciation to our friends and colleagues who contributed to this work and to us. In particular, we would like to acknowledge the significant contribution of Ren Wiebe. Ren worked closely with Liane and Vince as part of the "Snowdog" project team at Knightsbridge. Together, they did much of the early development of the Leadership Gap Analysis™. Thank you for your time, commitment and passion.

We would also like to acknowledge one another. Writing a book while managing the multiple demands of our work and home lives has not been easy. However, the commitment, sense of fun and encouragement displayed throughout the writing process made this a truly gratifying experience.

We also wish to offer our individual expressions of gratitude.

From David: Thank you to the many outstanding leaders in private and public sector organizations who have offered me insights, wisdom, stimulating dialogue and a forum to experiment with innovative ideas. Also, thank you to the leaders at the conferences and academic institutions who gave me the forum to speak about these ideas. In particular, I extend great appreciation to Dan Ondrack and Allison Ground of the Rotman School of Management, Paul Juniper of the Queen's University Industrial Relations Centre, Yoram Yahav of the Technion Institute of Management, and Lynn Johnston of CSTD. Finally, my family has been there for me throughout—to my son Joseph Weissgold, you are my source of great pride and a wonderful example for the next generation of leaders, and to my wife, Dr. Nora Gold, my true friend, partner and love, who has been a major inspiration, encouraging me to write my thoughts and share them with the world as she has so marvellously done through her writings of fiction and research. I am deeply grateful for your love and support.

From Vince: To my many clients and colleagues who I've had the pleasure to work with over the years. Thank you for your support and friendship. To my parents and in-laws who have always supported me in my endeavors. To my brother Robert, I admire the passion you bring to developing the next generation of leaders, as well as to Maria, John and

Rosanna. Thank you to my wonderful children Mateo, Tomas and Alessia. You are the inspiration in my life, the source of joy and pride. I am astonished by each of your unique gifts and look forward to seeing you each grow as young leaders. Finally, to my wife Elizabeth—once again you never cease to amaze me with your unending support and encouragement. My contribution to this project would not have been possible without you.

From Liane: To my parents and my brother, for instilling in me a passion for learning and a belief that I can do anything I put my mind to. I am the leader that I am because of you. To all those who inspired and believed in me along my journey—Mr. John Giandomenico, Dr. Mitch Rothstein, Dr. John Michela—thank you for your role in shaping the clay. To my colleagues and mentors Audra August, Nancy Gore, Teri Brown, Karen Wright, Ralph Shedletsky—thank you for seeing the strengths and bolstering the weaknesses. To my dear friends who give me respite when I need it: Tracey, Joe, Nancy, Stephanie, Allyson et al, thank you. To my family and my in-laws, for giving me a place to belong. To my daughters, Kira and Mackenzie, it is such a wonder and pleasure to watch you grow. Your size might be small, but your magic is vast—thank you for sharing it with me. Finally, to my husband Craig Easdon, you gave me my confidence, amplified every success and boosted me out of each valley. Thank you for accompanying me on this journey.

To all of you, our thanks and love.

David Weiss, Vince Molinaro and Liane Davey

Toronto, Ontario, Canada
August 2007

part one

LEADERSHIP

CHAPTER ONE

The Leadership Gap Persists

Building leadership capacity is mission critical. This is the conclusion of more and more senior executives who are making the connection between leadership capacity and competitive advantage. Unfortunately, many organizations have significant leadership gaps, which are undermining their ability to succeed. What is especially alarming is that despite significant investments in leadership development and other strategies to build leadership capacity, these gaps are not closing.

As organizations set out to build the leadership capacity they need for the future, they are often confronted with a series of questions: How can we build leadership capacity throughout the organization? How can we anticipate the type of leadership we will require in the future? How do we measure the leadership we have today? How will we know when we have bridged the leadership gap? Where do we start?

When organizations are confronted by these questions, they are sometimes overwhelmed by the challenge of building leadership capacity. Some are not concentrating on this issue because they are preoccupied with current struggles. Others have not yet focused their organizations on leadership because they are not satisfied with current approaches of how to build leadership capacity. Still other executives may believe that this is a "soft" issue that can be handled within the HR department. Quite to the contrary, we suggest that executives and HR professionals need to rally to address the leadership gap and not allow it to jeopardize their business success. Building leadership capacity must be one of the top business priorities for executives now and into the future.

Our intent in *Leadership Solutions* is to provide a comprehensive and compelling answer to this critical business issue. Part One of this book focuses on "leadership" and clarifies how organizations and individuals should think about leadership capacity; Part Two of this book focuses on "solutions" and describes the four-step leadership solutions pathway to build the leadership capacity required to achieve sustainable competitive advantage.

Let's begin with a story.

The CEO of a manufacturing company sits in an airport lounge, waiting for his flight back home. As he stares out the window at the bustling tarmac, he remembers sitting in the exact same spot last year. Then, as now, he had been in town to attend a board meeting. That meeting had focused on the directors' growing concern that the company's mandate for growth was in jeopardy. In the past the company had been successful by being the first to capitalize on sources of competitive advantage. They were the first to reengineer and use new supply chain processes to remove costs. Once others caught on to supply chain innovations, the company found huge gains by exploiting technology to automate key processes. But again, those gains had disappeared as other organizations copied their systems. At last year's board meeting, the board shared with the CEO that they believed the organization's leadership would be the next source of competitive advantage. They were unanimous that the CEO's top priority was to build the necessary leadership to drive the company's future growth. He was given 30 days to develop a strategy and a plan to address the company's leadership gap. When he left the meeting, he understood the board's concerns. Even though the company had experienced three years of consistent financial performance, there was an increasing understanding that the overall leadership capacity was not in place for the future. The CEO and members of the executive team had felt for some time that the company's leadership was too entrenched in departmental silos. While leaders were very strong in their technical or functional areas and were able to manage "business as usual," they were too internally focused. They were missing future growth opportunities in their markets, and the company was starting to fall behind its competitors. Employees felt their leaders were not strong people managers, and they had little confidence in them. The leaders themselves revealed that the company was not doing enough to support their own growth and development.

Now, one year later, the company had implemented the plan and had invested considerable resources in hopes of closing the leadership gap. In fact, benchmarking had shown that the company's annual budget for leadership development was higher than the industry average. Yet, the CEO had just faced the board again with little progress to report. The training and programs they had implemented weren't leading to changes in behavior on the job. Recent employee surveys showed no improvement in the engagement of employees—or of the leaders themselves. The boarding announcement startled the CEO. As he got ready to leave the lounge, he reflected with frustration on the persistent leadership gap and lack of clarity of what to do next. His top priority upon his return was to meet with the executive team, share the details of the board meeting and develop a new plan for the board—one that would be successful in closing the company's leadership gap. He was determined not to be in the same position again next year.

The above story is both a good news and bad news story. The good news is that the board of this company "gets it." They understand that leadership capacity has become the primary source of competitive advantage. They also understand that closing the leadership gap is one of the top business priorities and a challenge that they need to address in order to sustain the growth and success of the company. The CEO also seems to get it and demonstrates a commitment to building the leadership capacity required for the future.

The bad news is that despite investments made in building leadership capacity, the company still has a considerable leadership gap. Furthermore, there is a sense that the nature of the gap, if it persists, will put the company at risk of not being able to fulfil its growth mandate.

The experience of this CEO and organization is not unlike the experiences of many organizations in the private and public sectors. The competition has neutralized standard competitive advantages of operational excellence, product innovation and customer intimacy. The new competitive frontier has shifted to people—but not the over-simplified view of people as the organization's most important asset—which few really believed and even fewer acted on. Rather, the competitive frontier of people is specifically focused on leadership: what leaders do, how the organization fosters leadership talents and how organizations reinforce their leadership culture.

Leadership is the path to sustained competitive advantage because great leadership provides the vision to uncover each successive source of competitive advantage and the focus to realize the gains that will outpace the competition. Unfortunately, despite widespread investments companies have made to build leadership capacity, when all is said and done, the leadership gap still persists in many companies, and the next frontier in competitive advantage remains elusive.

EVIDENCE OF THE GAP

Since publishing *The Leadership Gap*, we have made numerous presentations to organizations. Many times, we polled the audience to describe the severity of the leadership gap. The questions we asked are:

- To what extent is the leadership gap in your organization a burning issue now?
- Five years from now, will the leadership gap be more, the same, or less of an issue for your organization? Please explain.

The responses to these questions have been consistent wherever we have traveled.

To what extent is leadership capacity a burning issue now?
80 percent of the respondents indicate it is a burning issue now.

Five years from now, will leadership capacity be more, or less, of an issue?
Approximately 50 percent indicate it will be more of a burning issue.
Approximately 20 percent indicate it will remain a burning issue as it is today.
Approximately 30 percent indicate it will be less of an issue—
because we will fix it now.

Approximately 80 percent of respondents say that leadership capacity is currently a burning issue. Even with strong agreement that there is a leadership gap now, a large majority of the people we talk to believe that in five years their organizations will be no better off (and perhaps worse off) than they are today. They cite reasons for their pessimistic view such as the increasing complexity of their business environment, which will make it more difficult to find leadership talent, and that attempts to resolve issues related to the leadership gap will be unsuccessful. Some examples of their responses include:

- *Even more important! Delayering of organizational structure, decentralization, demographics, lack of institutional learning/sharing, globalization, mobilization of people globally to centers of excellence, pace of mergers and acquisitions all exploding—therefore, the one with the leadership wins.*
- *Could be greater if we don't begin to take greater steps (immediate and substantial effort) to address gaps; if we do not change gears on what leadership is in our company, we will be in a position where the leadership gap will increase.*
- *Will get worse, i.e., change in demographics and the next generation will not want to take on leadership roles. It will be tougher if we do not build the capability to deal with it now.*

Approximately 30 percent of the people we ask believe that the leadership gap will be less of a burning issue in the next five years—primarily because they believe that their efforts to close the gap will be successful. Almost no respondents say that leadership capacity will be a non issue in five years.

WHY THE LEADERSHIP GAP PERSISTS

In our book, *The Leadership Gap*,[1] we described the nature of the leadership gap in some detail. Since writing that book, we've gained deeper insights into the dynamics perpetuating leadership gaps in organizations and the failure paths organizations sometimes take in implementing leadership solutions. We have found several reasons why organizations are struggling to close their leadership gaps.

Reasons the Leadership Gap Persists

1. Over-reliance on traditional views of leadership
2. No shared or well-defined view of leadership for the future
3. A void of leadership capacity metrics
4. Unclear accountability for leadership capacity
5. Fragmented solutions that are not sustained
6. Flat and lean organizations with fewer intermediate leadership positions
7. Poor supply of leaders

(1) Over-Reliance on Traditional Views of Leadership

Two traditional views of leadership are contributing to the persistence of the leadership gap:

The first is *charismatic leadership*, which has become a widely accepted view of leadership—actually, a collective default. The charismatic view overemphasizes the role of individual personality in leadership. Consider the results:

- Organizations become preoccupied with molding leaders into a prescribed style or having them emulate other successful leaders of the past. This is an approach that is seldom successful in changing leaders' behaviors.

- Organizations spend too much time and money on a small group of highly visible leaders at the top of the hierarchy. This causes them to neglect leadership at other levels and to ignore the collective forms of leadership that emerge in teams.

The second traditional view is the belief that it is important to select leaders from specific areas of expertise within the company. Organizations that hold this view are often led by a highly capable technical expert who comes from the organization's dominant function (e.g., consumer products companies that are led by brilliant marketers or professional service firms led by accountants). As organizations become increasingly complex, however, solutions cannot be found within a single perspective. Organizations with a strong legacy of hiring and promoting leaders based on superb technical or functional expertise will need leaders with wider perspectives. They must be capable of rising above their specific expertise to lead the company as a whole.

Traditional views of leadership lead to an overdependence on individuals and a narrow perspective of leadership. Organizations that continue to focus on these outdated models will not be able to build their leadership capacity quickly to stay ahead in today's dynamic and complex business environment.

(2) No Shared and Well-Defined View of Leadership for the Future

Although the following is a very specific example, it underscores the challenge faced by organizations that are trying to build leadership capacity without a shared and well-defined understanding of their leadership requirements for the future.

The VP of Marketing of a large manufacturing company was having an impromptu discussion with his CEO. That morning, they had each seen an article in the newspaper questioning whether organizations should be hiring MBAs or liberal arts graduates. The Marketing VP argued adamantly that the liberal arts grads didn't have the kind of work experience or skills required to get up to speed quickly. Not only that, but he also felt they didn't show the same confidence and self-assurance that was characteristic of the business students. Although the CEO agreed that those with a liberal arts background might need a little more training at the outset, he believed the key to success in their business was for leaders to be able to continually reframe the challenges facing the organization. He believed they must be comfortable with ambiguity and be flexible in finding creative solutions to challenges, which seemed to be the hallmark of a liberal arts education. He had had a few experiences that suggested MBAs were less comfortable in situations requiring these characteristics. Both sides had strong, valid arguments. The VP of Marketing shared his concern that the CEO was raising issues calling into question the basis of the leadership development program they were providing to their senior management group. In the end they agreed to get the rest of the team into the conversation and to come to a shared view.

Some of the factors that organizations like this one should consider in
coming to a shared view of leadership for the future are:

- *The impact of future external forces on the business*
  These forces can cause future leadership requirements to shift. Unfortunately, many organizations are struggling to anticipate how
  current trends in the market will affect their future environment.
  As a result they are unable to predict how their organizations will
  need to change in response.

- *The impact of future internal forces on the business*
  Internal forces are equally important. For example, if an organization evolves from early entrepreneurial stages or a new leader
  comes in and helps the organization emerge into a new era of
  growth, the leadership requirements will change.

Regardless of whether the forces for change come from outside or
from within the organization, being successful requires the right type of
leadership. Without a shared and well-defined view of leadership for the
future, the organization is left with only generic leadership models and
untailored programs that are less likely to resonate with leaders and much
less likely to close the leadership gap.

(3) A Void of Leadership Capacity Metrics

The following story illustrates another factor contributing to the persistent leadership gap: the void of leadership capacity metrics.

*A company retained a consulting firm to help them address critical
leadership gaps. As part of the initiative, the consultants interviewed
executives. One of the questions the consultants thought would be
the most mundane turned out to be the most intriguing: "How do you
measure leadership capacity, and how will you know if it's getting better?" The CEO at first struggled with his answer, and then went on to
say, "This place would feel different. I would know by walking around
and getting a different feel than I do now." The CFO responded with
precision by immediately listing measures from employee surveys,
leader retention rates and the percentage of internal promotions into
leadership roles. The VP of HR described similar measures, but he*

struggled because he wanted to answer the question less tactically. The VP of Sales didn't have any answers, but she shared her frustration that her fate hung on the results she produced every quarter, while the VP of HR was able to get away with hundreds of thousands of dollars of investments in programs for which he was not required to show the ROI. The other executives did not provide any other insights, other than agreeing unanimously that they expected HR to figure this out on behalf of the organization.

In research we conducted, we have found that in the future, line executives will place more and more emphasis on HR providing leadership capacity metrics—with leadership indicators becoming as important as turnover and employee engagement.[2] Even with the increasing exposure of the leadership gap at the executive table, few organizations have put metrics in place or even developed a strategy to identify the metrics for leadership capacity.

Without metrics, decisions about where to invest limited resources are often not based on data. Spending decisions are imprecise and not targeted to the skills that are most in need of development or to the individuals and teams that will most benefit from the investment. Furthermore, without good measures of leadership capacity, development efforts cannot be evaluated, and the impact of programs cannot be weighed against the hard and soft costs of implementation. The organization is vulnerable to squandering large sums of money on ineffective programs.

(4) Unclear Accountability for Leadership Capacity

As organizations have increased their awareness of the challenge of closing the leadership gap, boards and non-HR executives have become more accountable for owning leadership capacity within their organizations. More executives and board members are making the connection between strong leadership capacity and competitive advantage.

Still, we find a lack of clarity of what this accountability actually looks like. We have experienced a continuum of responses in client organizations. On the one extreme, we find what we refer to as the "Passionate CEO" who is often the sole driving force behind an organization's efforts at building leadership capacity. Although it's an important first step to have a CEO who understands the importance of leadership, we find there is too much accountability resting with one individual, and as we have seen countless times, once the passionate CEO departs the organization, things begin to crumble.

At the opposite end of the continuum, we still find examples of senior leaders who struggle to understand their accountability for leadership capacity. Many feel that time spent trying to develop leadership might distract the organization from achieving business results. Others resist accountability for leadership because they recognize the amount of time and effort that is required to develop leadership capacity well. In most cases, the underlying reason for not assuming accountability for leadership capacity is that a strong, short-term orientation wins out over the need to address a long-term business challenge.

The Human Resources function is equally culpable in failing to create meaningful accountability for leadership. On the one hand, we have seen HR leaders shy away from their responsibility to build leadership capacity. Often they are mired in the more immediate requirements of the day-to-day HR function. On the other hand, we have seen HR leaders try to single-handedly take on the mantle of leadership capacity. In our experience, when HR attempts to do so, they detract from the message of leadership as a broad strategic business issue, thus marginalizing the executive accountability for the leadership gap. Ideally, Human Resource leaders must help the organization articulate its vision of leadership and provide many of the tools to reinforce that vision (e.g., recruiting principles, reward mechanisms and development programs). As such, they can facilitate the process of building leadership capacity while ensuring that accountability for leadership remains in the hands of the CEO and the executive team.

Another disturbing trend we are encountering is the view of boards of directors that their only accountability for leadership capacity is to ensure the succession for the CEO's position. They create what we call the "In Case of Emergency, Break Glass" succession plan that at best turns one of the existing VPs into an interim manager until a legitimate search for a successor can be completed. Boards need to recognize that leadership capacity is an issue of risk mitigation for a corporation that extends beyond the role of the CEO. Just like boards have audit committees for financial issues, they now need to ensure the organization doesn't put itself at risk because of significant leadership gaps.

(5) Fragmented Solutions That Are Not Sustained

Many organizations attempt to implement a set of well-intended practices designed to close their leadership gap. Yet, we have found that often the practices do not complement one another. In the worst case scenario, the programs are actually in conflict because certain behaviors are encouraged by one program while being discouraged by another. Consider this example:

> A global technology company believed it had the right set of solutions in place to close its leadership gaps. Upon closer examination, it became apparent that what they were thinking of as a leadership solution was merely a compilation of separate interventions. The key leadership programs had been designed by four different vendors over several years with little coordination between them. One firm was retained to do the assessment of leaders. Another firm was retained to build the succession planning process. A third firm was hired to build new leadership competencies and incorporate them into the performance management process. Finally, an Ivy League MBA school was retained to deliver a residential leadership program to all the company's top one hundred leaders. Each program had its own branding, and each had its own messages and language about leadership. The uncoordinated approach sent conflicting messages to the organization, causing confusion and a lack of clarity around what was really required of leaders. Unfortunately, the executive team ignored the pleas from the VP of HR to stop some of the programs, arguing that they had been so costly to develop they didn't want to abandon them.

Building sufficient momentum to change leadership behaviors is difficult in the best of times, but when the organization's own programs send conflicting messages, it is very easy for leaders to just go about their business the way they always have.

Another common problem is that many organizations tend to place great emphasis on the launch of initiatives while ignoring the practices that will sustain their efforts over the long term. In many organizations, programs are professionally branded with binders and sweatshirts, but after some time, the "buzz" begins to fade. As a result all the initial energy fails to take hold and truly build the leadership capacity required.

A VP of Leadership Development referred to this phenomenon in her organization as the "leadership graveyard." She remarked, "Imagine a cemetery lined with tombstones, all with the titles of leadership programs of the past. Today they are only a faint memory in the mind of those participants."

Failing to implement a coordinated leadership solution or to sustain that solution over the long term will prevent an organization from creating a lasting improvement in its leadership capacity. In today's business environment, building leadership capacity is a long-term game. In fact, we believe it has emerged as a new organizational capability much like strategic planning and new product development have become core organizational capabilities. The organizations that are able to develop this capability the most quickly and sustain it will have an advantage over their competition.

(6) Flat and Lean Organizations with Fewer Intermediate Leadership Positions

The lean organization came about largely due to the large-scale restructuring and downsizing that occurred during the 1980s and early 1990s. Today's flatter and leaner organizations are more nimble and responsive. But for all the positive outcomes, one of the negative consequences of this delayering is that many intermediate leadership roles have been wiped out. In the past when organizations had more layers, leaders had many levels to climb up in their careers. Each level provided the opportunity for leaders to grow and expand their personal leadership capacity. Today, with fewer levels, the leaps in leadership roles can be quite sizeable. In some organizations, only four or five levels separate a first-line supervision role from an executive position.

As a result, leaders might take on fairly senior leadership roles without the proper experience. One CEO said, "We have many VPs in this company who don't even have the basics of Management 101."

Another unfortunate side effect of leaner organizations is that leaders have been forced to take on more of their own job responsibilities and have become working managers. Regardless of the leadership level, leaders are saddled with large mandates, pressing short-term demands, and often a more operational focus. This means leaders have no time, or very limited time, to coach and mentor their direct reports—never mind addressing their own development.

The risk to an organization is that there is little time or opportunity to lead the workforce effectively—let alone to build leadership capacity for the future. Leaders feel "permanently stretched" and feel they cannot afford any distractions or time away from their jobs to engage in their own development or to support the development of others.

(7) Poor Supply of Leaders

As the following story illustrates, organizations are being faced with a smaller pool of individuals for leadership positions:

> *The VP of Marketing and a young brand manager were having a career development discussion. The VP of Marketing told the young brand manager that she was planning to retire in the next year or two and that the executive team had asked her to play a role in grooming her successor. The VP told the brand manager how impressed she had been with her work—in particular, the leadership she had been displaying in her role. The VP believed the brand manager had what it took to be a senior leader in the company and strongly recommended she consider the career option. The young manager waited, and with a smile, replied, "I see how hard you work. The 94 weeks you work. The sacrifices you make in your personal life because of this job. Well, you know that isn't for me. I value my life balance too much to sacrifice everything for my job. I really appreciate your vote of confidence, but I'd like to continue to add value in my current role and am not interested in moving up the organization." The VP of Marketing was left confused and perplexed. She could not understand why the young brand manager would pass up such a great opportunity.*

This story is a good example of the two forces contributing to the poor supply of leaders for the future. First, as the baby boomer generation begins to reach their sixties, organizations will face an unprecedented rate of retirements from the leadership ranks. Second, not only are there fewer Generation X employees to take their places, but many of these Gen Xers might be unwilling to accept the mantle of leadership.

One of the most intriguing developments we have been witnessing consistently in organizations is the large number of what we refer to as "next generation" leaders who in fact are not interested in taking on senior leadership roles. In most cases these young individuals are motivated by a different set of values, which places greater emphasis on work-life balance.

Consider the example of a global technology company. It had undergone a rigorous process to identify 30 high-potential candidates. Each candidate was informed of the "honor." Each reacted in a lukewarm manner. The organization wanted to involve them in an accelerated leadership development program but found a lot of resistance. Once the organization probed a little deeper, they found that the thirty individuals did not want or desire the "high-potential" label. They did not see being chosen for leadership development as an honor but rather as a burden. Most saw it merely as extra work. The organization recognized they could not move ahead with the program until they first convinced the 30 individuals of the merits and benefits of being identified as high potentials.

Another variable to consider is that the next generation employees have more employment choices available to them than in the past. For example, the traditional career path, entering a company and slugging one's way to the top, isn't the only career path available today. If they choose, individuals can now set up their own businesses and become instant CEOs of their own organizations. Whereas past generations saw big corporations as providing job security, today's generation sees years of downsizing and terminations. This situation has left many people feeling that self-employment provides a more predictable future because it gives them the opportunity to be in control of their careers.

CLOSING THE LEADERSHIP GAP: THE FAILURE PATHS

Closing current leadership gaps and building the leadership capacity required for the future success of an organization is a critical business imperative. At times, the challenge can be so great for organizations that it appears overwhelming. In many cases this may lead organizations to respond by going down certain failure paths. On the surface each path appears to have merit, but we have discovered that each is likely to waste time, energy and limited resources. We have found three specific leadership solutions failure paths that prevent organizations from effectively closing the leadership gap.

Leadership Gap Failure Paths

Failure Path 1: Trying to Do It All
Failure Path 2: Over Reliance on Best Practices
Failure Path 3: The Quick Fix "Do It Now" Approach

Failure Path 1: Trying to Do It All

In many cases the complexity of building leadership capacity overwhelms organizations. They try to address issues of succession management, accelerated development, targeted programs for high potentials, etc. They believe they must do it all—and all at once.

In some cases they appoint one person in the company as the VP of Leadership Development or Chief Leadership Officer and give that individual sole accountability for leadership development. This approach fails because it does not recognize that all functions in the organization have accountability for leadership—or the reality that "it takes a village" to build leadership capacity in today's organizations.

In other cases, organizations in "trying to do it all," take a cross-functional, integrated, systemic view of leadership and try to change everything in the organization all at once. These organizations fail because the resources required to change everything all at once are too great. Either the initiative gains traction and distracts the organization from the actual work of the business (a sure path to failure) or the business wins out and leaders react to the overwhelming amount of change by ignoring the initiative. Consider the following example:

An organization launched a complex high-potential program lasting two years. It involved intensive learning sessions at an executive MBA program, one-on-one coaching and a significant action-learning project. In total, the investment was close to $1 million in hard costs alone. The investment was also considerable for the participants, as their involvement in the program took up to 30 percent of their time. During this period leaders in the program were also expected to maintain their job performance. After a year the program was cancelled

because almost all the leaders failed to achieve their personal busi-
ness goals and objectives. The program was so large and intensive
that it detracted from, rather than supported, the leaders' ability to hit
their performance targets.

The implications of the "doing it all" path are numerous. First, most organizations do not have the resources necessary to do it all. Second, this approach can also distract leaders from delivering on current performance expectations. Third, this approach can breed cynicism from the line leaders who see the declining business performance that occurs while leaders change their behavior wholesale. The line leaders may have a growing sense that the organization does not understand the demands of their business or lacks enough focus on driving results.

Failure Path 2: Over-Reliance on Best Practices

Some organizations respond to the challenge of closing their leadership gaps by first conducting extensive best-practices research. The underlying belief is that the elusive solution exists "out there," and the organization merely needs to find it and implement it. Consider the following example:

A new VP of HR had joined an organization with the primary mandate
of closing the company's leadership gap. As she met with her team
to review what they had been doing in this area, she learned the for-
mer VP had insisted that the first place to start was to put together an
internal team to conduct best practices research. The executive team
had disagreed, but the former VP of HR was a "purist" and pushed
through his idea. An internal "away team" was put in place and was
not seen or heard from again for several months. They spent weeks
researching companies, contacting them and arranging for invita-
tions to meet with them. It took several more weeks to visit the best-
practice companies and even longer to consolidate and make sense
of the reams of information they had collected. Almost nine months
passed by, and nothing was done within the organization to address
pressing leadership capacity issues. Once the team finally completed
their report, it consisted of a series of practices and interventions that,

though suitable for large, multi-national corporations, would not fit their organization. The former VP of HR lost all credibility with the executive team and was finally asked to leave. The CEO hired the new VP to develop a more effective approach.

Not only is best-practice research a very time-consuming process, but having done it, you are also likely to know more about the challenges facing someone else's organization than you are about those facing your own organization. In the worst case, this external focus results in team members who are enamored with the best-practice organizations and feel disheartened by the thought of returning to their organization to begin the overwhelming task of applying what they have learned.

We're not saying that best-practice research is not helpful. There are pockets of success and good ideas. Often, the organizations considered to have best practices had a wonderful time and place, an era with a great leader or the right conditions to grow leaders. More often than not, that era was not sustained as the leader moved on or the market conditions changed. In other instances, we've discovered that organizations who are contacted because they are seen as being best-practice organizations are quite surprised by the label.

Another challenge with best-practice research is that it deludes organizations into thinking they can close their leadership gap by simply implementing someone else's leadership solution. It is possible that you will find the "best practices," but simply lifting those practices and applying them in another organization won't work. Although leadership policies and practices can be copied, leadership culture and individual leaders cannot. As we will discuss in later chapters, the culture and the leader behaviors are just as important as (or more important than) the policies and practices themselves.

Best practices represent a snapshot in time. Although they may provide some valuable insights, rarely is there a complete solution that can be implemented from one organization to another. Rarely will a viable solution to building leadership capacity come from outside the organization. Use best-practice research to seek insights rather than solutions.

Failure Path 3: The Quick-Fix "Do It Now" Approach

When organizations need to change their leadership behaviors, they are often tempted to jump too quickly to solutions and to start "doing something" to address the serious organizational challenge. Organizations that embark on this third failure path believe that a "quick fix" solution will be enough to close their leadership gaps. Consider the following example:

> Over 40 percent of the company's leaders were in a position to retire over the next three years. In addition, many future leaders were exiting the company and joining competitor organizations, causing the supply of future leaders to dwindle. The company also had not made the necessary investments in leadership development, and it was now living with the consequences of that shortsightedness. The executives were worried. The CEO articulated the challenge by saying, "We're fighting a race against time." In response, a newly appointed Director of Talent Management needed to act fast. He partnered with a leading business school to develop a weeklong customized leadership development program. He thought this was a safe option and that even if this didn't work out, at least participants would get a diploma from the prestigious business school—something to put on their resume. Going against the recommendation of the business school, he decided against conducting a pilot session. They ran the first program with 30 leaders. The program received fairly negative feedback. It was seen as too academic, and although the business school was supposed to customize content, it became clear that it hadn't happened.

Organizations tend to jump too quickly to the potential solutions to change their leadership culture and behaviors. They don't take the time to understand their own strengths and weaknesses. Often, the result is less than desired or an out-and-out failure. This is because the quick fix is likely to try to repair something that wasn't broken or worse yet, to break something that was actually working. In the race to be seen taking action, organizations often skip the diagnostic phase and, in the end, get the lackluster results you might expect from any quick fix.

We have seen many different training courses and programs touted as the solution to the leadership gap. Regardless of the quality of a training curriculum, a new set of leadership competencies or a revised performance management system, no single solution will be able to change leadership behaviors over the long haul.

Quick-fix solutions have several negative outcomes. Adopting a quick-fix solution is usually exceedingly expensive, both in the cost to develop and deliver programs and in the time invested to roll the programs out to the organization's leaders. Quick-fix solutions fill everyone's calendar with various leadership development activities, which can often create a false sense of security that something is being done to address the leadership gap. Unfortunately, when the changes in behavior aren't sustained, quick-fix solutions contribute to a growing cynicism in the organization about the value of leadership development initiatives—making it that much harder to create traction for the next initiative, even if it has the necessary metrics and forethought to back it up.

CONCLUDING COMMENTS

Imagine for a moment that you are preparing for your annual general meeting of investors. Answer the following question: How confident would investors be in the future success of the company if they knew that a critical mass of the company's leaders believed in the importance of leadership and was working diligently to build the leadership capacity throughout the organization? They would probably feel fairly confident. They would know the company was well on its way to delivering real value for its customers and shareholders. They might be confident enough to buy more of the company's stock.

Now imagine the exact opposite. What if they knew the company was in the dark about its leadership capacity—with no way of measuring or knowing where it stood? What if the lack of a clear vision for the future had caused the organization to implement a series of disconnected programs that never became embedded in the organization? What impact would this have on the company's ability to achieve its vision? At this stage, investors might be feeling fairly uncertain, even nervous, about their investment.

Let's play out the worst possible scenario for a moment. The functional mindset is so strongly ingrained that the leaders are unable to resolve conflicts between different parts of the organization. With no clear accountability for leadership, executives are spending considerable time focusing internally to deal with leader resistance, instead of being externally focused on delivering value to customers. With such a dismal track record of infighting at the top, high-potential young employees are not interested in taking on leadership roles. How confident would investors feel now? They probably would be thinking about calling their brokers to sell the stock.

Fortunately (or unfortunately), investors are only starting to appreciate the importance of leadership as a key to creating and sustaining value. Had they been paying attention earlier, they might have been discouraged by the many early failed attempts to overcome the leadership gap.

We need a new leadership solution. We need a successful pathway to a sustainable leadership solution that will achieve business transformation through leadership, and that is precisely what this book intends to achieve. So read on!

CHAPTER TWO

Leadership Capacity

The young child was frustrated—he tried to solve the puzzle maze, but it seemed impossible. Over and over he traced his pencil from the starting point through the maze, and each time he reached the same roadblock. Only after many tries did the teacher lean over and say to him, "Try it another way." So the child thought about it for a while—he turned the paper sideways and then upside down. He began to draw a line starting from the box marked "finish," and he was surprised to find that he had no trouble finding his way through the maze from the finish to the start. He had learned that whenever he reached an impassable roadblock, he should say to himself, "Try it another way," and then do it.

Organizations have a similar challenge as they try to discover their leadership solution. They have been continually tracing the same pathway and finding the same roadblocks. Many of their early attempts to implement leadership solutions have failed dismally for one or more of the reasons described in Chapter 1.

Our intent in *Leadership Solutions* is much like the teacher's message to the child with the maze—"try it another way." Don't keep following the failure paths of the past—find a new leadership solution.

THE TRADITIONAL APPROACH TO LEADERSHIP

What comes to mind when you think of the word "leadership"?

Below are some of the most common responses from leaders when we ask this question. Select the responses that come to your mind.

- ❏ A series of personal traits (e.g., having vision, charisma, courage, focus on results) required for successful leadership
- ❏ Images of great leaders (e.g., John F. Kennedy, Sir Winston Churchill, Martin Luther King, Mother Teresa, Nelson Mandela)
- ❏ Images of high-status and powerful leaders who are well known in the business world (e.g., Bill Gates, Jack Welch, Oprah Winfrey, Michael Dell)
- ❏ Individuals who have directly influenced or affected your life in positive ways (e.g., teachers, former supervisors, colleagues)
- ❏ Poor examples of leadership (e.g., ineffective political figures, inadequate bosses, business leaders involved in high-profile scandals)
- ❏ Your own leadership role and the challenges you currently face as a leader
- ❏ Something you learned or experienced in a classroom-based leadership development program

We have found that the choices in this simple quiz are quite telling of the state of leadership in today's organizations. If you review the checklist above, you will find one common theme runs throughout—a focus on the personal side of leadership.

We conducted another simple exercise recently. We did a search on amazon.com under the word "leadership" that resulted in a staggering 183,380 titles.[1] When we scanned the list of titles, once again we saw a predominate focus on the personal element of leadership. For example, many of the books focus on charismatic leadership featuring leaders who have accomplished great things in their companies. Also, a large number of titles provide insights to help leaders improve as functional managers of core business disciplines such as marketing, sales, human resources or finance.

These two little exercises point out how leaders and their organizations are still holding onto the traditional views of leadership and approaches to leadership development. This traditional view overemphasizes the personal aspects of leadership, which are increasingly becoming insufficient to describe the kind of leadership required in the twenty-first century.

It is important to note that the traditional approach worked in the past because most leaders were expected to be good functional managers and technical experts. They were expected to engage in many standard managerial practices, such as planning, organizing, delegating and evaluating within their own functional areas. Typically, the smartest and most technically savvy leaders were the ones who were promoted and given legitimate power and authority to lead. In the traditional view, nirvana was having technically savvy leaders who were also good people managers. The traditional approach made sense for the times. It was a useful guide for organizations. However, this approach is no longer sufficient. In fact, the traditional approach to leadership can create problems.

LEADERSHIP ISN'T WHAT IT USED TO BE

Chapter 1 presented the results of our research that shows many executives are forecasting they will have an unacceptably low level of leadership talent available to meet their future needs. Some of the more frequently cited reasons are:

- Too few leaders who understand the complexities of organizations and who have the experience to know how to resolve these complexities.
- The departure of older "baby boomer" managers from the workforce and the loss of their institutional knowledge. Coupled with the loss of mid-level leadership roles as hierarchies have been flattened, these departures have reduced the availability of talented leaders.
- The unattractiveness to potential leaders of investing in building a career in large organizations because they have viable alternatives, such as freelancing or building an independent small business (either in the marketplace or through the Internet).
- The emerging reality that younger-generation employees do not find traditional leadership roles enticing. They see them as being too demanding and in conflict with their personal values for greater life balance. As a result, few younger workers are choosing leadership roles.

These leadership challenges are further exacerbated by the threats of an increasingly complex business climate. This climate, too, is expected to place greater demands and pressures on organizations and leaders. They will have to navigate in a highly competitive and ever-changing environment. Consider the following story:

> The leadership group of a company in the aerospace industry held a three-day strategy session to discuss the future of their business. The past decade had been unprecedented in terms of the change and uncertainty within the industry. As the leaders tried to anticipate the future business environment, they had a sense that it would only intensify and become even more complex. They engaged in an environmental scan activity, where in small groups they identified emerging trends (economic, social, political, technological, customer and organizational) that they believed might impact their company in the future. Each group posted their ideas, and the leaders were asked to review them. The sheer number of trends and issues overwhelmed many leaders. Others commented on how the trends appeared to be interdependent and connected to one another. They discussed how they needed to be mindful of all the trends and issues and their interrelationships when making decisions about the future. The group was then asked to reflect on the implications of the trends and issues on their roles as leaders. Some raised the point that they needed to act more cohesively as a leadership group with a collective view of the future climate. Others stated they needed to be clear about the kind of leadership that was going to make them successful in the future. One leader summed up the group's thinking best when she said, "When I look at all the trends and issues, it is clear in my mind that leadership isn't what it used to be."

The closing comment in this story captures the main sentiment expressed by many leaders in today's organizations. As they look to their future, they see a business climate with a multitude of complex issues, opportunities and uncertainties. As they consider what the future business climate will mean to their roles as leaders, they understand that what they need from leadership is not what it used to be—they know they need something new. The leadership required to succeed in tomorrow's business environment is not what made leaders and organizations successful in the past. It is less dependent on great leadership from individuals and more dependent on the leadership capacity of the whole organization.

Research conducted at Knightsbridge also found a significant shift in the expectations that organizations have of their current and future leaders.[2] In discussions with boards, C-suite executives and senior HR practitioners, Knightsbridge found that the emerging kinds of behaviors and expectations that organizations require and value from their leaders are changing. The emerging expectations are that leaders must:

- Align and engage employees around a strategy that delivers value to the customer.

- Take an enterprise-wide perspective of their role to emphasize success for the whole company, not just their functional areas.

- Build strong relationships with customers, employees and external stakeholders through openness and dialogue.

- Help employees deal effectively with ambiguity, uncertainty and conflict associated with the increasingly complex business environment.

- Build strong leadership capacity within their organizations by growing and developing future leaders.

- Model the values of the organization, rather than being self-absorbed with their own personal egos and agenda.

As we review this list, two key points are particularly interesting. First, we can see a shift away from the traditional approach to leadership that relied on functional, technical and charismatic leadership. Second, it is clear that organizations need leaders who can respond to organization-wide challenges and who are well-rounded holistic leaders.

The research of Dr. Ronald Heifetz[3] suggests that the need for a different kind of leader is tied to the types of challenges leaders face today. In the past, leaders encountered technical challenges. He describes the nature of technical problems:

- They typically have clear answers and solutions.

- They are fairly straightforward to contend with because there are generally few competing variables, and, therefore, a few "correct" technical solutions will suffice.

- Leaders are able to generate answers and solutions based largely on their previous technical or functional expertise and experience.
- Leaders can implement their technical solutions through the exercise of their formal power and authority within the organization.

These technical challenges can be addressed by calling on functional or technical expertise. In contrast, Heifetz argues that leaders today are confronted with an onslaught of issues representing what he refers to as "adaptive challenges." These challenges are very different from the technical problems just described. Here are some of their characteristics of how leaders need to react or respond to adaptive challenges:

- Leaders need to restrain their impulse to jump to conclusions. Their prior technical or functional experience or expertise may be of little guidance in responding to adaptive challenges.
- Leaders need to ask the right questions, create deeper conversations and influence key stakeholders to reach consensus on the best possible choices and decisions.
- Leaders cannot respond to adaptive challenges by merely exercising their power and authority.

The message is clear—the traditional approach to leadership is no longer a viable solution for organizations. Only a more comprehensive approach to leadership will help organizations contend with the complex, ambiguous and interdependent challenges presented by the business environment.

LEADERSHIP CAPACITY: THE NEW ORGANIZATIONAL CAPABILITY

Over the past 20 years, the idea of organizational capability has taken hold as an important concept in business. Ulrich and Lake define organizational capability as "the ability of a firm to manage people to get a competitive advantage."[4] We have expanded the definition of organizational capability to refer to the ability of an organization to maintain a state of readiness to implement its evolving business strategies quickly and repeatedly to create and sustain competitive advantage.

Building leadership capacity is the new strategic organizational capability. Our forecast is that building leadership capacity will be the primary business and organizational challenge facing executives over the next decade.

Therefore, leadership capacity will demand attention and action on the part of executives and all leaders. However, the challenge they will face is that the traditional approach to build leadership capacity is no longer effective. Organizations need to discover a new approach to define, measure and build leadership capacity.

Organizations will overcome their leadership gap when they build the leadership capacity they require.

We know the idea of "leadership capacity" is new for many business leaders. Perhaps a manufacturing analogy will help clarify what we mean by leadership capacity.[5] Manufacturing executives use the term *capacity utilization* to describe the extent of their potential production capacity that is in use at any given point.

In manufacturing, capacity utilization has two parts:

- *Machine capacity:* A mathematical calculation based, for example, on how fast a piece of equipment runs or how many gallons per hour can go through the machine in a specified time.

- *Human capacity:* The availability of trained staff to run the machinery (e.g., one, two or three shifts per day, for five to seven days per week).

Manufacturing executives try to ensure they have the required human capacity to use their machines to their maximum capacity. They do a great deal of analysis to determine a sensible capacity utilization number required to run a manufacturing facility. For example, some very capital-intensive industries that run continuously would expect to have capacity utilization above 90 percent. Other industries that have seasonal or flexible production may expect capacity utilization of between 50 and 70 percent.

Now consider how the term "capacity" can be used to understand what businesses need from their leadership talent. An effective business derives its overall capacity from two sources:

- ***Organizational leadership capacity:*** Each business has various products and/or services that need to flow through its organization to deliver value to its external customers or stakeholders. An organization needs to develop processes and tools to increase the effectiveness of how its leadership works with these products and/ or services. These processes and tools are the "machinery" of leadership capacity.

- *Individual leadership capacity:* The organization requires a current and future cadre of leaders who are trained, capable and willing to make effective business decisions and to lead people to optimize the available organizational capacity. These capable and willing people create the "human side" of leadership capacity. Leadership capacity is enhanced by the following:
  - Leaders who are fully engaged and aligned to the core purpose and vision of the business.
  - Organizational practices and programs that help make individual leaders more effective. Some examples of these programs include: well-designed recruiting and selection profiles, orientation and development programs, cross-functional planning exercises, coaching and mentoring.

The organization's leadership culture creates and embeds expectations that further reinforce a more effective type of leadership. Organizations need to ensure they have the level of leadership capacity required to execute their strategies. Talented individual leaders, supported by effective organizational practices, in a reinforcing leadership culture, are able to propel businesses to achieve their strategic goals. In contrast, organizations with insufficient leadership capacity to meet their business needs are unable to drive the alignment and engagement of employees to the strategic direction, which can put the entire business at risk.

All organizations should determine the level of leadership capacity they require to propel their business forward. Unless they achieve that level, the resulting gap in leadership capacity will very likely cause a significant erosion of their business. Some organizations are attempting to build a level of leadership capacity beyond the minimum requirements. These organizations realize they may need to have back-up leadership resources available for various reasons—perhaps their leaders may choose not to take on certain roles or they won't live up to their expectations, or they may choose to leave the organization.

Consider the cost to the following company that needed to modify its business strategy because of its limitations in leadership capacity:

A pharmaceutical company was expanding its product offerings and anticipated strong growth over the next few years. They had identified an opportunity to combine one of their strong consumer products categories (facial cleansers) with their expertise in prescription pharmaceuticals. Their strategy required that they combine parts of two separate business units to form a third unit that would focus on patented drugs for facial cleansing.

They held a strategy meeting to discuss the need to restructure the organization to have a new stand-alone business focused on these products. After several hours of planning, they opened up the discussion to a risk analysis of this change and why it might not succeed. Two major risks emerged from the discussion: that regulators might not list the new patented drugs and that physicians might not develop awareness of the new drugs to replace competitive products. After some discussion they agreed that these risks were manageable. The CEO then said, "I agree that we need to create the new business quickly, but who will lead it?" The executives looked around the room at each other. Each of the executives was overloaded already with business challenges. Their leaders at the next level were not ready to take on a full business responsibility; they were too focused on their own functional areas, and they had limited experience and exposure as leaders of a complete business unit. The executive group considered hiring someone from the outside, but they decided that that would not work—the required business leader needed too much inside knowledge to amalgamate parts of two businesses to form a third viable business.

After some deliberation, the CEO decided they would implement the strategy—but slowly. He decided to run the new business as a virtual business for the interim period without formally restructuring into one business unit. Three directors, one from R and D, another from government relations and a third from sales and marketing, would share the leadership from within their different business units with joint performance targets for the new virtual business. They would need unanimous agreement to move forward on any of their new business ideas.

Although some executives questioned the slowness of the strategy for the new business, the CEO explained that his leadership approach achieved the objective of launching the business. At the same time, it reduced the risk of inexperienced senior leaders making decisions that were inappropriate. He anticipated that the three directors would counterbalance each other's ideas. Because they would have to achieve unanimous agreement on direction, they would be forced to reach a more conservative, cautiously planned direction for the new business. The CEO also felt this process would develop the three directors and give them a more holistic perspective. Hopefully, one of them would rise to the top and eventually be ready to take over the entire business.

Although the approach was slower, it was manageable from a risk perspective. The organization simply did not have the leadership capacity to take it any faster. The anticipated lost revenue opportunity of the slow-down strategy was approximately 30 percent of the fore-casted business revenue for the first two years.

After this discussion, the CEO began expressing his concern that the leadership gap could limit future growth decisions as well. He became a strong advocate for investing in leadership capacity. He directly experienced the cost of not having the talent with the broad holistic leadership skills who could lead the new business. His target for leadership capacity was simple—he never again wanted to be in the position of having to alter a business strategy because of the risk associated with insufficient leadership capacity.

Stories like this one of insufficient leadership capacity are becoming commonplace. Good business strategies are delayed because organizations do not have the leadership capacity to lead in new business arenas. The lack of the required leadership capacity is damaging organizations' ability to expedite their strategic direction effectively and at the desired speed. In some cases it has altered strategy entirely. As a result, businesses must build a meaningful leadership solution that generates the leadership capacity required to meet current and future business needs.

CONCLUDING COMMENTS

Building leadership capacity is forecasted to be the primary business and organizational challenge facing executives for the next decade. In essence, it has become the new organizational capability. In response to this challenge, a business needs to have a good grasp of the leadership capacity required and the nature of their leadership gap. Unfortunately, we find that many leaders and their organizations are still holding a traditional approach to leadership, one that focuses on building the skills of a few individual leaders at the expense of building the leadership capacity of the whole organization.

Paradoxically, although many organizations have a leadership capacity gap, at the same time many Western societies report unemployment data that include many middle managers who were released from their companies. Indeed, there are enough people to fill the open leadership positions; it's just that the available people are not suited for the holistic leadership roles. Most of these leaders have been socialized in a traditional functional approach to leadership. They have been trained to excel at their functional roles and not to pay attention to their holistic leadership responsibilities.

The purpose of *Leadership Solutions* is to outline precisely what is required to build leadership capacity in organizations and to identify what individual leaders will need to bridge the leadership gap. The remainder of Part One of this book is dedicated to exploring the full nature of leadership capacity, beginning with the next chapter that focuses on the three dimensions of leadership capacity. Part Two introduces the leadership pathway that describes the four steps of how organizations and individual leaders can build the leadership capacity they require.

CHAPTER THREE

The Three Dimensions of Leadership Capacity

In *The Leadership Gap*, we said that building leadership capacity requires a dual response—from both individual leaders and their organizations. Leaders must take personal responsibility for behaving holistically, and organizations must encourage the development of leadership capacity by implementing supportive practices and by fostering a strong leadership culture.

Although many organizations are developing leaders through training, coaching or stretch assignments (focusing on individual leaders), most are missing the opportunity to build leadership capacity through improved organizational practices and strengthened leadership culture. They have yet to embrace the idea that leadership capacity exists beyond the individual leader.

In this chapter, we examine the following:

- The three dimensions of leadership capacity
- The impact of each dimension on the ability of individual leaders and organizations to build leadership capacity (using a case study)
- The role that organizational practices and leadership culture play in supporting the emergence of holistic leadership

By the end of this chapter, we hope you will have a greater appreciation of all three dimensions of leadership capacity and a greater awareness of the opportunities to build this capacity in your organization.

THE THREE DIMENSIONS OF LEADERSHIP CAPACITY

Imagine a novice gardener who has decided to grow beautiful flowers in her garden. Before she begins planting, she reads about which plant varieties will grow well, and she enlists the help of an expert at the garden center to help her pick several kinds of seeds. She brings the seeds home, plants them in her garden, dutifully waters them and waits for them to sprout.

She, like many inexperienced gardeners, believes these are the key steps to growing a beautiful garden. To a certain extent, she is right. Because of the high quality of the seeds, some will indeed sprout and eventually bloom. But the experienced gardener knows that plants require more than just watering. Fertilizing, weeding, pruning, clipping and staking are also key in helping the flowers stay strong and beautiful. But it's not just what the gardener does that matters; it's also the quality of the environment—the nutrients in the soil, the hours of sunshine and the amount of rain. All these factors enhance the beauty and resilience of the garden.

The same is true of growing leaders and building leadership capacity. Choosing the right talent and "feeding" leaders with training is the starting point. But there are many ways to support leaders in their development. In some cases, it is instituting practices that encourage leaders to behave holistically. In other cases, it is working to foster an environment where leaders have positive experiences and interactions that reinforce a more integrative way of leading. Developing individual behaviors, instituting organizational practices and fostering a supportive leadership culture—these are the three dimensions of leadership capacity, as represented in Figure 3.1 on page 37.

1. ***The Individual Leader Dimension***: This is the extent to which leaders demonstrate holistic leadership behaviors. The individual dimension has been the dominant view of leadership in the past. Like the gardener who plants her seeds and waters them with care, the organization benefits from developing individual leaders. (In Chapters 4 and 5, we explore the individual dimension in some detail by examining six elements individual leaders must pay attention to and five capabilities they need in order to lead holistically.)

Figure 3.1 *The Three Dimensions of Leadership Capacity*

2. ***The Organizational Practices Dimension:*** This is the extent to
   which an organization's practices affect holistic leadership. In recent years, we have seen more organizations devote attention to
   the practices (such as succession management) that will help them
   build leadership capacity. What we have not seen is the leveraging
   of practices (such as business planning or budgeting) for which the
   primary purpose is something other than leadership development.
   These practices can be potent supports or equally potent barriers
   to the development of holistic leadership. (We examine these ideas
   in more detail in Chapter 6.)

3. ***The Leadership Culture Dimension:*** This is the way in which the
   norms, values and standards in the organization shape leaders'
   behaviors. As the quality of the soil or the availability of sunlight
   affects plants, the environment in organizations has a major effect
   on the way leaders develop. Like the air around us, culture is
   invisible to the eye, and because of its intangible nature, it has been
   difficult for organizations either to appreciate it or to influence
   it. But despite the challenge, it is fundamental for organizations

to deliberately manage their leadership culture. (We discuss the leadership culture dimension in more detail in Chapter 7.)

THE THREE DIMENSIONS OF LEADERSHIP CAPACITY IN ACTION: A CASE EXAMPLE

To better understand the three dimensions of leadership capacity, it is helpful to illustrate a typical experience of someone who is attempting to become a holistic leader. This scenario demonstrates how the three dimensions of leadership capacity can play out in an organization.

John is the Director of Customer Relationship Management (CRM) for a technology company. In a recent performance review, Margaret, John's manager, informed him that he was seen as the only director who could replace her. As part of the succession planning program, Margaret told him that he would need to take part in a company-sponsored "mandatory" leadership development program.

John was concerned about taking four days out of his hectic schedule to attend the program, but he didn't have a choice. He attended the program, and much to his surprise, he enjoyed it. The program stressed the need for leaders to be more holistic in their approach to leadership. He found the combination of theory, case examples and role-plays extremely helpful. In the concluding exercise, the leaders shared some of the insights they had gained. John told the group he was overwhelmed by the realization that he had been spending too much time doing work that his employees could do and trying to control them rather than lead them. He recognized he led with "blinders on," only focused on his own area and mandate, without having enough understanding of the rest of the organization.

The program was a wake-up call for John. He knew he had to change if he was going to be a more holistic leader. He returned home energized from the four-day leadership program and spent the weekend reflecting on what he had learned. He shared some of his new ideas with his wife and prepared to "turn over a new leaf" the following week.

Monday morning John went in to work especially early, eager to share his new approach with his team and excited about what he was sure would be a positive response. He brought the team together, told them about what he had learned and discussed the ideas with them. Over the following weeks, John worked hard to involve the team in more decision making, to be explicit about his expectations and to recognize and reward each employee in a way that was suited to them—all lessons he had taken away from the leadership program. He also developed a plan to begin to reach out within the organization and learn about other parts of the business.

Let's take a moment and reflect on what has happened so far in John's situation. This scenario is actually one we encounter frequently in our work with leaders. We find that in many cases organizations build their leadership capacity primarily by equipping leaders with new knowledge, skills and insights. The assumption is that new knowledge and skills will generate the desired behavior change. This approach focuses solely on the first dimension of leadership capacity—individual behavior of leaders.

In this case, even though John was initially skeptical about attending the mandatory program, in the end he found it to be valuable. As a good leader, he demonstrated the capability and the willingness to become a holistic leader.

Before we continue, ask yourself what other factors might have affected John's ability to change his leadership approach. What could help John sustain his new leadership behaviors?

Let's revisit John two months later.

As time passed, John's management style slowly began to regress. Rather than sharing his expectations and then allowing the team to develop their own ways of solving the problems, he was directing them. Instead of involving the team in discussions about important topics, he was first making up his mind and then communicating his decisions.

John was feeling quite frustrated by the fact that he was reverting back to his old ways. Part of his frustration was that he found it challenging to find the time in his day-to-day role to reflect on his leadership and to try to be a more intentional holistic leader. He found the pressures in his job actually got in the way of his ability to lead more holistically.

One day, Samantha, one of John's team members who had worked with him for a long time, invited him to go for a cup of coffee. Samantha told John candidly she was disappointed that all of the positive changes she had seen in him following the training program had vanished. She talked about the negative impact it was having on the other team members as their newfound autonomy was being revoked. John appreciated the feedback, but he felt deflated.

It was troubling to him because he genuinely believed that the changes were important, that they would make him a better leader and, ultimately, that they would improve the team's performance. As they talked, John began to realize that several different forces were making it tough for him to sustain the changes. The first was the reaction of Margaret, his manager. When John had shared his belief that the team could develop their own approach if given the goal, Margaret balked at the suggestion and argued emphatically that employees just need to be told what to do. She also reinforced that since John was the "CRM guru," he should spend more time delivering on his projects and less time "poking his nose" around other parts of the organization. Margaret viewed these actions as a distraction to John. She wanted him "focused" on the mandate she set for him. John felt conflicted because the direction he received from Margaret was completely the opposite of what he had learned in the leadership development course. Not only was Margaret not supporting his new behaviors, she was actually thwarting his attempts to give greater autonomy to his staff.

Samantha asked John why he had stopped involving the team in decision making because they had been particularly pleased when he consulted them about key issues. John reflected for a minute and then told her how the planning timelines were being shortened this year and how the business unit leadership required that he make the important decisions on his own while attending the company's business planning session. By working on the business plan at the management offsite, John lost the opportunity to consult the team mid-stream. Furthermore, the business planning process was highly fragmented, in that each business unit developed its own plan, in isolation from other units. John reflected again, "It's like we hold our business plans close to our chest before we present them at the management offsite.

This seems to foster competition among leaders, rather than encouraging us to discuss the business as a whole."

After an hour of conversation, both John and Samantha realized why John's new approach had not been sustained. Although he honestly believed that his new skills would help him be a more effective leader, many forces in the organization were pushing him back toward his old habits. By the time they finished their coffee, it was clear to them that it isn't enough to send leaders to a training program on how to be individual leaders—it is just as important that they return to an organization that has both the organizational practices and the leadership culture that support the new behaviors.

The Case of John: Key Lessons

Using the three dimensions of leadership capacity as a guide, let's analyze John's case.

1. ***The Individual Leader Dimension:*** As we have already discussed, many organizations see leadership primarily from the individual dimension. The result is a considerable investment of energy and resources to train individual leaders. In John's case, the training program was received positively, and his motivation to become a holistic leader was high. He was particularly inspired by messages about team leadership and also by new approaches to connecting with his colleagues. However, John's attempts to put what he learned into practice were confronted with powerful counterbalancing forces from the existing organizational practices and leadership culture.

2. ***The Organizational Practices Dimension:*** The organizational practices, such as the company's performance management process, contradicted the messages in the leadership development program. The business planning process did not foster cross-departmental collaboration because it was functionally driven and not holistic in nature. To make matters worse, the business-planning process and offsite limited the opportunity for John to consult with his team throughout decision-making sessions, which would have contributed to both the alignment and engagement of his team and probably to the quality of his decisions.

3. *The Leadership Culture Dimension:* The norms of the existing leadership culture encouraged behaviors that were different from those John was taught in the leadership program, which taught the importance of holistic leadership, building teams and working across organizational boundaries. On the other hand, his manager insisted on the need for him to be the CRM guru and focus on his individual contribution to achieving business results—severely limiting his efforts at organizational leadership. Moreover, the leadership culture reinforced internal competition and lack of trust among departments. This undermined the organization's ability to build the holistic leadership it required for future success.

The Case of John: The Implications

Stories similar to John's are commonplace. Organizations send their leaders off to inspiring, life-altering training programs; then they return to an organization that does not support them in applying the skills they have learned. The often costly investment[1] in training provides little return, and the employees are left feeling they will never have the kind of leadership they are looking for. The programs do not demonstrate long-term results.

Do you believe the company gained a return on its investment by sending John to the leadership development program? Probably not.

This same story is multiplied hundreds of times in John's company as other leaders take part in the leadership program, with similar outcomes when they return to their jobs. The implications are quite simple: If organizations continue to think about their leadership capacity from only one dimension, they risk squandering their investment. They will likely fail to build the level of leadership capacity required for future success. It is imperative that organizations understand the aspects of leadership that exist beyond the individual leader—that they see all three dimensions of leadership capacity.

CONCLUDING COMMENTS

The three dimensions of leadership capacity do not exist in isolation from one another. The individual dimension affects and is affected by the organizational dimension, which affects and is influenced by the leadership culture dimension. The next four chapters of Part One describe the three dimensions of leadership capacity in greater detail: the individual leader dimension (Chapters 4 and 5), the organizational practices dimension (Chapter 6) and the leadership culture dimension (Chapter 7). Part Two then uses the foundation established in Part One to describe the four-step pathway to build leadership capacity.

CHAPTER FOUR

The Individual Leader Dimension:
The Holistic View of Leadership

The participants in a leadership seminar were asked a common question: "What is the difference between management and leadership?" One person joked that the answer is simple: "Management is bad and leadership is good—so call yourself a leader." Another person asked if there really is a difference or is it just that the word "leadership" has a better brand?

Eventually the group brainstormed a list of words to describe management and leadership. They determined that management includes day-to-day results, operational efficiency, production, accountability, implementation—it's about the present and about evaluating what has been done to be able to do things better.

In contrast, they decided that leadership requires the capability for vision, inspiration, focus on opportunities, anticipation, developing leaders' potential—it's about the future and anticipating what needs to be done to remain (or to become) successful.

One participant remarked, "Management focuses on the function—the details of getting the job done." Another participant said, "I agree that management focuses on function. And I think leadership focuses on the whole business." The facilitator then pointed out, "Each of you knows your management responsibility really well; however, the challenge you face is learning to lead your businesses holistically." This is the central challenge facing leaders and their organizations today: to understand the concept of holistic leadership and to foster it within their enterprises.

Just as the facilitator felt the group was coming to a new level of understanding of leadership, the sales director said, "My job of selling into our large accounts is so huge that I don't even have time to manage my staff. Where am I going to find the time to devote to leadership?" The tone in the room changed quickly. Everyone could empathize with the question.

The facilitator had heard this refrain many times before. "I share your concern about your personal accountabilities detracting from your ability to effectively manage your function, but I'd like to propose a slightly different way of looking at leadership." He explained to the group that leadership is not a set of activities, but rather, it is a way of thinking, a perspective that influences what you pay attention to. He challenged the group to become more holistic leaders, not by adding meetings to their calendars, but by paying attention to different things in the meetings they already attend. One participant raised her hand, "So leadership is more of a lens through which you view the world." "Exactly," the facilitator replied, knowing his point was getting through.

This chapter and Chapter 5 explain the individual leader behavior dimension of leadership capacity (Figure 4.1).

Figure 4.1 *The Three Dimensions of Leadership Capacity*

The purpose of this chapter is to explore holistic leadership—what it is and why it is important. We will consider the following:

- The problems that arise when functional management becomes functional leadership
- A tale of two leaders that demonstrates the difference between functional management and holistic leadership
- The six elements of holistic leadership

By the end of this exploration, you should have a thorough grasp of what holistic leadership is and why it is central to building leadership capacity.

As the participants in the seminar came to realize, functional management is very important to the success of an organization. But a serious problem arises when leaders lead from the functional vantage point. A "functional leadership" mindset overemphasizes the importance of the function. As a result, the leader does not pay attention to the entire business and makes decisions based only on what makes sense for the leader's department.

Often, functional leaders rationalize this approach, arguing that particular issues outside the realm of their specific function are "someone else's responsibility." They don't want their teams to be distracted by these other issues. Functional leadership fosters and reinforces the "silo mentality." That is why we conclude that functional leadership is actually dysfunctional leadership.

HOLISTIC LEADERSHIP IN ACTION: A TALE OF TWO LEADERS

Here are stories of two plant managers who work for the same manufacturing company: Functional Frank and Holistic Holly. Both are effective leaders. However, one's strength in functional management causes him to take a functional view of leadership, while the other successfully manages her function guided by her holistic view of leadership.

The Tale of Functional Frank

Frank manages approximately 300 employees and has a team of six production managers. He has a solid background rooted in engineering and total quality management.

He runs a fairly "tight ship." His plant consistently hits production quotas and has one of the top safety records within the company. He is very data-oriented in his approach to running the plant and credits his success to the fact that he "knows his stuff."

Frank is devoted to "his" plant. He is typically at work early each morning reading all the reports from the previous night's shift. He also puts in long days and is happy to come in during the night shift if there is a problem.

Frank is so fact-based that he tends to spend most of his time in his small office on the production floor. His desk is usually piled high with papers. He's often quoted as saying, "Everything I need to run this plant I get through these daily reports." The numerous reports provide regular status and metrics of the plant's operation. He comes out of the office only when he needs to solve a problem. He likes to resolve matters quickly and does so by telling his people which steps to take.

In his weekly team meetings with his production managers, he does most of the talking. The team spends the greater part of the meetings poring over reports and data. When problems arise, Frank typically dictates the solution based on his vast experience and expertise.

Despite his many strengths, Frank's devotion to his plant comes at the expense of his tolerance for what he refers to as "external distractions" from head office. Whether it is the latest "harebrained" campaign from sales, a communication from the executive team or a new finance policy, Frank largely ignores the directions from above. He rarely shares information coming from the head office with his managers because he wants them focused on hitting their quotas, versus being distracted by head office "noise." Frank also has little regard for "fluffy HR stuff," so he rarely supports corporate HR programs, such as training and performance management. The recent employee survey indicated that employee engagement was lower compared to other plants, but Frank didn't believe this to be a factor in the running of his plant.

Throughout the company, Frank's plant is viewed as "Frank's world." It is isolated from the rest of the company. Few ever are allowed to go into the plant. Few actually want to, given the reception they typically receive from Frank. Many at head office acknowledge his shortcomings, but because of his tenure and the fact that the plant's performance is relatively strong, Frank is left alone. So Frank marches on, diligently doing his job, day after day.

The Tale of Holistic Holly

Holly is a plant manager for the same manufacturing company. Her plant has a similar number of production managers and employees, and she has a background similar to Frank's, with the same engineering pedigree. Holly also runs a highly productive plant, with a very strong safety record.

Like Frank, Holly is also data-oriented, but says, "By the time I see bad numbers, it's too late for me to do something—numbers don't tell the whole story." So rather than running the plant from her office, Holly frequently walks around the plant, taking time to chat with production managers and supervisors and line employees.

Holly also believes that the "customer is king." She manages to spend time with external customers, either visiting them at their sites or having them come into the plant for tours. During the tours she ensures that employees have an opportunity to interact with customers. She believes strongly that "employees need to have a clear understanding of how their job affects the customer."

Holly also is very devoted to her work. However, her devotion is to the company as a whole. She appreciates that her plant does not exist in isolation—it is part of a larger company. So Holly is always looking for ways to understand the company's big picture, its strategy and how other departments function and support one another. She arranges to have her production managers devote a small percentage of time working on corporate initiatives. It is not something that is expected from a plant, but it is something that Holly believes is good business. "It helps my production managers to be less insular and to see how their work contributes to the grand scheme of things. It also helps the plant, because the production managers make sure the programs coming from corporate make sense in the real world."

Her management team meetings tend to focus on both strategic and operational issues. She does not dominate the conversation but rather places accountability on the production managers to raise issues and provide potential solutions. She also believes it is important to set a good example of teamwork, so she strives to run good meetings so that her production managers will do the same with their teams.

Holly also is a big believer in direct communication with staff. She frequently holds small town hall meetings before employees begin their shifts to keep them abreast of corporate strategy, customer expectations and the plant's performance.

The Tale of Two Leaders: The Insights

The way in which Frank and Holly lead their two plants is very different and can be attributed to the difference in what they pay attention to. If you examined only the results of the two leaders, you might not see much difference. Both Frank and Holly run very strong plants and achieve the desired business results.

Frank is a strong functional or technical manager. He drives strong results through his own hard work and keeps his team single-mindedly focused on hitting quotas. These are both positive qualities, but his approach has limitations. He fails to pay attention to building the capabilities of those around him. He's the expert; he always has the answer. He also fails to appreciate the need to operate as part of a large company. His approach artificially creates an "us versus them" relationship, which is counterproductive to the success of the whole company.

When leaders like Frank continue to rely on functional leadership, a number of risks emerge that can jeopardize the current or future success of their organizations.

- *Leaders may lead with "blinders" on:* Blinders have utility with horses because they prevent them from being distracted or spooked. Blinders also are a good metaphor of what can happen with functional leaders. Frank is too focused on his own plant. He undervalues or underestimates the importance of thinking about his plant in relation to the entire company. A situation or an idea viewed only from a single perspective often does not open itself to creative possibilities. And in today's world, organizations need leaders who can think creatively.

- *Silos become entrenched in the organization:* When leaders lead primarily through their functional expertise, they may not develop strong knowledge or appreciation of the workings of the organization as a whole. We find in these organizations that leaders view organizational disciplines (e.g., sales, manufacturing, R&D, operations, marketing, finance, human resources) as separate and distinct from one another. This in turn may lead to strong boundaries, artificial divisions or "silos" and even destructive internal competition between functional groups. Frank sees his plant as an island unto itself. Though this may serve Frank's interest, it is not in the best interest of the company.

- *Leaders may fail to lead in the interest of the whole enterprise:* When leaders are deeply entrenched in a functional perspective, they fail to leverage the value and contribution of all the functions or disciplines. They behave more as heads of their functions than as true leaders representing the whole organization. We have observed this dynamic frequently during executive decision making when one executive says to another: "Take off your functional hat and put on your corporate hat." When functional interests conflict, the potential risk to organizations is that in complex situations, the leaders may not be able to evaluate the best overall course of action for the business.

When we consider Holly's approach, it is evident that she has a broader perspective than Frank. She balances the need to drive for results with the need to build the capability of her team. She wants to understand the company as a whole and where her plant fits into the grand scheme of things. She also knows that it isn't enough for her to be the only one to operate in this way. She gives her production managers and employees the chance to gain a broader perspective by meeting customers. She also directs her production managers to take part in company-wide projects.

Now consider a talent review process conducted by the senior executives at this manufacturing company. Which individual would they pick as a high-potential leader? In most cases, the executives see only the results, and the results for Frank and Holly are equivalent. The executives probably could not differentiate between Frank and Holly's performance. However, if they investigated each one's leadership approach, they would discover that although Frank is a good functional and technical manager, Holly sees the holistic picture and has the makings of a great leader. So Holly is the high-potential leadership talent.

Now consider if you were a production manager or plant employee and had the choice to work for Holly or Frank—which one would you pick? Most would agree that Holly would be the better choice. As a production manager or employee, you would have a richer experience—filled with greater opportunities to grow and develop. You also would feel part of a real team.

Which leader is adding more value to the organization? Although Frank and Holly are contributing equally to the current success of the business, Holly is actually adding much more to the long-term value of the organization. For example, Holly's results are likely to be sustained longer because Frank risks losing good employees who become disengaged by his management style. In contrast, Holly is not only increasing the likelihood that her employees will stay, she's building their skills so that they will have more to contribute in the future. Great managers add value for today; great leaders add value for tomorrow.

The quote, "Tell me what you pay attention to, and I'll tell you who you are"[1] can certainly be applied to Frank and Holly. Holly is guided by a different approach to leadership than Frank, and this makes all the difference. She may not be any smarter than Frank or have greater technical expertise. However, Holly pays attention to and values a more holistic rather than a functional view of leadership. In the next section we will continue our discussion by exploring the six elements of holistic leadership, in order to give you a better understanding of what holistic leaders pay attention to in their leadership roles and why they are important to the success of their organizations.

THE SIX ELEMENTS OF HOLISTIC LEADERSHIP

In *The Leadership Gap*, we introduced the Holistic Leadership Framework (see Figure 4.2 on the following page),[2] which presents a set of six integrated elements. The six elements guide and shape how holistic leaders like Holly contend with a myriad of opportunities and challenges they face.

Holistic leadership is the kind of leadership required for sustained future competitive advantage.[3] We choose the term "holistic" to mean a

Figure 4.2 *The Holistic Leadership Framework*

more whole and complete way of thinking about leadership capacity.[4] The traditional approach to leadership overemphasizes the functional aspects of leadership. In doing so, it misses other critical leadership elements essential to success in the new business environment.

Holistic leadership requires leaders to focus on the entire business by paying attention to all of the six elements of holistic leadership:

1. *Customer Leadership*—delivering value to the external customer

2. *Business Strategy Leadership*—creating and implementing a business strategy that gives competitive advantage

3. *Culture and Values Leadership*—capitalizing on the role of culture and values in making the organization successful

4. *Organizational Leadership*—transcending functional boundaries to bring the resources of the enterprise together

5. *Team Leadership*—building strong teams where the whole is greater than the sum of its parts

6. *Personal Leadership*—projecting effective personal leadership and modeling the values of their organizations

One leader in a business told us that her company already focuses on all six elements of holistic leadership. She then proceeded to draw a chart (Figure 4.3) that assigns accountability for each element to a specific group.

Element	Authority/Responsibility
Customer Leadership	Sales & Marketing
Business Strategy Leadership	Executives
Culture & Values Leadership	Human Resources
Organizational Leadership	Diffusion of Responsibility
Team Leadership	Individual Leaders
Personal Leadership	Individual Leaders

Figure 4.3 *The Incorrect Assignment of Elements to Functional Areas*

The flaw with this approach is that it creates a false assumption that the holistic leadership elements are the accountability of specific functions (and thus don't need to be attended to by others). The chart suggests that the only leaders who are responsible for customer leadership are Sales and Marketing—that only HR is accountable for culture and values and that only the executives are accountable for business strategy.

Based on this kind of thinking, it is not surprising that the topics in most leadership development seminars focus on team leadership and personal leadership. The designers of the programs could argue that customer leadership and business strategy are not relevant in a company-wide curriculum because they are not applicable to all leaders. It also should not be a surprise that silo behavior persists in these kinds of companies because no one is paying attention to seamless cross-functional collaboration, which we refer to as "organizational leadership."

Organizations that distribute accountability to specific functions for the elements of leadership then reach another faulty assumption: that only the executives should be holistic leaders. We take the diametrically opposite position—*all* leaders need to be holistic leaders. All leaders need to pay attention to the customer, to business strategy, to the culture and values, to cross-functional organizational collaboration, as well as to their teams and their personal behaviors. Every leader needs to think as a holistic leader, paying attention to all of these issues as they fulfill their functional management responsibilities.

HOLISTIC LEADERSHIP ELEMENTS

This section will answer some fundamental questions about each of the six elements of holistic leadership: What is it? Why is it important? What should holistic leaders pay attention to?

As you read this section, remember that the six elements are deeply integrated and dependent on one another in a dynamic rather than static process. Although we present each element separately, think of how each supports and interacts with the others. Also, on a personal level, ask yourself:

- To what extent do I personally pay attention to each of the six elements that make up the Holistic Leadership Framework?
- How could I use the six elements to broaden the perspectives and enhance the effectiveness of the leaders within my organization?

Customer Leadership

What Is It?

Customer leadership is the central element of our Holistic Leadership Framework. We define it as the extent to which all leaders, no matter where they work in the organization, align around a common understanding of how to deliver value to the external customer. For some of the leaders we have worked with (especially those accustomed to the traditional approach to leadership), this represents a radical departure in the way they think about leadership. Instead of beginning leadership development by focusing on the technical expertise of leaders or their personal traits, we begin with the customer. This starting point leads to an entirely different discussion about the kind of leadership required for sustainable competitive advantage.

Why Is Customer Leadership Important?

Almost all organizations in all sectors and industries are facing increased expectations from their customers. These increased expectations are, in turn, increasing the pressure on leaders to be responsive to customer needs. For leadership capacity to truly be a source of competitive advantage for organizations, it must be rooted in the continual creation of value for the external customer.

Customer needs are continually shifting and evolving. By beginning with customer leadership first, organizations and their leaders are forced to continually think externally about the business and the leadership required for success.

The traditional approach to leadership, with its inward focus on leaders' personal traits or technical expertise, had merit in the past, when the business climate was more stable. However, in today's world, the approach is far too insular.[5] Leaders who focus exclusively on the personal element may find one day that they have finally become the perfect leader for the business climate that existed 10 years ago.

Customer leadership strengthens an organization's leadership capacity. When organizations get customer leadership right, their customers often reward them with increased loyalty and sustained competitive advantage.

Leaders who wish to deliver this kind of value must demonstrate the agility to adapt and respond quickly to marketplace opportunities, be comfortable with blurred reporting lines and adaptable to cross-functional team approaches.

What Should Holistic Leaders Pay Attention To?

When customer leadership is strong, holistic leaders pay attention to the following:

- Understanding the customers' emerging needs and expectations
- Ensuring these needs guide decision-making and action regardless of where they work in the organization (e.g., manufacturing, R&D, sales, HR, finance)
- Spending a significant amount of energy tailoring solutions to customers' specific needs (e.g., providing a less expensive product or service if cost is the most important factor, or providing the needed customization if the customer has unique specifications)
- Implementing only those changes that are customer driven
- Hearing the customer's "voice" in everything they do and acting as "customer advocates" within their organization

Business Strategy Leadership

What Is It?

With an understanding of the voice of the customer, leaders must be able to develop and implement an effective business strategy. They must demonstrate strategic agility and create an intense focus on the strategy within the organization. This includes developing strategies and implementing plans that lead to competitive advantage and drive strong customer leadership.

Why Is Business Strategy Leadership Important?

In the traditional approach of leadership capacity, business strategy was seen as a core process reserved for only the "smartest leaders" in an organization. This meant that the strategic planning process was conducted primarily by either the senior executives or by a corporate planning department. However, the speed of change in the business environment today makes it necessary for all leaders in the organization to understand and contribute to business strategy. Furthermore, organizations are too large and complex for a small group of executives to understand intimately all aspects of the business. As a result, all leaders need to think strategically and be ready to react quickly. They need the ability to align their actions and the direction of their teams to the business strategy.

What Should Holistic Leaders Pay Attention To?

When business strategy leadership is strong, holistic leaders pay attention to the following:

- Developing customer-focused strategies that create competitive advantage for the entire business
- Focusing their organization on the targeted set of strategic initiatives and reducing the amount of non-aligned work that does not support the strategic direction
- Anticipating threats that could affect the implementation of the strategy and preparing a response in the event the threats become reality

- Mobilizing the organization to achieve the strategy, helping employees understand the strategy and inspiring them to give their maximum effort
- Continually evaluating the effectiveness of their work to ensure it supports the strategy and making course corrections as required

Culture and Values Leadership

What Is It?

Culture and values represent an enduring force that can shape an organization's ability to sustain competitive advantage. Leaders must focus on building the culture and values that the organization requires to drive customer leadership and, ultimately, to achieve the desired business outcomes.

Why Is Culture and Values Leadership Important?

This leadership element is important because culture and values help align and engage employees to implement the organization's business strategy. Culture and values also play an important role in attracting the right talent to the organization. Holistic leaders understand the crucial role that culture and values play in guiding day-to-day behaviors and decisions. They know that culture and values are not simply the purview of the HR department, but rather, the responsibility of every leader in the organization.

What Should Holistic Leaders Pay Attention To?

When culture and values leadership is strong, holistic leaders pay attention to the following:

- Leading culture change by shifting employees' mindset and rewarding new behaviors that exemplify the desired culture
- Recognizing and celebrating employees' demonstrations of the values and putting those who understand and exhibit the values in critical positions

- Selecting, developing and promoting others who live the values
- Using the culture and values to create a compelling place to work
- Driving employee engagement by creating environments that encourage employees to personally invest in their work
- Committing to being role models of the culture and values

Organizational Leadership

What Is It?

Organizational leadership refers to the ability of leaders to transcend functional boundaries and align and engage the organization to focus on delivering customer value and achieving business goals. Traditionally, functional leaders did a good job of leading their part of the organization (or team)—we refer to this as "leading within the box."

Holistic leaders balance the need to manage within their box with the need to "lead outside the box." This is the world of organizational leadership, and it requires leaders to balance functional or departmental demands with the horizontal holistic demands across functional boundaries.

Why Is Organizational Leadership Important?

Leaders today are expected to have an enterprise-wide perspective and work together seamlessly across organizational boundaries. This means that leaders need to balance two aspects of high performance: alignment and engagement. *Alignment* is the degree to which business units, departments and teams are able to work together efficiently, moving the entire organization in lock step. *Engagement* refers to the personal investment of employees in their roles and in their organization.

Holistic leaders recognize that the path to long-term, sustained success comes from attending to both alignment and engagement. Unlike managing within the box, organizational leadership requires leaders to marshal people over whom they don't have direct control. To be successful, leaders need to be able to influence key stakeholders (e.g., employees, fellow leaders, suppliers, advocacy groups and regulators) even when they don't report to them.

What Should Holistic Leaders Pay Attention To?

When organizational leadership is strong, holistic leaders pay attention to the following:

- Working in the interest of the whole enterprise, rather than just their functional areas
- Promoting alignment by building relationships and influencing key stakeholders across organizational boundaries
- Fostering integration across the organization through shared learning among departments, joint planning and problem solving, common processes and collaboration on specific cross-functional initiatives
- Leading up and down (vertically) and across the organization (horizontally) by working together with other leaders to break down functional silos
- Considering the "ripple effects" of their actions on other parts of the organization

Team Leadership

What Is It?

In many organizations, the promise of teams is elusive. Team leadership refers to harnessing the potential of each team member to create a whole that is greater than the sum of its parts. It involves those fundamentals that build and motivate productive work groups.

Why Is Team Leadership Important?

In Chapter 2 we said that the complexity of the business climate presents leaders with adaptive challenges.[6] These challenges typically do not have easy answers. As a result, organizations cannot rely on a few minds at the top to resolve adaptive challenges. Teams are required, because they ensure that organizations are able to bring collective intelligence to bear on the opportunities and challenges of a complex business environment.

What Should Holistic Leaders Pay Attention To?

When team leadership is strong, holistic leaders pay attention to the following:

- Helping individuals on the team get to know one another and to "gel" as a team
- Leading the team to create commitments that guide the team's behavior and performance
- Measuring the team against shared team goals and encouraging individual team members to share goals with each other
- Helping team members understand the interdependencies with one another
- Establishing a clear decision-making process for the team
- Applying individual and team coaching to ensure understanding of the holistic challenges and to enhance team performance

Personal Leadership

What Is It?

Personal leadership is the final element of the Holistic Leadership Framework, and it refers to the ability of leaders to lead in a more reflective and contemplative manner so they can effectively manage the pressures they face on a day-to-day basis. Leaders slow down and become more purposeful in their practice of leadership.

Why Is Personal Leadership Important?

Leaders today move quickly to respond to pressure situations and hypercompetition. Often leaders are under so much pressure that they have little time to sit back and approach their practice of leadership in a measured, thoughtful manner. The element of personal leadership helps leaders be more deliberate so they can effectively manage the pressures they face daily.

What Should Holistic Leaders Pay Attention To?

When personal leadership is strong, holistic leaders pay attention to the following:

- Cultivating personal credibility and earning the respect of others by achieving results
- Practicing humility by relating to others in their organizations without being arrogant or self-absorbed
- Acquiring a personal perspective and finding new ways of seeing the adaptive challenges of the business
- Helping other leaders develop by sharing insights and experiences and by giving them opportunities to lead
- Developing shared understanding of critical business issues in day-to-day conversations
- Exercising balance to ensure others have the energy and focus to be at their best both at work and in their personal lives

HOLISTIC LEADERSHIP Q&A

The facilitator in our story at the beginning of this chapter encouraged the participants to ask questions at the end of the seminar. He knew that holistic leadership would be a tough concept to grasp for those who had been promoted repeatedly for their technical expertise. The questions and his answers are listed below:

1. Do we need both management and leadership?
Of course we do. We need functional management and also holistic leadership.

2. Why is functional leadership dysfunctional?
We already have functional management. If we add functional leadership, we will further focus the leader exclusively on the function, which will entrench the silo mentality and reduce alignment to the overall business direction.

3. Can I be a functional manager without holistic leadership?
Yes. That is the problem we find in many organizations. Too many leaders are functional managers exclusively. You can plan and execute

the activities of a particular function without necessarily paying attention to all six elements of holistic leadership. But remember, if you stay focused on your functional view, you will only be a manager and not an effective leader. It is time for all leaders to raise the bar and practice holistic leadership.

4. Can I be a holistic leader even if I am not managing a function?
Yes. All employees need to be holistic leaders. At times, some leaders are exclusively holistic leaders, such as project leaders of cross-functional teams, corporate resources servicing the entire company and all leaders who participate in developing the business strategy for the entire organization.

5. How much time should I devote to functional management and to holistic leadership? What is the formula?
The answer is 100 percent to both functional management and holistic leadership. As you engage in your functional management role, you have an opportunity to simultaneously pay attention to the six elements. The holistic leadership perspective should shape how you make functional management decisions on a daily basis.

CONCLUDING COMMENTS

Increasingly, leaders in all organizations are being expected to change how they lead. The expectation is that they will expand their focus from functional management to include an emphasis on the holistic view of leadership. Leaders need to personally commit to making the transition. The next chapter explores the skills and behaviors that holistic leaders call on to bring to life each of the elements of the Holistic Leadership Framework.

CHAPTER FIVE

The Individual Leader Dimension:
The Five Capabilities of Holistic Leaders

Leaders today are being challenged to change how they lead. This change requires them to expand their focus from functional management to holistic leadership. How can leaders effectively make this transition?

There are essentially two steps:

1. Begin by paying attention to the six elements of holistic leadership: customer, strategy, culture and values, organizational, team and personal leadership.
2. Understand and apply the five capabilities of holistic leadership to the six elements. These five capabilities are the skills that leaders call on to bring each of the six elements to life.

In Chapter 4, we explored in detail the first step by examining the six elements of holistic leadership. In this chapter, we continue the discussion by describing the five capabilities of holistic leadership and why they are important for leaders and their organizations. We conclude the chapter with the 30-Cell Grid of Holistic Leadership Behaviors, which is a comprehensive map of holistic leadership. The grid details the behaviors of holistic leaders by describing how leaders apply their skills (capabilities) in the different areas (elements) they are paying attention to.

THE FIVE CAPABILITIES: WHAT HOLISTIC LEADERS NEED TO BE GOOD AT

We will begin our exploration of the five capabilities with an example of a leader challenged with the task of transitioning to holistic leadership.

Mark was a 36-year-old former category manager who had just been appointed the VP of Marketing at a large packaged goods company. He was extremely intelligent and respected by everyone for his abilities. Recently, he had won acclaim for turning the company's number one product line from a third place market share to first. Since Mark was a new executive, the company provided him with an executive coach for the first 100 days in his new role. This was a common practice to ensure that new executives started on the right path.

The executive coach assigned to Mark had a direct style. He began the first session with a compelling question: "What do you think you need to be 'good at' as a new executive in this company?" Mark was not expecting the question but responded quickly by saying, "I need to develop a good marketing strategy and to manage my department to effectively deliver on our strategy." The coach replied, "Your answer is only partially correct. You described your functional management responsibility. This is what has made you successful in the past. However, you will find it will no longer be enough for you to succeed in the future." While intrigued by what the coach had said, Mark had an impatient streak and commented, "Well, give me the checklist of things I need to be good at, so I can start doing them right away." The coach remarked, "I wish it were that simple. What we're talking about is more fundamental than a checklist."

The coach then described the six elements of holistic leadership and the relationship between functional management and holistic leadership. Mark was keen to succeed in his new role, so he listened intently. As the session ended, the coach asked Mark to summarize what he had heard about holistic leadership. Mark replied, "The bottom line is that I need to start paying attention to different things now. My success will not be solely a result of my marketing expertise. I need to think about leadership more holistically. I need to first determine customer needs and competitive challenges to help create the marketing strategy. I then need to work cross-functionally to align the organization and engage my team with the strategy." The coach then gave Mark an assignment. His task was to start paying attention to the six elements of holistic leadership. Mark agreed to do this and to report back at their next session.

The coach began the next coaching session by asking Mark, "We spent a lot of time in our last session talking about the types of things leaders need to pay attention to; was that helpful?" Mark answered immediately, "It was helpful, and I did look at things differently the past couple of weeks. But I can't help but feel that all I'm doing is observing. I'm not an observer; I'm a doer. I don't want to be paying close attention while the train goes off the tracks—I want to keep the train on the tracks. I need to know what to do—not just what to pay attention to." "All right," the coach replied. "At the first session, I gave you part of the answer—the six elements of holistic leadership. Before I can get anywhere near the type of leadership checklist you're looking for, we need to talk about another important idea—what leaders are 'good at.'" The coach then wrote on the whiteboard, "The five capabilities of holistic leaders."

Many leaders in today's organizations are confronted with the same challenge Mark encountered—to successfully transition to a more holistic approach to leadership. As we have stated, leaders need to begin by paying attention to the six elements. They then need an understanding of what holistic leaders do and what they are good at. We call these skills the "five capabilities of holistic leaders," and they are presented in Figure 5.1:

Figure 5.1 *The Five Capabilities of Holistic Leaders*

These five capabilities apply across all elements of holistic leadership. As with the elements, any single capability is not sufficient to produce holistic leadership. But when the capabilities are all demonstrated and are used to support all six elements, they form an integrated approach to leadership.

In the section below, we describe the five capabilities in detail. For each, we provide a definition of the capability, a description of why the capability is important, and some examples of what holistic leaders are good at when they are strong in that capability as applied in the six holistic leadership elements.

Capability 1: Sensing

What Is the Capability of "Sensing"?

Sensing is the leader's ability to understand the perspectives of others. It involves collecting information from a variety of sources and using that information to recognize and anticipate what stakeholders value, need and want. The key sensing skills are considering, communicating and anticipating.

Leaders who engage in sensing spend a great deal of time talking to others, asking open-ended questions and actively listening to ensure they comprehend other people's intended meaning. Strong sensors try to "walk a mile in the other person's shoes," not only to see their view of the world, but also to imagine the impact of different courses of action.

> The key sensing abilities are considering, communicating and anticipating.

Why Is "Sensing" Important?

Sensing is important because it provides leaders with the data to guide their actions and decisions. Without current information about the internal and external environment, leaders may have an insular perspective or base decisions on false or outdated assumptions.

Consider how sensing is important as applied in the holistic leadership elements:

- *Customer Leadership:* Being effective at the capability of sensing is essential to customer leadership. Some leaders are too inwardly focused and do not consider the current and emerging needs of external customers; their insular perspective reduces the likelihood that they will deliver the value the customer is looking for.

- *Business Strategy Leadership:* Being capable at sensing also is essential for leaders in the area of business strategy. They must be able to explore, understand and anticipate the changes in the business environment that will affect their organization so that they can develop the kind of strategy that delivers competitive advantage.

- *Culture and Values Leadership:* Sensing is also fundamental to help the leader know the pulse of the organization and to pick up on any subtle shifts in the culture that might be of concern.

- *Organizational Leadership:* Organizational leadership requires a leader to have an appreciation of the perspectives of different departments and functions, and allows for greater cooperation and reduced conflict.

- *Team Leadership:* A leader needs to have strong sensing abilities to understand team members' points of view and to predict which motivational strategies will be most effective for different individuals. Sensing also allows a team leader to pick up on group dynamics that can undermine effective team functioning.

- *Personal Leadership:* Sensing allows leaders to understand how they are perceived and the impact their actions have on those around them. The ability of leaders to anticipate how others are reacting to them is critical because it underlies their ability to tailor their approach to the situation.

Leading without sensing is like trying to drive a car wearing a blindfold and ear plugs. It is possible, but there are significant risks. In organizations where sensing capabilities are poor, elaborate strategies can be defended and well implemented, but the result can often be "a solution in search of a problem." Strong sensing anchors the approach to the needs of the situation.

How to Apply Sensing Capabilities to the Holistic Leadership Elements	
Customer Leadership	Define what is important to the customer.
Business Strategy Leadership	Stay attuned to the myriad of different business drivers and know what business trends will have the most significant impact over time.
Culture & Values Leadership	Remain in sync with what is important in the organization and with a broad cross-section of the organization's employees.
Organizational Leadership	Appreciate the different perspectives of others from different parts of the organization.
Team Leadership	Perceive the individual and team dynamics at play and the impact that members of the team have on one another.
Personal Leadership	Show an awareness of styles of others and alter your own style to suit different individuals and situations.

Capability 2: Creating

What Is the Capability of "Creating"?

Creating is the ability of leaders to build new solutions in response to situations and to what they have learned from sensing the environment. Creating involves developing innovative approaches that correspond to the needs of the situation and the stakeholders. The key creating skills are building, defining and envisioning. Leaders who are good at creating are able to imagine the future, to work in the abstract and to deal with hypothetical scenarios. They innovate and strategize new ways of adding value that might not be apparent to others. They "play out" their approach and extrapolate the impact it will have on the organization and its customers.

> The key creating skills are building, defining and envisioning.

Why Is "Creating" Important?

Creating capabilities are critical because they help leaders respond effectively to marketplace opportunities. Consider how creating capabilities are important as applied in the holistic leadership elements:

- *Customer Leadership:* Without strong creating skills among leaders, competitors will consistently be first to market with innovative products and services that ensure customer satisfaction.

- *Business Strategy Leadership:* The ability to define and create a new reality underpins the development of a strategy that leads to competitive advantage.

- *Culture and Values Leadership:* Culturally, creating is important because leaders must be deliberate about the type of organizational culture that will support the achievement of the strategy. Without a strong vision of the desired culture, the organization is likely to languish with the default culture that has emerged over time.

- *Organizational Leadership:* Organizationally, leaders must be able to build the type of structure that will support the strategy. Beyond visualizing the formal vertical structures that are required, they must be able to identify the lateral mechanisms that support communication and decision making across the boundaries of the organization.

- *Team Leadership:* Creating abilities enable leaders to employ different types and compositions of teams depending on the situation. The ability to build varied types of teams increases the organization's flexibility and reduces the likelihood that the organization will under- or over-resource a given opportunity.

- *Personal Leadership:* It is important for leaders to be self-reflective and deliberate about the type of leader they want to be—in essence to "create" a personal brand that maximizes their contributions to the organization.

Without strong creating capabilities, leaders are unable to develop appropriate approaches to solve the challenges of a complex business environment. Instead, they rely on the strategies that have worked in the past. Although some organizations have succeeded by copying the innovative strategies of their competition, without strong creating abilities, leaders and their organizations must be resigned to the position of follower.

How to Apply Creating Capabilities to the Holistic Leadership Elements	
Customer Leadership	Develop the right products and services to ensure customer satisfaction.
Business Strategy Leadership	Develop a strategy that optimizes the use of the organization's resources to succeed in the business environment.
Culture & Values Leadership	Describe the culture in a way that will engage employees and align them with the organization's strategic objectives.
Organizational Leadership	Design the right structure and processes to support strategy execution.
Team Leadership	Compose different team structures for different situations.
Personal Leadership	Envision the type of leader they would like to be and the path that will take them there.

Capability 3: Implementing

What Is the Capability of "Implementing"?

Implementing is the ability of the leader to mobilize resources and people to execute on the plans that were created. It involves applying appropriate methods of communication and motivation to move people to action and embed a solution within the organization. The key implementing skills are rallying, deploying and executing to turn plans into action. Leaders who are good at implementing are able to marshal resources to direct toward their activities. They communicate effectively to motivate people to take action. Implementing skills include the ability to delegate and to be comfortable in holding people accountable to their commitments.

> The key implementing skills are rallying, deploying and executing.

Why Is "Implementing" Important?

Implementing is a fundamental leadership skill because it is the ability that supports forward motion. If sensing allows leaders to see the lay of the land, and creating allows leaders to define a vision of the future, implementing is the skill that takes them there.

Consider how implementing is important as applied in the holistic leadership elements:

- *Customer Leadership:* Implementing is especially important in the area of new product development, where it can mean the difference between an innovation that revolutionizes the industry and a creative idea that never reaches the market. A leader with strong implementing capability brings these new approaches to the market in a way that meets the needs of the customer.

- *Business Strategy Leadership:* Without strong implementing capabilities, the leader is unable to convert strategies into action.

- *Culture and Values Leadership:* Culturally, implementing is critical because it allows the leader to understand which structures and processes will help move the organization in the desired direction. A leader who is a strong implementer will know how to shift mindsets, to reinforce the right behaviors, and to isolate and eliminate countercultural behaviors to initiate and sustain culture change.

- *Organizational Leadership:* Implementing is important because it enables the leader to bring the sterile organization chart to life. The leader must mobilize individuals into a vibrant and dynamic organization where the structures facilitate communication and action that will drive the company forward.

- *Team Leadership:* At the team level, implementing is about action and accountability. It is important for leaders to have implementing skills so that they can set clear expectations, establish well-aligned objectives and continuously motivate team members to achieve goals.

- *Personal Leadership:* Rather than having a relentless drive to produce short-term results, good implementers know how to manage their energy to sustain long-term performance.

Without strong implementing skills, leaders are unlikely to drive great performance. They will likely struggle to produce results or will burn out by pushing too hard for too long. Either way, poor implementers will have difficulty building credibility in the organization.

How to Apply Implementing Capabilities to the Holistic Leadership Elements	
Customer Leadership	Bring new approaches to the market in a way that best meets the needs of the customer.
Business Strategy Leadership	Effectively cascade strategy into increasingly more specific and relevant operational plans and mobilize the organization to achieve its priorities.
Culture & Values Leadership	Set the structures and processes that can be used to transform culture and institutionalize a new set of behaviours.
Organizational Leadership	Bring together diverse groups to work toward a common goal.
Team Leadership	Build clear expectations and accountability and use feedback and coaching to enhance results.
Personal Leadership	Exhibit strong initiative and use various techniques to preserve energy and sustain performance.

Capability 4: Connecting

What Is the Capability of "Connecting"?

Connecting is the ability of the leader to build relationships with different stakeholder groups. It involves building trust, influencing expectations and establishing a candid discourse. The key connecting skills are communicating, relating and influencing. Leaders who are good at connecting are able to build an effective dialogue with others. Through this dialogue, they create a common understanding and shared goals. Leaders who are strong connectors are able to empathize and gain the trust of others.

> The key connecting skills are communicating, relating and influencing.

Why Is "Connecting" Important?

Connecting is an important capability of leaders because it allows them to keep diverse stakeholders engaged. Consider how connecting is important as applied in each of the holistic leadership elements:

- *Customer Leadership:* Leaders who have connecting skills create rapport with customers, shape and manage their expectations and build customer loyalty. While strong creating abilities lure customers in with well-designed products and services, leaders with connecting abilities develop the emotional attachment that will keep customers coming back. This emotional connection is the primary goal of branding initiatives, which started in packaged goods companies but have become pervasive in most industries today.

- *Business Strategy Leadership:* A parallel exists in the area of strategy leadership where implementation skills help the leader move employees into action but connecting skills elicit employees' commitment to and passion for the achievement of the strategy. Without strong connecting abilities, leaders will at best capture the head and hands and will not unlock the discretionary effort that comes when you engage the hearts of employees.

- *Culture and Values Leadership:* Within the organization, leaders' connecting abilities underlie shared goals and a sense of camaraderie across different parts of the organization. Connecting allows the leader to build cross-functional relationships based on trust and mutual understanding.

- *Organizational Leadership:* Organizations need to forge strong connections across the business to inspire employees to think of the organization as one large team. In the absence of connecting skills, these overtures seem forced and contrived.

- *Team Leadership:* At the team level, leaders who have connecting skills develop a degree of cohesiveness that is important for effective team functioning. Without cohesiveness, the team will become mired in conflict and will make little progress toward its goals. Furthermore, because many employees today look to their workplace to provide a sense of community, a leader with weak connecting skills risks losing the best and the brightest talent.

- *Personal Leadership:* For individual leaders, connecting abilities are fundamental to building trusting, long-term relationships with stakeholders.

Inadequate connecting capabilities can have serious consequences. For example, in a large professional services firm, the head of a tax practice was known as a guru because of his technical expertise. However, he also was known as a recluse, typically remaining in his office pouring over files and writing memos on key issues. On the few occasions when he granted a meeting, his staff felt he was cold and uninviting. He behaved the same way when he dealt with customers. His inability to connect limited his overall impact in the organization. If he had been a better connector, his expertise could have been leveraged even further to benefit customers and employees.

Without strong connecting capabilities, leaders will struggle to enlist the help of others and will be forced to attempt to accomplish tasks alone. In today's complex business environments, going it alone will seldom be an effective strategy.

How to Apply Connecting Capabilities to the Holistic Leadership Elements	
Customer Leadership	Build genuine dialogue with customers, earn their trust and influence their expectations.
Business Strategy Leadership	Develop shared goals and engage people across the organization in activities that are mutually beneficial.
Culture & Values Leadership	Model the behaviors of the desired culture and values in interactions.
Organizational Leadership	Earn the trust of others and benefit from a strong network within the organization.
Team Leadership	Garner the respect of team members and use that position of trust to open up communication about shared expectations.
Personal Leadership	Live up to commitments, ask for support from others and provide support to others when needed.

Capability 5: Advocating

What Is the Capability of "Advocating"?

Advocating is the ability of leaders to lobby for a stakeholder group or a particular interest and to ensure their position is taken into account in decision making. Advocating involves promoting another's interest and using persuasion to change individuals' decisions and actions. The key advocating skills are promoting, lobbying and defending. Leaders who are good at advocating are comfortable defending unpopular opinions. They are very persuasive and are able to debate and convince others of the merit of their point of view.

> The key advocating abilities are promoting, lobbying and defending.

Why Is "Advocating" Important?

Advocating capabilities are growing in importance in organizations. As heated competition makes survival and success increasingly challenging, leaders must push their organizations to evolve and adapt. Consider how advocating is important as applied to the holistic leadership elements:

- *Customer Leadership:* Success depends on providing greater value in the eyes of the customer and being able to provide it with increasing efficiency. But even excellent strategies can be met with resistance and cynicism. Only those leaders who are able to staunchly defend the case for change and convince others in the organization to make decisions based on the best interest of the customer will move their organizations forward.

- *Business Strategy Leadership:* Without strong advocating skills, there is little passion for issues. Leaders appear to be complacent and passively accept "order" without challenge. Debate on key strategic issues is kept to a minimum, and the opportunity to forge a new path is lost.

- *Culture and Values Leadership:* Leaders can reinforce culture and values leadership by exercising strong advocating abilities. While organizations sometimes view the merit of a decision strictly from the financial or customer perspectives, leaders must advocate on behalf of the organization and its culture. Even financially sound decisions that would contravene the organization's values or reinforce undesired behaviors must be challenged and their risk considered. Some of the most respected companies have earned their reputations because leaders have been willing to make the right decision in the face of difficult situations.

- *Organizational Leadership:* Leaders need to rise above their own functional perspectives and advocate to other leaders the importance of alignment across functional boundaries. Leaders also need to advocate within their own functions so that they fully appreciate how their function contributes to the entire organization.

- *Team Leadership:* At the team level, advocacy is a critical skill that supports the leader in securing resources and opportunities. In organizations where leaders have poor advocating skills, good ideas can go unexplored because no one has the gumption to fight for them. Moreover, if team members feel that their leader won't "go to bat" for them, they will lose respect for the leader and their engagement will suffer.

- *Personal Leadership:* Individual leaders must have the self-confidence to promote their own interests and abilities. When leaders are comfortable discussing their own strengths and career goals, the organization can more effectively manage talent. The savviest of leaders today demonstrate the courage to stand up for their convictions and the capability to influence others. Without strong advocating capabilities, leaders will not be able to promote what is important to them and instead will be pulled in multiple directions by others who are more steadfast in supporting their own ideas.

How to Apply Advocating Capabilities to the Holistic Leadership Elements	
Customer Leadership	Present the needs and the values of the customer and convince individuals to make decisions based on the best interest of the customer.
Business Strategy Leadership	Ensure that strategic alignment is a key criterion for all decision making in the organization.
Culture & Values Leadership	Effectively lobby others to consider the cultural implications of business decisions and to ensure programs and policies are aligned with the desired culture of the organization.
Organizational Leadership	Encourage integrative thinking and encourage decision-making that integrates cross-functional opportunities and issues.
Team Leadership	Build the credibility of the team and garner resources that support the team's activities.
Personal Leadership	Communicate one's desires and expectations and credibly articulate one's value to the organization.

Revisiting Mark's Coaching Sessions

Let's take a moment to revisit the case of Mark and examine his understanding of the five capabilities described above.

The coach began the meeting by saying, "After our last meeting I asked you to reflect on our discussion on holistic leadership and the five capabilities. What insights have you had over the past month regarding holistic leadership?" Mark paused and then said, "It is interesting—I often find myself immediately diving into my functional management role. So now that I have learned to become aware of this, I force myself to start paying attention to the six elements." The coach asked, "What happened when you began to apply the five capabilities in your leadership role?" Mark replied, "First, I recognized that I always thought about leadership as implementing—driving the troops forward. I didn't think as much about the other capabilities such as connecting. I just figured that people who have the right personalities to be leaders are good at connecting with others. I've always been good at that, so I take it for granted. But the other capabilities you talked about—sensing, creating and advocating—I hadn't really even thought about those skills. I think I'm pretty good at advocating— I'm not afraid to stand up for what I believe in. But I'm not sure that I'm very good at sensing and creating. I'm always being taken by surprise by things. Some of my colleagues laugh at me because I'm always saying 'really?' Maybe I have my head down too often rather than staying plugged in to what's going on around me."

Mark added, "I understand what I need to 'pay attention to' and what I need to be 'good at,' but I'm still struggling a little with what I need to do specifically to be a great leader." The coach agreed and said: "Applying your leadership capabilities to each of the different elements leads you to the behaviors you need to be a great leader. Let's conduct a 360° peer, supervisor and direct-reports feedback survey to assess how you are doing. The survey is built on the 30-Cell Grid of Holistic Leadership Behaviors."

THE 30-CELL GRID OF HOLISTIC LEADERSHIP BEHAVIORS

In the descriptions of each of the five capabilities, we discussed how they are applied in each of the six holistic elements. The result is a set of thirty behaviors, which are provided in our 30-cell grid (see Figure 5.2 on page 82). This grid provides the basis for leaders to assess strengths in both the elements of holistic leadership and the capabilities. It can also highlight opportunities for more effective leadership.

As you review the description of each of the cells, are there areas where you had not previously thought about applying one of the capabilities?

Mark's Holistic Leadership Dashboard

Mark and the coach met to review Mark's 360° report that assessed his effectiveness on the individual leader dimension of leadership capacity.

Mark and the coach spent some time discussing the report and what it means. The coach then summarized Mark's behavioral patterns: "First, your colleagues think you're the guy to give a job to when it needs to get done, but they worry that you don't think things through before you jump in. You are a strong implementer across all six elements. However, your colleagues see the need for you to spend more time 'sensing' the lay of the land when lots of stakeholders are involved in a situation." Mark's coach helped him get a deeper understanding of the various patterns that can emerge for a leader and the implications for creating a developmental plan.

Patterns of Strengths and Weaknesses

The 30-cell grid provides leaders with tremendous insights into the current state of their holistic leadership. Three patterns can emerge for leaders who use this valuable tool:

1. ***Leaders have particular strengths (or weaknesses) in a given element.***

   This pattern is evident if leaders demonstrate all the behaviors in one element (one column of the grid). For example, a leader might be a highly effective team leader and bring all the capabilities (sensing, creating, implementing, connecting, advocating) to bear to get the most from his or her team. This pattern also is evident when leaders do not demonstrate all the behaviors in an element. For example, a leader might lack capabilities in the area of organizational leadership and be unable to use strengths to forge connections across boundaries in the organization. Leaders who are weak in a given element need to increase the attention they pay to that area and to leverage their capabilities to add value in that domain.

2. *Leaders are strong (or weak) in one of the capabilities.*
In this case, it is not that leaders are neglecting one or more of the elements. Instead, they are lacking one or more of the fundamental skills—across the board. For example, leaders might be highly effective creators but might lack ability to execute those ideas—demonstrating weak implementing capabilities. Leaders who are weak in one or more of the capabilities have different options for strengthening those skills. One option is to develop their skills by taking a training program, being coached or taking on specific assignments. For leaders who do not feel they can increase their skills sufficiently, there is the option of teaming with others who have strength in the complementary capabilities—building a complete package with two people who have different abilities.

3. *Leaders are not leveraging certain capabilities in individual cells in the grid.*
In this case, there is no element that leaders are neglecting to pay attention to. Nor is there a capability that they lack. Instead, there are skills that they are not leveraging in one or more areas. For example, leaders might be relatively strong in the strategy element but somewhat weaker in applying their sensing capabilities to strategy. This is often evident in leaders who don't spend sufficient time and attention scanning the external environment before developing strategy. Leaders who are weak in a particular cell can benefit tremendously from an awareness of their weakness. Because they are already demonstrating the skill in other areas, it is a relatively minor adjustment to apply those skills to a new element. They can get a large return for a reasonably small investment in their development.

Mark's Final Coaching Meeting

"It really is coming together," Mark said with some relief. "I understand now that holistic leadership is about paying attention to a few key areas and using a core set of capabilities to add value in each of those areas." "Yes, that's exactly what we've been talking about over the past few months," the coach replied. "I think you are seeing now that great leadership is more than just a checklist. I will never be able to predict all the opportunities you will have where the five capabilities

	Customer Leadership	Business Strategy Leadership	Culture & Values Leadership	Organizational Leadership	Team Leadership	Personal Leadership
						The 30-Cell Grid of Holistic Leadership Behaviors: The Individual Dimension
Sensing	Knows what is important to the customer (and what will be important in the future) and knows how the customer will react in response to different situations.	Is attuned to myriad different business drivers and knows what trends will have the most significant impacts over time.	Is in sync with the employees and has an astute awareness of the dynamics of the organization.	Appreciates the positions of others who have different perspectives because they come from different parts of the organization.	Demonstrates sensitivity to the individual and team dynamics at play and the impact that members of the team have on one another.	Is aware of the styles of others and is able to alter his style to suit different individuals and situations.
Creating	Develops the right products and services to ensure customer satisfaction.	Responds to environmental context and optimizes the organizational response given the available internal capacity.	Describes the way of doing things that will engage employees and align them with the strategic objectives of the organization.	Envisions the dynamics of the organization and chooses the right configuration to optimize business processes.	Uses different team structures for different situations and dynamically changes the structure or processes to adapt to changes in the environment.	Is deliberate in her actions and is self-reflective in evaluating her current and future impact.
Implementing	Brings new approaches to the market in a way that best meets the needs of the customer.	Cascades strategy into increasingly specific and relevant operational plans and mobilizes the organization to achieve its priorities.	Knows all the levers that can be used to transform culture and uses these levers to institutionalize the desired behaviors.	Is aware of the interdependencies between groups and is able to bring groups together to work toward a common goal.	Builds clear expectations and accountability and uses feedback and coaching to enhance results.	Shows strong initiative and uses various techniques to preserve his energy and sustain performance.

	Customer Leadership	Business Strategy Leadership	Culture & Values Leadership	Organizational Leadership	Team Leadership	Personal Leadership
Connecting	Builds genuine dialogue with customers, earns their trust and influences their expectations.	Develops shared goals and engages people across the organization in activities that are mutually beneficial.	Models the desired culture and values in their interactions with others.	Earns the trust of others and benefits from a strong network within the organization.	Earns the respect of team members and uses that position of trust to open up communication about shared expectations and engages in candid conversations with individuals on the team.	Lives up to commitments, asks for support from others and provides support to others when needed.
Advocating	Presents the needs and the values of the customer to others in the organization and convinces individuals to make decisions based on the best interest of the customer.	Ensures that strategic alignment is a key criterion for all decision making in the organization.	Effectively lobbies others to consider the cultural implications of business decisions and ensures programs and policies are aligned with the desired culture of the organization.	Encourages integrative thinking and resists decision making that neglects cross-functional issues.	Builds the credibility of the team and garners resources and support for the team's activities.	Clearly communicates his desires and expectations and defends his value to the organization from a position of credibility.

Figure 5.2 *The 30-Cell Grid of Holistic Leadership Behaviors: The Individual Dimension*

will be important. But I can tell you that if you keep paying attention to customers, to culture and values, and to the other elements, you'll find hundreds of opportunities to apply these capabilities—and an infinite number of chances to demonstrate behaviorally that you're a great leader." Mark and his coach continued their discussion. Together they created another 100-day plan to ensure that Mark continued his success as a holistic leader.

CONCLUDING COMMENTS

Many organizations that are just starting their leadership capacity journey find the five capabilities useful to describe the necessary skills for individual leaders and to clarify how they will build leadership capacity. When using the five capabilities with organizations that already have leadership competency models, we find it helpful to map their existing competencies onto the higher-order capabilities, often with two or three distinct competencies together representing each capability.[1]

The 30-Cell Grid of Holistic Leadership Behaviors is an extremely useful tool, helping leaders to see the behavioral pathway for building their individual leadership capacity. Chapters 6 and 7 explore the next two dimensions of leadership capacity—going beyond individual leadership, to organizational practices and the organization's leadership culture.

The Organizational Practices Dimension

Leaders cannot be expected to develop leadership capacity on their own. The organization must support this development by creating a context for it. In this chapter we describe the organizational practices that are explicitly designed to build this capacity (refer to Figure 6.1 on the following page). The organizational practices dimension includes all official practices, programs and policies and their impact on leadership capacity. It includes two main categories of organizational practices:

1. Those that are specifically intended to build leadership capacity, such as leadership development, succession management, embedding leadership in the organization and ensuring executive accountability for leadership capacity.
2. Those that indirectly enhance or restrict the ability of an organization to close its leadership gap and to build its leadership capacity.

CATEGORY 1: ORGANIZATIONAL PRACTICES THAT ARE SPECIFICALLY INTENDED TO BUILD LEADERSHIP CAPACITY

In *The Leadership Gap*, we described in detail the four critical success factors or organizational practices that directly contribute to building leadership capacity for competitive advantage.[1] Figure 6.2, on the next page, depicts these organizational practices.

Figure 6.1   *The Three Dimensions of Leadership Capacity*

Figure 6.2   *Organizational Practices to Build Leadership Capacity*

1. Integrated Leadership Development

Typical leadership development sessions focus on leaders' personal development. These standard courses are useful to help leaders reflect on their personal roles as leaders and how they can improve their individual contributions. However, the value of leadership development significantly increases when the learning concepts are expanded to include their role in leading the team and the organization. Ideally, leadership development programs reinforce an integrated approach that combines personal leadership development with the organization's environmental challenges and its business focus.

The organizational practice of leadership development further increases its value when it extends beyond formal training to a comprehensive strategy for development. This includes alternative opportunities for learning such as special assignments or secondments, individual and team assessment and coaching, formal and informal mentoring, experience-based opportunities and support for networking and communities of interest. But simply introducing these alternative learning methods will not create the desired effect if they are implemented in a fragmented manner. Instead, when organizations use different learning methods in tandem, they maximize the enhancement of learning and the return on investment. Organizations need to implement their leadership development practices in an integrated manner—ensuring that each method is aligned to the overall strategy and is complementing the messages and activities of the other methods.

Consider the following description of an integrated leadership development approach:

A medium-sized electronics manufacturer invested wisely by developing a robust integrated leadership development program. The program's foundation was built on regular assessments of high-potential managers. The company also developed an in-house leadership program that gave managers the opportunity to discuss strategic issues with the company's owner. They also provided external coaches to help managers grow as leaders and to prepare them to assume more substantial roles. This approach was cohesive, with each element adding value to the other.

We will expand the concept of the term "integrated" in Chapter 11 when we consider the need for even broader integrated leadership solutions.

2. Succession Management: Focus on Critical Positions and Key Talent

Most organizations that do succession planning see it as an administrative task of completing required forms rather than as an organizational practice designed to build leadership capacity.[2] Many of these succession planning efforts produce sub-par results. Often, the approach is too generic and focused only on back-filling for executive positions. Organizations need to take a more strategic approach. They need to recognize succession management as a risk-reduction exercise to lessen the threat of not filling critical positions or of losing high-performing talent.

The organizational practice of succession management needs to be future-focused and anticipate the critical skills that will be required to be successful in the future. For example:

> *An organization emerging from bankruptcy had an incumbent chief financial officer (CFO) who was an expert in renegotiating debt, meeting creditor targets with extreme fiscal control and increasing shareholder confidence. However, the succession management process revealed that the anticipated future high-growth business needed a different kind of CFO who would have expertise in growth organizations and in managing the changing cultural environment. The organization needed to contribute to building leadership capacity through its succession management practice by identifying the future requirements of executives and not just the replacement of the current executives.*

Ideally, organizations conduct succession management as a cross-functional practice rather than as a departmental administrative task. All leaders have key talent on their radar; the entire organization—not just specific departments—"owns" high-potential leaders. The executive team reviews critical leadership talent and conducts meaningful and thorough talent reviews.

3. Embed Leadership in the Organization

Organizations that recruit and promote leaders based solely on their technical skills reinforce the functional mindset rather than holistic leadership and miss the opportunity to build leadership capacity. The recruitment and promotion processes can contribute to or diminish the leadership capacity in an organization depending on whether those with holistic leadership capabilities are promoted through the organization or not. If those who have achieved results in an unsustainable way (driving employees too hard, creating conflict instead of cooperation, etc.) are promoted, a strong message is embedded that what you achieve is more important than how you achieve it.

The organizational practice of "embedding leadership" is a process of ensuring that leadership capacity becomes an integral part of the very fabric of the organization. Organizations need to focus relentlessly on "embedding holistic leadership."

One way organizations embed leadership is by making it a part of their "employment brand" so that prospective leaders have a strong and significant expectation of what it is like to work in their organizations. A brand is the visual, emotional, rational and cultural image that one associates with an organization or a product. It packages all aspects of the employment agreement under an integrated set of symbols and key messages. The brand creates a statement to the prospective employee of the work experience that an organization commits to deliver. Integrating messages into the employment brand about the way the organization leads will signal to new and incumbent leaders how they must behave to fulfill the promise of the employment brand.

Another way to embed holistic leadership is through high-profile strategic leadership programs. Consider the following example:

After divesting one of its non-core businesses, a large financial institution needed to transform itself to become more customer-focused and results-oriented. The senior executives realized the transformation could only occur if all the leaders shared a similar belief and understanding about the new kind of leadership needed for the organization to succeed. Prior to the divestiture, leaders operated more as managers of their own business units and departments. After the divestiture, the leaders' entrenched silo behavior became a barrier for the company to move forward. The company needed leaders throughout the organization to align and engage employees to the new business strategy. Leaders needed to work across organizational boundaries and lead together for the benefit of the entire enterprise. The company was able to successfully embed leadership by launching a high-profile strategic learning program targeted to all the company's leaders. The executives and leaders learned to work more effectively as holistic leaders, rather than just as functional managers. They were able to align themselves to the new vision of the organization, to understand the importance of working across organizational boundaries and to engage employees to the new business strategy.

4. Executive Accountability for Leadership Capacity

Historically, the accountability for leadership capacity was either solely with the HR function or held informally by a CEO who was personally passionate about the issue. Neither of these approaches is sustainable; the entire executive team needs to own the accountability for leadership capacity. Many organizations are now formalizing the accountability for leadership capacity through such practices as executives owning talent reviews, executives getting involved in teaching leadership development programs and board committees taking responsibility for the key talent pipeline. Executives are measuring how well they are currently meeting their leadership capacity needs and developing solutions to meet their future needs.

The accountability for leadership capacity also extends beyond executives. Organizations need to put practices in place that foster accountability of all leaders to build their own and their teams' leadership capacity.

CATEGORY 2: ORGANIZATIONAL PRACTICES THAT INDIRECTLY AFFECT THE LEADERSHIP GAP

Category two organizational practices are fundamental practices that organizations use to run their businesses. They are often designed and implemented without any thought for how they affect the development of leadership capacity. Yet they have real impact on this capacity and represent an untapped opportunity (and an under-appreciated threat) for organizations. Each organizational practice sends strong messages about how leaders are expected to lead.

Organizational practices that focus employees' energy on the entire business rather than on functional areas and on creating competitive advantage by delivering customer value are useful to reinforce leadership capacity. Figure 6.3 lists the seven organizational practices in this category that have the greatest potential to be highly leveraged by organizations.

Seven Organizational Practices That Can Be Leveraged to Build Leadership Capacity

1. Customer Service and Sales Management
2. Business Planning
3. Innovation Processes
4. Organizational Design
5. Performance Management
6. Metrics and Rewards
7. Budgeting and Financial Management

Figure 6.3 *Seven Organizational Practices That Can Be Leveraged to Build Leadership Capacity*

1. Customer Service and Sales Management

Most organizations want all employees who are in contact with customers to take personal responsibility for customer satisfaction. Organizations need to further leverage this practice to embed holistic leadership throughout the business. Customer service and sales management should reinforce cross-functional discussions about the customer to help build customer leadership. They also should ensure that the different functional areas are aligned to deliver customer value and thereby reinforce organizational leadership. Eventually, as leaders start taking responsibility for customer satisfaction, they will become more effective at sensing the needs of the customer and aligning product and service development with business strategy.

Customer service and sales management organizational practices should also support the practice of sharing customer data among employees. This practice will allow leaders to:

- Co-create solutions with customers to better meet customer needs, strengthen the customer relationship and deliver increased value
- Be prepared to respond to customer complaints with highly responsive recovery teams
- Empower employees to lobby and advocate on behalf of the customer in all decision making

Effective customer service and sales management practices will increase the leadership focus on customer loyalty and enhance the speed and efficiency with which products and processes are brought to market.

2. Business Planning

The business planning process starts with the organization's vision and purpose and translates the vision into a set of strategies and tactics that deliver competitive advantage. Business planning also includes the process by which organizational goals are cascaded to create functional, team and individual objectives. The business planning process is the main avenue for aligning employees around customer value. If the customer is not at the center of the planning process, it will be difficult for leaders to drive customer value as other outcomes take precedence.

In addition to its role in supporting customer leadership, business planning also is important in promoting the other elements of holistic leadership. The planning process is the primary tool supporting leaders in creating business strategy leadership, as it helps them architect a plan, balance priorities, plan for contingencies, deploy tactics, and evaluate and revise the approach. Business planning also is a very effective alignment tool supporting the creation of leadership capacity.[3]

Business strategy practices should also be leveraged to help the organization's key talent understand the holistic challenges the organization faces. It includes the following:

- Searching for non-traditional competitors and new markets and providing the market intelligence to foresee changes before they occur
- Knowing your customers very well and sensing or anticipating their changes in direction

- Making strategic planning and business decisions with an understanding of the implications on the whole system
- Constructing strategy teams to include the right people, the right functions and the right hierarchical levels

3. Innovation Processes

"Innovation processes" is a broad term for all the organizational practices that move the organization forward and encourage the creativity of all leaders. Some organizations have decided to control innovation and designate a department that is accountable for new ideas. Often, this results in a belief that only the innovation department is allowed to be creative. The outcome is many lost ideas because employees don't share them with their organizations. Innovation practices that are effective drive innovation throughout the organization, whereas innovation processes that are isolated, disjointed or misaligned squander the organization's energy.

Organizations need to support innovation processes that disrupt complacency[4] to ensure employees and leadership generate new ideas that deliver greater value to customers and shareholders. The innovation processes should encourage all leaders to discover the following:

- Highly valued customer-focused enhancements (such as new product or new service development)
- Methods that deliver greater shareholder and stakeholder value
- Creative ways to improve internal processes that make the organization more efficient and effective
- Workplace changes to enhance employee engagement and the experience of working in the organization
- Approaches to further embed holistic leadership and build leadership capacity

4. Organization Design

The organization design[5] practice includes all policies and practices that stipulate how the employees in an organization work with one another and with external stakeholders. As such, these practices set out the vertical relationships (e.g., number of levels, span of control) and the horizontal relationships (e.g., cross-functional teams, project teams).

Organization design can play an important role in supporting or detracting from holistic leadership because it determines how the leaders in the organization are structured to interact with each other. The organization design should support cross-boundary communication and an understanding of the entire organization.

This practice also specifies how leaders are expected to interact with customers. For example, organizational design can structure a customer relationship management approach with a single point of contact, or, alternatively, it can support a product/service-based model with multiple points of contact for each customer. The latter approach would encourage a broader cadre of leaders to understand customer needs.

5. Performance Management

Performance management encompasses all the practices associated with individual goal setting, feedback, and coaching and evaluation. Performance management can be a highly effective tool in building leadership capacity when it emphasizes the tangible outcomes (what leaders need to achieve) and also how outcomes are achieved. In contrast, performance management practices that do not include the manner by which results are delivered may ignore dysfunctional and unsustainable behaviors that sometimes are used to drive results in the short term.

The performance management practice needs to include clear goals that link all the elements of the holistic leadership framework. This is achieved through cascading the vision and strategy and creating clear lines of sight to the customer. It also includes focusing on accomplishing goals and establishing accountability for achieving results. The performance management organizational practice guides leaders to appropriately differentiate performance and accountabilities and to deal effectively with performance-related issues.

6. Metrics and Rewards

The metrics and rewards practice is the organization's main tool for defining and reinforcing desired behaviors. Metrics include all the ways by which the organization evaluates its overall performance, a sub-group within the organization or an individual. The types of metrics an organization uses send very strong messages about the relative importance of different outcomes. For example, organizations that measure customer satisfaction or customer value signal to employees that the customer is important.[6] Similarly, the behaviors or outcomes that organizations recognize and reward are more likely to be seen as important. Thus, rewards that promote cross-functional cooperation or demonstration of the organization's culture and values support holistic leadership.

A balanced scorecard[7] is an effective organizational practice that achieves a clear line of sight of metrics from the organization's vision, its departmental objectives and team and individual performance plans. The balanced scorecard should be leveraged to help leaders begin to think and act holistically as they focus on and deliver their accountabilities.[8]

When metrics and rewards are effective, leaders are compelled to inform other leaders in the organization about decisions that are required. However, if the wrong behaviors are measured and rewarded, the organizational practice of metrics and rewards can also promote dysfunctional behaviors. Organizations sometimes inadvertently measure and reward behaviors that advance the cause of one individual or group but detract from the success of the whole. For example, individual bonuses for performance are sometimes achieved at the expense of team and organizational performance. Also, some rewards drive a short-term focus and diminish the importance of longer-term targets. The measures and rewards need to be thought through carefully so that they motivate the desired leadership behaviors.

7. Budgeting and Financial Management

A budget sends a very important message about the priorities and expectations of leaders. Many organizations are ineffective at leveraging the budgeting and financial management practice for the development of leadership capacity. The presence or absence of financial resources will speak more loudly to leaders about what the organization values. Most leaders will adhere to the budget rather than the strategy when there is an inconsistency or conflict between the articulated strategy and the allocation of financial resources.

Some methods to leverage budgeting to build leadership capacity include:

- Build the business and financial acumen of all leaders and teams so they can understand the financial implications and trade-offs that need to be considered.
- Help leaders understand how to balance priorities to allocate scarce resources to the organization's greatest areas of strategic need.

Budgeting is a powerful organizational practice that needs to be carefully designed. In some cases, when this process is ineffective, it can sub-optimize the performance of an organization and its leadership. For example:

> *One organization had invested in new finance software and hired a new director for the finance department. The department was attempting to implement an organizational practice based on instituting financial controls. The controls could have contributed to developing leadership capacity and business acumen. Instead, they over-controlled the leaders, who then began resenting the extent of administrative reporting that was required. Eventually, several leaders confronted the new director of finance at a meeting. They pointed out that not only were the systems cumbersome, but the finance department was over-controlling. It took the finance department another year before they were able to begin to achieve some adherence to a modified version of the financial system and to recover their credibility.*

When budgeting and financial management are handled effectively, leaders understand decisions and know how to act upon them. The leaders do not allocate financial resources to activities that are misaligned to the strategy. The organization becomes more effective at allocating the budget to foster holistic leadership. The organizational practices support the budgeting and financial management process with face-to-face meetings when required, by implementing technology to foster ongoing communications, and by leveraging technology for knowledge management and work flow effectiveness.

THE 30-CELL GRID FOR THE ORGANIZATIONAL PRACTICES DIMENSION

In Chapter 5 we presented the 30-cell grid for the individual leader dimension. There also is a parallel 30-cell grid (see Figure 6.4 on the following page) for the organizational practices dimension and for the leadership culture dimension (discussed in the next chapter). Each cell describes the norms and standards that support the corresponding leadership behavior. The organizational practices dimension 30-cell grid also reinforces that some organizational practices are designed to directly build leadership capacity and other practices are equally effective in indirectly building leadership capacity.

An Example of How Organizational Practices Can Build Leadership Capacity

Here is an example of how an organizational practice can help an organization close its leadership capacity gap:

> An insurance company prided itself on the high level of service it provided to its customers. In fact, delivering value to the customer was a core value. During a recent executive meeting, the CEO expressed a high degree of frustration that many leaders in the organization were not focused on the external customer. Most directed their energy to their departmental plans, and he did not see enough discussions about delivering value to the customer.
>
> The first potential solution that surfaced was to develop a leadership program that helped leaders understand customer dynamics. The VP of HR was frustrated that every time an issue with the organization's leaders came up, all eyes turned to him. To redirect the conversation to what he believed would be a more fruitful topic, he asked an interesting question: "How do we collect customer data now, and what do we do with it?" The VP of Marketing said, "You know the answer—we are always conducting surveys and focus groups with our customers, and we produce monthly reports." Another VP asked, "But where do those reports go?" The VP of Marketing replied, "Well, they go to the customer account reps and product managers in

The 30-Cell Grid of Holistic Leadership: The Organizational Practices Dimension

	Customer Leadership	Business Strategy Leadership	Culture & Values Leadership	Organizational Leadership	Team Leadership	Personal Leadership
Sensing	Collects information from current and potential customers and disseminates that information throughout the organization.	Formally examines the competitive landscape and makes environmental scanning a fundamental part of the strategic planning process.	Uses a variety of formal and informal tools to understand the culture and the needs and perceptions of employees.	Provides opportunities for employees to understand the perspectives and needs of others in different parts of the organization.	Provides the tools for individuals or teams to better understand one another and to acquire perspective on how to function effectively.	Provides the tools to leaders to help them reflect on and understand their own strengths and weaknesses.
Creating	Puts the customer at the center of new product and service development and builds solutions to respond to emerging customer needs.	Makes strategic planning an inclusive, ongoing process that focuses on building customer value and competitive advantage.	Articulates a desired culture and values that will support the business strategy.	Builds organizational structures that support a focus on the customer and promote dialogue across boundaries of the organization.	Uses and supports a variety of different types of teams, depending on what is best suited to the situation.	Provides programs such as mentoring and coaching to help leaders develop their skills and set a career path.
Implementing	Makes ongoing changes at all customer touch points to continually bring increased value to the customer.	Effectively cascades the business strategy to all levels of the organization, creating alignment of individual activities and focus on high-value activities.	Uses a variety of levers (e.g., performance management, recruitment) to reinforce the desired culture.	Establishes shared goals and metrics and creates opportunities to communicate and move talent throughout the organization.	Clearly communicates team goals and effectively manages the performance of teams.	Provides the tools and accountability to help individuals optimize their productivity and contribution.

Connecting	Provides opportunities and forums to interact with the customer and to shape customer expectations.	Ensures employees stay in touch with key stakeholders both inside and outside the organization (e.g., industry associations).	Provides opportunities for employees to connect with one another and to promote the desired culture and values.	Creates opportunities for communication across the organization and encourages interaction with leaders at all levels.	Provides formal and informal opportunities for team members to interact and build effective working relationships.	Provides the formal and informal opportunities for leaders to build relationships that will help them to be successful.
Advocating	Empowers employees to respond to the needs of customers and to lobby on behalf of the customer in all decision making.	Uses decision making processes to ensure resources are not allocated to activities that are not aligned to the business strategy.	Uses alignment with the desired culture and values as key criteria in decision making.	Ensures that the best interest of the whole organization is taken into account in decision making rather than letting the needs or best interest of one group take precedence.	Provides forums for teams to lobby on their own behalf to secure required resources to meet team goals.	Provides an opportunity for leaders to express their career interests and to help the leader develop in the areas that will increase their value to the organization.

Figure 6.4 *The 30-Cell Grid of Holistic Leadership: The Organizational Practices Dimension*

Marketing." The CEO asked, "Why don't we share these reports more
broadly with all of our leaders?" The VP of Marketing said, "I don't
know, maybe because no one ever asked."

Many leaders within this organization were not focused on their
customers—largely because they never received customer data. Even
though the organization collected it, no one had ever thought to leverage
that practice by sharing it with leaders beyond the marketing department.
Circulating the customer data more broadly was a simple yet powerful
solution. It did not involve a tremendous investment of time or money
(unlike the proposed solution to train leaders on customer dynamics). And
this solution quickly yielded a change in leader behaviors. Each part of the
organization could identify and act on opportunities to increase customer
value—the ultimate goal of holistic leadership.

Three key lessons in this example merit discussion:

- Leadership capacity does indeed exist beyond the individual
  dimension. In this example, the organizational practices not only
  affected leadership capacity, but they also were critical in closing a
  gap in customer leadership.
- Even if organizational practices are not designed or intended to
  build leadership capacity, they can affect the ability of leaders
  to lead holistically. In this particular case, leaders at the insurance
  company might have had the right intentions, but ultimately the
  organization's practices did not support customer leadership.
- Organizational practices can impact on one particular cell (see Figure 6.4 above)— in the above case it impacts primarily on customer
  sensing. The restricted availability of information about the customer was reducing the leaders' ability in all parts of the business
  to focus on customer value.

Now imagine how the practices in your organization touch the 30
behaviors on the grid—either supporting leaders in leading holistically
or reinforcing traditional and siloed approaches to leadership. The more
you think about the different cells in the 30-cell grid—such as Business
Strategy Implementing or Organizational Leadership Connecting—the
more practices you will see as potential opportunities to build leadership
capacity.

> Organizations need enhanced awareness of how their organizational practices impact their leadership capacity.

ENHANCING AWARENESS OF HOW ORGANIZATIONAL PRACTICES AFFECT LEADERSHIP CAPACITY

The table below presents a series of questions to help you enhance your awareness of the organizational practices that affect leadership capacity. For ease of presentation, we have organized the questions to align with the six elements of holistic leadership. (Many practices, though, support more than one element.)

Enhancing Awareness of How Organizational Practices Impact Leadership Capacity	
Element of Holistic Leadership	Organizational Practices
Customer Leadership	❑ Are customer data distributed widely among leaders and employees? ❑ Does the organization clearly communicate customer "touch points" to all employees? ❑ Does the organization make all decisions with an understanding of customer impact? ❑ Do customer metrics drive organizational changes/process improvements to increase customer value?
Business Strategy Leadership	❑ Does strategic planning help to build the strategic and financial acumen of leaders? ❑ Are all objectives aligned from the top of the organization to each individual's performance objectives? ❑ Does the planning process for enabling functions (e.g., Finance, IT, HR) support the business units?

Continued

Element of Holistic Leadership	Organizational Practices
Culture & Values Leadership	❑ Do your organizational practices shape the culture and values? ❑ Does the organization collect and respond to feedback from employees? ❑ Does the organization have an employment brand that is aligned with the business brand and does the employment brand attract and retain talent?
Organizational Leadership	❑ Is the organizational structure designed to promote cross-functional planning, collaboration and communication? ❑ Does the change management approach give as much attention to the people-transition aspects of change as it does to the business aspects of change? ❑ Has the organization leveraged succession management so that it is a key organizational practice to de-risk the organization and to develop future leadership?
Team Leadership	❑ Are teams aligned around common and agreed upon goals that support the overall business strategy? ❑ Does the organization provide tools (e.g., team assessments, development, and coaching) to promote effective team dynamics? ❑ Are cross-functional teams used to bring together divergent groups from within the organization?
Personal Leadership	❑ Do leaders have access to mentors and coaches? ❑ Are formalized leadership programs delivering the intended value and building the leadership capacity required for future success? ❑ Does your organization foster diversity in leaders?

Figure 6.5 *Enhancing Awareness of How Organizational Practices Impact Leadership Capacity*

CONCLUDING COMMENTS

Leaders cannot be expected to develop leadership capacity on their own. The organization needs to create the context that supports this development.

Many businesses emphasize the organizational practices that are explicitly designed to build leadership capacity, such as succession management, leadership development, embedding leadership in the organization and ensuring executive accountability. Often these organizations need to sharpen their focus on these practices. In contrast, most organizations are not considering how they can leverage organizational practices that are not specifically designed to build leadership capacity. We view these practices as the hidden jewel that needs to be nurtured and leveraged as described in this chapter and in Chapter 11, "Act to Build Capacity."

The next chapter explains the third dimension of leadership capacity: the leadership culture dimension. This dimension is perhaps the most difficult to influence, but it also has the most enduring impact on an organization's leadership capacity.

CHAPTER SEVEN

The Leadership Culture Dimension

This chapter explores leadership culture as the third dimension of holistic leadership (Figure 7.1). We will begin with a case example of a regulated monopoly company that needed to evolve its leadership culture in order to build the leadership capacity it required.

Figure 7.1 *The Three Dimensions of Leadership Capacity*

This organization was attempting to transform itself from being a bureaucratic and inwardly focused company to one that was more nimble, competitive and customer-centered. In preparation for deregulation, it undertook a five-day residential leadership development program. The goal was to help leaders understand the transformation taking place and to help them internalize a new set of leadership behaviors. At first, the program met with considerable resistance. Over time, as leaders began to realize the value of the program, beliefs and perceptions began to change.

After about a year of running a series of intensive weeklong programs, the top 200 leaders were taking part in a semiannual strategy session. Upon entering the room, the CEO was struck by the different mood of the leaders in the room; he began his opening remarks by acknowledging the "change in the room." In fact, all 200 leaders (most of whom had already participated in the leadership program) had the same reaction. Things just felt different. There was more optimism; more alignment around customer needs, greater receptivity to change and more collegiality—essentially there was a different leadership culture in the room.

What "changed in the room" in this example? We argue that it was more than a series of intensive leadership programs that created this change. It was more than a change in individual behavior; it was essentially a transformation of the company's leadership culture. An organization's leadership culture is a critical but often underestimated dimension of holistic leadership. What is leadership culture?

It includes the organization's values, traditions, mythology and expectations of behavior about leadership. Although organizational practices provide explicit guidance in each of these areas, the leadership cultural dimension is focused on the implicit rules that guide leadership behavior.

The cultural dimension is much less tangible than the individual or organizational dimensions because culture is, for the most part, impossible to see directly. But even though leadership culture is intangible, it certainly is real. Consider again the gardening analogy introduced in Chapter 3. The nutrients in the gardener's soil can't be seen with the naked eye, but they have a tremendous impact on the growth of the flower.

An abundance of the right nutrients yields beautiful blossoms, but too little of an important ingredient or too much of a harmful one and the flower will not grow. The same is true of the environment for leadership. It can be vibrant and rich—supporting the development of leaders. It can be hostile and challenging—actually decreasing the likelihood that leaders will act holistically. Or it can be neutral or nondescript—with little to offer in support of leaders.

Evidence of the leadership culture is provided by the way people behave and by the nature of the organization's formal practices. Both will reflect the accepted way of doing things. But leadership culture is not simply a function of behaviors and practices. It has its own unique characteristics that can be self-sustaining and self-perpetuating. This is why we have defined it as a third dimension of holistic leadership.

One helpful way of thinking about leadership culture that shows how it differs from organizational practices is to imagine a scenario where all of an organization's managers and leaders are away at an offsite meeting. The employees left behind are quite likely to break the rules (ignoring organizational practices and policies), but they are unlikely to contravene the leadership culture. In some cases, the culture is so strong that the organization's explicit rules (organizational practices) will be ignored in favor of actions that are in line with the implicit rules.

As difficult as it is to see and understand the leadership culture, it is even more difficult to change it. An organization's values and norms evolve over time and are not easily altered. A change in the leadership culture can be supported by changes to individual behaviors (getting leaders to act in accordance with the desired culture) and by changes to organizational practices (changing the explicit rules of the organization in hopes of influencing the implicit rules). Although changes in individuals' behavior or changes to organizational practices may slowly shift the culture, it is likely that the leadership culture will endure longer than behaviors and practices.

Think about your career as a leader and the different organizations in which you have worked.

- How would you describe the leadership cultures of the organizations in which you have worked? Were they strong or weak? Positive or negative?

- Did these organizations deliberately try to envision and create a desired leadership culture?
- Think about your current organization. Is the leadership culture in place now sufficient to sustain your organization's future success?

THE THREE TYPES OF LEADERSHIP CULTURES

As you reflected on the questions about your experiences with leadership cultures, you probably came to the realization that every organization has a leadership culture. Some of these cultures facilitate holistic leadership. Others inhibit it by reinforcing functional leadership. Organizations need to understand leadership cultures and to be strategic and deliberate in creating theirs. Edgar Schein observes, "The bottom line for leaders is that if they do not become conscious of the cultures in which they are embedded, those cultures will manage them."[1]

Let's consider the three types of leadership cultures and their characteristics.

The Three Types of Leadership Cultures

1. The Weakly Embedded Leadership Culture
2. The Strongly Embedded Functional Leadership Culture
3. The Strongly Embedded Holistic Leadership Culture

---

1. The Weakly Embedded Leadership Culture

Some organizations have weakly embedded leadership cultures that are hard to characterize and have little presence in the organization. There may be a lack of positive stories or examples of leadership, unclear expectations about the role of leaders, and little support and mentoring of young leaders.

There are several risks to an organization with a weak leadership culture:

- *The leadership culture may become rooted strongly in the charismatic leadership of one individual:* If a leadership culture is not intentionally defined and shaped, the style of a single charismatic leader may set the tone. For example, in one organization with a weak leadership culture, a default culture began to emerge as one strong and dynamic leader began to gain prominence. Over time, a mythology was established that amplified the leader's contribution. The leader's personality and style became the dominant view of leadership. It shaped whom the organization promoted into leadership roles and who became an executive. Within the organization, other leaders tried to emulate the charismatic leader's behaviors. Though this was at first seen as a strength, over time, it became a weakness of the company. As the business environment changed, a new approach to leadership was required. The prevailing culture was so dependent on the charismatic leader that it prevented the organization from effectively making the change.

- *Leaders may default to functional leadership and lead primarily within their departments and business units:* If an organization does not define and manage the leadership culture it needs, then leaders may simply focus on their functional areas. Without a strong integrating force supporting a holistic leadership culture, leaders promote the behavior that has made them successful at lower levels—strong functional management. The resulting functional leadership culture is not likely to help the organization be successful or enable it to close its leadership gap.

- *The lack of an organization-wide understanding of leadership may lead to unwritten rules:* Leadership behaviors that are not in the best interest of the organization may prevail. The unwritten rules might be communicated through who gets promotions and who is chosen to do high-profile projects. Favoritism may be commonplace with no mechanisms in the organizational practices to address these issues. Whereas a strong holistic leadership culture would reject these dysfunctional behaviors and practices, in a weak culture, they persist.

- *Inconsistent employee experience:* In the absence of a strong leadership culture, there may be a high degree of variability in how employees are led; those in one part of the organization may experience a very different approach to leadership from those in other areas. This inconsistency may erode employee engagement.

Here are some questions to help you identify whether your organization has a weakly embedded culture:

Checklist to Assess If Your Organization Has a Weakly Embedded Leadership Culture

❑ Would you describe your leadership culture to be dull and mundane, lacking vitality?

❑ Do leaders struggle to articulate the kind of leadership culture required for your organization to succeed today and in the future?

❑ Is there no unifying force aligning the organization's practices for building leadership capacity with the behaviors of individual leaders?

❑ Are you concerned that the standards of leadership today will not be sufficient to sustain the future success of your organization?

❑ Does your organization lack a leadership culture that distinguishes it from others?

If several of these characteristics describe your day-to-day experience as a leader, then chances are your organization has a weakly embedded leadership culture. The bad news is that you are not benefiting from a leadership culture that supports the development of holistic leaders. The good news is that at least your culture is not working at odds with holistic leadership and, therefore, may be malleable. In contrast, the strongly embedded functional leadership culture is often very resistant to change. We turn to that scenario now.

2. The Strongly Embedded Functional Leadership Culture

The second type of leadership culture is strongly embedded in the organization, but the norms and standards promote a solely functional approach to leadership.

This checklist can help you identify whether your organization has a functional leadership culture that is strongly embedded:

Checklist to Assess If Your Organization Has a Strongly Embedded Functional Leadership Culture

❏ Do senior leaders behave as the heads of their functions rather than as true leaders of the whole organization? Do leaders at all levels appear to be more engaged in their function than in the success of the broader organization?

❏ Do one or two functional perspectives dominate the leadership culture? For example, does the leadership culture focus exclusively on sales or marketing, or R&D? Are other important functional areas excluded or undervalued?

❏ Are departmental or vertical structures of the organization entrenched, with little opportunity for cross-functional activities? Does this perpetuate functional silos that underemphasize the interdependencies across different parts of the organization?

❏ Does the organization have a rigid chain of command that influences where ideas are generated, how decisions are made and who can speak to whom?

❏ Do deeply held functional perspectives allow only a narrow understanding of business issues and opportunities? Do leaders have difficulty dealing with the complexity of the business environment in which they are operating?

If several of the characteristics feel familiar to you and seem to describe your day-to-day experience as a leader, then chances are your organization has a strongly embedded functional leadership culture.

How did this happen? Some organizations value that approach and foster it intentionally. (Even if it is functional, a strong leadership culture brings clarity to an organization—everyone knows the approach to leadership that is desired.) In slow-moving industries with relatively straightforward challenges, strong functional leadership might be effective. Think of this situation as an organization that can be "managed" but doesn't need to be "led."

Although this might be sufficient for some exceptional cases, our contention is that a functional leadership culture that is strongly embedded is no longer what is required for sustained competitive advantage. In fact, holding on to this kind of leadership culture has significant risks:

- *Functional areas may compete to dominate the leadership culture.* One company had two strong executives—one led Marketing and the other led Research and Development. Those in Marketing saw themselves as the leaders of the company because they were the owners of the sales strategy. The people in R&D saw themselves as the leaders because they developed new products for customers. Both VPs were very capable, but they had created a false competition between parts of the organization. The functional leadership culture was actually derailing the overall success of the company.

- *The leadership culture may not be open to new leaders with different approaches:* This type of leadership culture is particularly challenging for new leaders who join the organization and encounter a series of unspoken rules that govern the way leaders lead. For example, a new middle manager within a healthcare institution saw the need to bring an interdisciplinary group of healthcare professionals together to resolve an internal operational issue. The head of medicine reprimanded the manager because he had failed to acknowledge the role of the department of medicine within the hierarchy of the hospital. The interdisciplinary approach was seen as a threat, and the process was shut down.

- *Some leaders may feel trapped in the organization:* Leaders who believe in holistic leadership but find it impossible to advance this perspective in the organization may struggle with the leadership culture. The risk is that these leaders may disengage or leave the organization, thereby reducing the ranks the organization is trying to build and widening the leadership gap.

- *The organization is unable to respond to its business environment:* Functional leadership can create rigidity within the organization and an over-reliance on solutions that have worked in the past. Without the ability to transcend functional silos, the organization is unable to identify novel solutions that would enable them to have competitive advantage. Over the long term, the organization's ability to sustain success is jeopardized.

- *The approach to leadership is inconsistent with how employees want to be led:* In today's organizations, employees have high expectations of the quality of leadership. Employees want to be led rather than managed. In organizations with strongly embedded functional leadership cultures, employees may have too little opportunity to create their own solutions to problems. They may be stifled by the inability or unwillingness of the leaders to stop doing everything and start leading. This may result in high-potential employees leaving organizations with functional leadership cultures to move to those that support holistic leadership.

If organizations are to be successful, they need to create and embed a holistic leadership culture. For some it will mean evolving from a weakly embedded leadership culture. For others, it will mean a major transition from a strongly embedded functional culture. Either way, organizations need to understand the characteristics of holistic leadership cultures and strive to bring them about.

3. The Strongly Embedded Holistic Leadership Culture

In a strongly embedded holistic leadership culture, the organization works intentionally to create an environment where leaders have an integrated view of the enterprise and can focus the organization's resources on creating customer value. Holistic leadership is valued and seen as a source of competitive advantage. When a holistic leadership culture is strong, everyone from front-line supervisors to the board of directors shares these views. In the next checklist, we present a series of questions to help you identify whether or not your organization has a strongly embedded holistic leadership culture. The questions are aligned to the six elements of the holistic leadership framework.

Whether your organization's culture was cultivated deliberately or whether it emerged in the absence of a more defined alternative, that culture is affecting individual behaviors and the practices your organization puts in place. To support individual leaders in shifting to holistic behaviors, the leadership culture must set high standards and encourage leaders to lead in the best interest of the whole organization.

	Customer Leadership	Business Strategy Leadership	Culture & Values Leadership	Organizational Leadership	Team Leadership	Personal Leadership
Sensing	Expectation that all employees think about and talk about the customer and share what they know.	Leadership culture expects its leaders to be continually scanning their environments and identifying threats and opportunities.	Leaders proactively look for information and seek feedback about the work environment and employee perceptions.	Leaders are finding out what is happening cross-departmentally with total openness and candor.	Leaders understand the importance of team dynamics and ensure that they understand each other's perspectives – it's okay to ask.	Leaders are expected to be open to feedback and reflective in their roles as leaders.
Creating	Expectation that innovation is valued and encouraged – no matter where ideas come from.	Leaders are passionate about directing their efforts on delivering competitive advantage and customer value.	Leaders understand that culture can be a competitive advantage.	All leaders are open to the best structure to satisfy business needs, versus preserving their departments.	Leaders are flexible in forming and "unforming" as they design and implement teams with the "flexibility to do the right thing."	Leaders take initiative to develop their careers and know where they are going.
Implementing	People expect continuous culture improvement – always looking to do things better.	Leaders have a shared sense of ownership for achieving the strategy.	Leaders naturally think about the impact and cultural implications of all business decisions and view opportunities to build it.	Leaders are automatically thinking about how the changes they make affect other parts of the organization.	Leaders take shared ownership of the team's mandate.	Leaders commit to achieving results.

The 30-Cell Grid of Holistic Leadership: The Leadership Culture Dimension

Connecting	People are expected to strengthen customer relationships to drive trust and loyalty.	Leaders are expected to forge relationships across organization to work together.	Leaders have a total openness to diversity and where a person comes from has no impact on idea generation.	Leaders value relationship building and different perspectives across departments.	Leaders value the need of team members to get to know each other, and enjoy each other's company.	Leaders are open to sharing ideas and learning from each other.
Advocating	People are expected to respond to the needs of customers and to lobby on behalf of customers in decisions.	Leaders can advocate both for what to do and what not to do. Culture doesn't support saying something for the sake of argument.	Leaders advocate for direction and for decisions that are culturally based, even if there are conflicts with business decisions.	Leaders ensure the best interests of the whole organization are taken into account in decision-making, rather than the needs of one group.	Leaders are able to defend their positions.	Leaders are able to stand up for themselves without repercussion to their careers.

Figure 7.2 *The 30-Cell Grid of Holistic Leadership: The Leadership Culture Dimension*

The Characteristics of Strongly Embedded Holistic Leadership Cultures	
Customer Leadership	❏ Is the customer the focal point of the culture—is there relentless attention to customer value? ❏ Do leaders have clarity about who the customer is and what the customer values? ❏ Is the customer continually discussed in conversations among leaders and employees?
Business Strategy Leadership	❏ Are leaders continually striving to create new sources of competitive advantage? ❏ Are leaders aligned and engaged around the company's business strategy? Do they have the common drive to execute and implement it? ❏ Do leaders see leadership capacity as a strategic source of competitive advantage and invest in it during both the ups and the downs of the business cycle?
Culture & Values Leadership	❏ Does the leadership culture promote a genuine "community of leaders" where politics is kept to a minimum and the culture is supportive (rather than a "sink or swim" environment)? ❏ Do leaders model and demonstrate the values in how they behave and in how they make decisions? ❏ Do employees across the organization have a consistent experience (being led by leaders who share a common set of expectations about leadership)?
Organizational Leadership	❏ Are leaders in the organization committed to the idea of "one company"? ❏ Do they demonstrate an awareness of the whole organization and its parts? ❏ Are leaders free of "unwritten rules" that prevent them from working cross-functionally?
Team Leadership	❏ Do team leaders promote the goal of leveraging the talents of team members for the betterment of the team and the organization? ❏ Does the organization encourage the use of enterprise-wide teams? ❏ Do team members lead in the interest of the whole organization, rather than solely for the success of their specific team?

Personal Leadership	❏ Are all leaders clear about what leadership means and what expectations the organization has of them in their roles? ❏ Do leaders take accountability not only for their own development but also for the development of their colleagues? ❏ Do leaders have the courage to give each other candid and constructive feedback and help other leaders address issues that may derail them in their careers? ❏ Do leaders demonstrate a high degree of personal maturity?

THE 30-CELL GRID FOR THE LEADERSHIP CULTURE DIMENSION

Figure 7.2 on page 114 shows the 30-cell grid for leadership culture. It parallels the 30-cell grids we provided for leadership behavior in Chapter 5 and for organizational practices in Chapter 6. Each cell describes the norms and standards that support building a strongly embedded holistic leadership culture that will contribute to building the required level of leadership capacity.

CONCLUDING COMMENTS

The three dimensions of leadership capacity are related, but they are not exact copies of each other—the leader behaviors, organizational practices and leadership culture all have different characteristics. But it is important that you do not underestimate the impact of having all three dimensions aligned and driving increased leadership capacity. Leaders acting holistically begin to define the standards for their colleagues and for the next generation of leaders. Sound organizational practices shape and reinforce the right behaviors and encourage more holistic behaviors. Both behaviors and practices influence the nature of the leadership culture. In turn, the leadership culture influences how leaders behave and the types of practices the organization develops. When aligned, the individual behaviors, organizational practices and leadership culture become a self-sustaining engine to build leadership capacity.

We have now completed Part One of this book that describes the persistent challenge of the leadership gap and why building leadership capacity in the three dimensions of individual leader behaviors, organizational practices and leadership culture is essential to overcoming the gap. In Part Two, we lay out the four-step pathway to build leadership capacity in your organization.

part two

SOLUTIONS

The Pathway Forward

"This represents the most important work that I can do as an executive."

These are the words expressed recently to us by a CEO of a large investment company. He was about to embark on a rigorous process of building leadership capacity to ensure the sustained competitive advantage of his organization.

This CEO is part of a growing number of senior executives who understand that one of their primary mandates is to assume accountability for building leadership capacity. This book is focused on mapping out how executives and their organizations can effectively assume this responsibility and master the capability required to build leadership capacity for future success.

In Part One we provided a foundation to help you understand holistic leadership and its importance for building leadership capacity. A thoughtful process for building this capacity is required. It is based on a clear view of holistic leadership as well as a comprehensive appreciation of the three dimensions of leadership capacity: (1) behaviors of individual leaders, (2) organizational practices and (3) leadership culture.

In Part Two we will describe a method for going forward that we call the "Leadership Solutions Pathway." This pathway is a four-step process (see Figure 8.1 on the next page).

THE LEADERSHIP SOLUTIONS PATHWAY

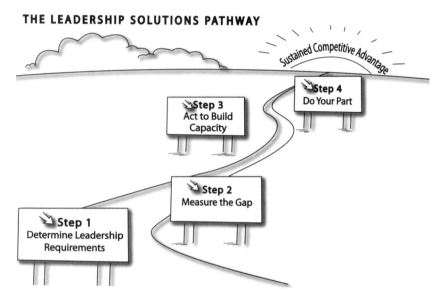

Figure 8.1 *The Leadership Solutions Pathway*

This process is not "one size fits all." Every organization and every leader must respond to their specific situations and tailor their leadership solutions accordingly. They must define their own pathways to meet their requirements for leadership capacity. We have referred to this as the dual response required on the part of organizations and their leaders to close the leadership gap.

AN OVERVIEW OF THE LEADERSHIP SOLUTIONS PATHWAY

In Chapter 2, we stated that building leadership capacity will be a primary business and organizational challenge facing executives for the next decade. Therefore, leadership capacity will demand attention and action on the part of executives and all leaders.

However, as we discussed, the challenge they will face is that traditional approaches are no longer effective. Organizations and their leaders need to implement practices and processes to define, measure and build leadership capacity for competitive advantage. The Leadership Solutions Pathway provides the much needed road map that organizations require. Let's briefly consider the four steps of this pathway:

Step 1: Determine Leadership Requirements

Organizations must focus on the specific leadership capacity requirements that are most critical to their ability to achieve their business goals and to create a competitive advantage. They must factor in everything they know about their external environment and its emerging business needs so that they can choose the nature and extent of the leadership capacity required to sustain their competitive advantage. They need the leadership capacity that meets or exceeds the demands of the external environment—but they should be wise about not going to extremes and creating an unrealistic pipe dream. As one leader said after an innovative idea did not catch on with customers, "One step ahead and I'm a genius; two steps ahead and I'm delusional."

Four actions determine leadership requirements for the future:

- Know your current situation and how your approach to leadership development evolved.
- Consider the future changes in the external environment that will affect your business. Situations such as the consolidation of competitors, increasing regulation or changing customer needs affect the type of leadership that will be effective.
- Predict how the changes in the external environment will require your organization to alter its organizational practices, leadership culture and your overall leadership capacity requirements.
- Engage your leaders in validating the leadership requirements to ensure that these requirements are relevant and that you gain the necessary support and buy-in.

Chapter 9 describes the process required to determine your leadership requirements—i.e., to define the vision of leadership capacity that you want for your organization to ensure your future success.

Step 2: Measure the Gap

Once organizations define the leadership capacity they need for their specific business aspirations, they must measure their current capacity and then compare it with the capacity required in the future.

In many situations, organizations seem to be content to develop leadership capacity without assessing their current state. In this step we recommend a thorough measurement approach to guide the organization to set its priorities and to determine what needs to be done. For example, if your requirements for leadership capacity center on changing customer dynamics and you identify that you are weak in customer leadership, then you will be able to pinpoint that area as the focus for leadership capacity development.

Organizations measure their current leadership capacity by determining how they are doing in the three dimensions of leadership capacity described in Chapter 3. These are:

- Individual leaders dimension: Assess the individual leaders and measure their current skills and behaviors to see which areas are already strong and which need to be developed.
- Organizational practices dimension: Assess the organization's programs, policies and practices and the extent to which they support the development of holistic leadership.
- Leadership culture dimension: Assess the extent to which the organization's norms and values create an expectation of holistic leadership.

In Chapter 10 we describe the Leadership Gap Analysis™, our diagnostic process to measure the three dimensions of leadership capacity. This process represents a focused approach that leads to the better deployment of limited organizational resources. Armed with data gathered from this process, organizations will be able to take targeted action to build the leadership capacity required for the future.

Step 3: Act to Build Capacity

The third step is to start moving the business forward to the desired leadership capacity in the precise areas diagnosed in Step 2. Only after the first two steps of the pathway are completed can organizations take meaningful and targeted actions that will move them to build the leadership capacity they require. For many organizations, the desire to accelerate the development of this capacity is driven by the aging workforce, increasing competitive pressures and the focus on the bottom line. Most organizations cannot wait patiently for a new recruiting profile to seed the organization with holistic leaders. Instead, depending on the severity of the needs and their available resources, they must choose the precise areas requiring improvement and the most efficient ways to rapidly meet their leadership capacity.

Chapter 11 describes the four actions that will enable organizations to take the necessary action to build capacity:

- Target areas that have the greatest necessity for improvement.
- Integrate the multiple initiatives to ensure each is aligned to the overall targeted approach to building leadership capacity.
- Accelerate implementation by leveraging all of the dimensions of leadership capacity to create behavior change as quickly as possible.
- Evolve the leadership solution as conditions change.

Step 4: Do Your Part

In the opening of this chapter we explained that building leadership capacity must be a strategic imperative for executives. They must take the accountability to address the issue as they would address any other major threat to the ongoing success of their business. However, this accountability is not just an executive accountability. All leaders also have accountability for building their own personal leadership capacity.

Chapter 12 describes how an individual leader would apply the four steps of the Leadership Solutions Pathway and how they must be engaged with each step of the process:

- Step 1—Define your leadership requirements: Understand the external environment in which they operate. Individual leaders need to then determine their own leadership requirements for their future success.
- Step 2—Measure your gaps: Assess individual strengths and developmental areas to pinpoint the ways they need to develop and refine their personal leadership.
- Step 3—Act to build your leadership capacity: Formulate a plan that will focus on primary gaps and how they will develop their skills in pursuit of their personal vision and then act on that plan.

- Step 4—Do your part in support of your organization's efforts to build leadership capacity: Actively support the organization's journey along the Leadership Solutions Pathway. An essential factor in organizations' success in building leadership capacity is the willingness of each leader to travel down that pathway with the organization. Making this transformation successful requires a mutual commitment from the organization and its individual leaders.

THE IMPERATIVE TO SHAPE YOUR FUTURE

Chapter 13 concludes the book by emphasizing the imperative to shape your own future. It begins by reviewing the seven leadership gap issues identified in Chapter 1, and how each was addressed throughout this book. The chapter concludes by identifying the imperatives of building effective leadership solutions for executives, boards of directors, HR professionals and our society.

CONCLUDING COMMENTS

The Leadership Solutions Pathway lays out a focused and systematic way to bridge the leadership gap and to build the leadership capacity organizations need. It provides a process for organizations to follow to determine their leadership requirements, measure their current leadership capacity strengths and gaps, take targeted action and then sustain the gains that are made. This approach puts organizations in the best position to implement precise actions to transform their leadership capacity. It also prepares them to sustain and evolve the positive changes within a constantly changing internal and external environment.

The next five chapters take you on this pathway to discover how executives must accept accountability to build their organizations' leadership capacity. These chapters also describe the personal accountability individual leaders need to take to build their own leadership capacity and also to support their organization's initiatives to build this capacity. Together, the organization and all of its leaders can overcome the gap and build the leadership capacity they require for sustainable benefit to their customers, employees, shareholders and themselves.

CHAPTER NINE

Step 1: Determine Leadership Requirements

"First say to yourself what you would be; and then do what you have to do."
—Epictetus

Knowing where you are going makes the journey easier. That is the basis of the first step in the Leadership Solutions Pathway (Figure 9.1). Rather than starting with action, start with a clear view of your organization's leadership requirements.

THE LEADERSHIP SOLUTIONS PATHWAY

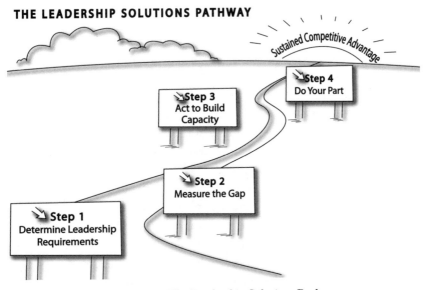

Figure 9.1 *The Leadership Solutions Pathway*

In this chapter we explore how the external environment shapes the type of leadership capacity an organization requires. Next, we describe the five key actions an organization can use to determine its unique leadership needs. Throughout the chapter, we provide a case example that illustrates how one organization implemented each of the five actions of Step 1.

THE EXTERNAL ENVIRONMENT DEFINES LEADERSHIP REQUIREMENTS FOR THE FUTURE

Leadership is one of the most thought about and researched topics in business, and yet the term has no commonly accepted definition. While many scholars and business thinkers see this as a problem, we do not. Although there may be some aspects of leadership that are common to all organizations, the definition of leadership is largely dependent on an organization's own unique business environment and its response to that environment. Some of the categories of environmental changes include:

- Societal norms and values
- Customer expectations
- Competitive forces and industry trends
- Technological innovations
- Political or regulatory dynamics

Rather than seeking a common definition of leadership, we presented a process in our book *The Leadership Gap* that explains how an organization can assess the external environment and develop a strategy and organizational structure in response. Once the strategy is clear, it can be translated into the requisite leadership capacity. That is, the organization must define the nature of leadership required to marshal the desired strategic response.

However, an organization's environment is not static. It changes repeatedly, if not constantly. As the external environment changes, it creates pressure on an organization to consider whether it needs a new strategic response (a new strategy and structure) to continue to be successful. If the organization implements a new strategic response, then new leadership capacity will probably be required. Figure 9.2 on the following page illustrates this continuum and the relationship between the external environment—the strategic response—and the leadership capacity requirements.[1]

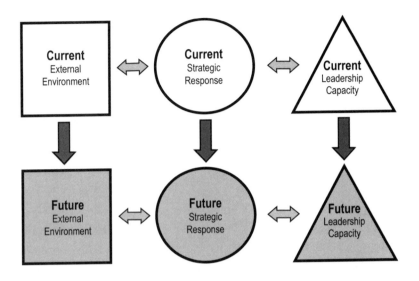

Figure 9.2 *Changes in the External Environment and Their Impact on Leadership Capacity Requirements*

For many organizations, holistic leadership has become the kind of leadership capacity required for sustained competitive advantage. Chapters 4 and 5 of this book devoted considerable attention to describing the six elements and five capabilities of holistic leadership, which are essential to success in new business environments. But holistic leadership has a unique definition in each organization. Therefore, organizations must take the time to explore their future leadership requirements and define the type of holistic leadership they will need to succeed.

THE FIVE ACTIONS TO DETERMINE LEADERSHIP REQUIREMENTS

Organizations should take five key actions to determine their leadership requirements:

- Action 1: Understand Your Organization's Current State
- Action 2: Explore the External Environment in Your Future State
- Action 3: Identify Your Future Strategic Response
- Action 4: Articulate Your Future Leadership Capacity Requirements
- Action 5: Validate Your Assessment of Future Leadership Requirements

Throughout our discussion, we will use a case study of a consulting engineering firm and illustrate how it applied the five actions to determine its leadership requirements.

Here's the background about the company:

Four years ago, a large European firm of consulting engineers found that it had reached a plateau in its growth. It had been successful by winning many of the large infrastructure projects in its home country, but the appetite for major infrastructure projects was waning. After careful analysis, the leaders determined that they needed to implement an ambitious strategy to leverage their infrastructure expertise in developing countries around the world. Their strategy was to acquire mid-sized, best-in-class engineering firms that specialized in transportation infrastructure projects in developing countries.

Initially, the implications of the strategy for most of the firm's leaders were minimal. Leaders who came with acquired companies continued to operate within their original countries and focused on securing and delivering projects tailored to the local demands. The organization benefited from some enhancements to the management and financial practices, which allowed for better monitoring of the firm's performance. They were also able to get a return on investment through successfully leveraging their best-in-class technologies. These technologies were exportable to developing countries with some minor adjustments for regulatory and local municipal requirements. The senior executives were satisfied with the incremental change, but they knew they would need a greater level of leadership in their global operations to fuel the next round of growth.

This case example describes the business challenge that a growing number of businesses are experiencing worldwide—future success is increasingly based on having the right level of leadership capacity in place. In this example, the executives of the engineering firm were hopeful that they could transform their firm's leadership capacity to meet their business needs; however, they did not know for sure if this would be successful.

Action 1: Understand Your Organization's Current State

Before you determine what you need for the future, it is important to understand where you are currently. This process involves exploring the dynamics that generated your current state, which is defined by the external environment, your organization's strategic response and its leadership capacity (illustrated in Figure 9.3).

Figure 9.3 *Current State: The Current External Environment, Strategic Response and Its Leadership Capacity Requirements*

In Figure 9.4 on the following page we present a set of questions designed to help you arrive at an understanding of your organization's current level of leadership capacity. Not all of the questions will be relevant in all cases, but use those that apply to stimulate discussion.

The outcome of Action 1 is that the organization's leaders create a common understanding of their organization's current state and how the current type of leadership came to be. With this clearly understood, it is then possible for the leaders to begin exploring their organization's *future state*.

Case Study: Action 1

Let's revisit our case study and see how the engineering firm gained a better understanding of the conditions that led to the current state of leadership capacity.

Current External Environment	Current Strategic Response	Current Leadership Capacity
• What are the key trends and drivers in your current environment? • What are the customer dynamics that you are currently facing? • What are the competitive dynamics in your marketplace? • What are the current political, economic, social, technological and regulatory trends?	• What strategies are you using to respond to your current external environment? • To what extent does your strategy position you for success in your current environment? • To what extent does your organizational structure position you for success in executing your strategy? • How have your organizational metrics focused you on successful strategy execution?	• What are the current leadership requirements to effectively implement your strategic response and enable you to succeed in the external environment? • To what extent does your strategic response identify the ways in which your organization acquires, promotes, recognizes, develops and exits leadership talent? • How widely understood is your organization's current approach to building the required leadership capacity? • To what extent does your organization have in place a strongly embedded leadership culture that will support your success?

Figure 9.4 *Questions about the Current State of Leadership Capacity*

The leaders met and began with Action 1: Understand Your Current State of Leadership Capacity. They used some of the questions from Figure 9.4 as prompts to guide their thinking. The team summarized the highlights of their discussion in Figure 9.5.

As a result of their discussion, the executives came to a common understanding that their current strategy had been a good response to their current business environment. They could also see that new environmental trends were creating opportunities that would require a new strategic response and a whole new type of leadership capacity.

Current External Environment	Current Strategic Response	Current Leadership Capacity
▪ Fewer transportation projects being initiated in local markets.	▪ Acquire midsized firms to create local footprints in emerging markets.	▪ Leaders reflect the different cultures and operating styles of their home countries.
▪ Industry consolidation has left four major players, each equally capable of delivering on large-scale projects.	▪ Acquisitions integrated on financial and technology systems but allowed to operate autonomously in their local markets.	▪ Leaders are exceptionally strong technical experts.
▪ Emerging markets are investing heavily in transportation as they become increasingly urbanized.	▪ Attempts are being made to market and sell as "one firm" with a single brand worldwide to compete and win global contracts.	▪ Success has been built upon strong relationships with local governments and business leaders.
▪ International development in Africa and South America is providing funding for transportation.	▪ Organizational metrics reinforce regional structure and drive project management excellence at the local level.	▪ There is little or no strategy guiding the attraction, retention and development of leaders.
▪ Mobile technology and satellite imagery are allowing work to be managed remotely.		▪ There is no unified leadership culture and very few opportunities for leaders to interact with their colleagues from other regions.

Figure 9.5 *Case Study Summary Table*

With a solid understanding of how the environment has shaped your current leadership capacity, you can look to the horizon and begin to anticipate the future environment.

Action 2: Explore the External Environment in Your Future State

In Action 2 you look specifically to the future and map out the trends that you believe will define the environment of the future. A thorough understanding of the emerging environment will be the basis for your next strategic response and your requirement for leadership (see Figure 9.6 on the following page).

Figure 9.6 *Future State: The External Environment, the Strategic Response and Its Impact on the Required Leadership Response*

The future environment for your organization may differ from the current environment due to one or more of the following scenarios:

- *External changes to the environment:* In this scenario your organization may not have changed, but the environment around it has changed significantly. This can be due to external factors such as changing customer needs, increasing (or decreasing) competitive pressures, shifting political or economic forces, or even technological advances that reshape the market in which the organization operates.

- *Your organization successfully reshaped the environment:* In this scenario your organization is the source of the changes in the environment. This can be due to its influence on how business is done in your market through customer intimacy, product innovation or operational excellence.[2] Ideally, your impact on the environment was designed to give you a competitive advantage that cannot be easily replicated by your competition.

- *Your organization's growth or decline moves it into a new environment:* It is also possible that the external environment has not changed but rather the changes in your organization have shifted it into a new environment. For example, the growth or decline of your business could place your organization in a different environment than your current one. In the case of the engineering firm, growth has transformed it into a global organization that will now be affected by global, rather than just regional, trends.

As an executive team, create a list of all the trends you can think of in the external environment. Even trends that seem irrelevant at first might have an impact, so don't be too selective. Compare the future environment to the current one:

- Is the change from the current to the future external environment significant enough to require your attention?
- Will the strategy and structure need to change to capitalize on opportunities in the environment and to mitigate threats?
- Will the leadership capacity need to change to support the changing strategic response?

If the answer to any of these three questions is "yes" then proceed to Action 3 to define the implications of the changing environment on your strategic response.

Case Study: Action 2

Let's return to the case study of the engineering firm.

The executives held a follow-up meeting to discuss Action 2. As they discussed the major trends affecting their business, several themes emerged.

- *Competitive Forces:* Consolidation in the industry was creating strong competition. In countries with the capital to invest in infrastructure, the competition was focusing on innovation and quality, rather than on price. In developing countries, price competitiveness was still an issue.
- *Political and Economic Trends:* Increasing regulatory controls were raising the cost of projects and constraining profitability. Personal relationships and strong regulatory affairs capabilities were becoming much more important.
- *Social Trends:* The company wanted to work in cities and countries with larger populations. Although general labor was readily accessible in these countries, skilled workers were scarce. Working in countries with different religious and cultural customs would require greater sensitivity to issues such as the role of women on local projects.
- *Technology Advances:* Video and web conferencing, mobile computers and satellite telephones would soon allow the firm to

manage projects from anywhere in the world. This would reduce the necessity for travel and mitigate the risk of projects in unstable regions.

- **Customer Needs:** Customer needs were diverging. In the developed world, there were fewer new projects but more projects to upgrade infrastructure. Upgrading was significantly more complex to manage because the projects needed to accommodate constant traffic even during construction. In the developing world, the projects were simpler, but the governments were motivated to use local workers to create jobs and build capability. Finally, the firm was beginning to see work from large multinational organizations that were beginning to outsource their engineering work in an effort to reduce their own costs. As the executives examined all the trends, they realized their organization had to contend with some threats. It was also positioned to take advantage of growth opportunities. They felt poised to leverage their success with local governments and ready to expand to the private sector to secure large multinational transportation projects.

Now, let's consider the next action organizations must take in determining future leadership requirements.

Action 3: Identify Your Future Strategic Response

After executives discuss the various trends affecting the future external environment, they then need to plan their strategic response. Most often, this response is reflected in changes such as the following:

- **Revise the business strategy**—to capitalize on the opportunities and to mitigate the risks inherent in the external environment.
- **Evolve customer relationships**—to enhance the level of customer value and create enduring customer relationships.[3]
- **Restructure the organization's vertical reporting relationships**—to facilitate more effective communication and focus on the activities set out in the strategy.
- **Put in place lateral teams or processes that cut across the vertical structure**—to foster dialogue between groups with common

interests across the organization. For example, if vertical structures are based on functional areas, lateral teams might be organized around products or customer segments.

- *Develop external vendor and outsourcing relationships*—to increase focus on core competencies and create efficiencies in non-core areas.

- *Revamp the metrics used to evaluate success*—to focus the organization on what needs to be achieved in the new environment.

The organization needs to build the structure to support strategy execution:

- *Structure always follows strategy*: Develop the strategy to respond to the environment before you consider the changes that might be required to the organizational structure.

- *Lateral processes and teams are as important as the vertical structure*: If the organization's vertical structure is too powerful, a silo effect can occur, with the potential of limiting the success of lateral teams that work cross-functionally. Two guidelines for ensuring that lateral teams and projects have the opportunity to succeed are: 1) create lateral teams and processes for groups that naturally talk to each other and work together and 2) establish clear reporting relationships to ensure lateral processes are embedded in the new organizational structure.

- *Have an agile structure so that it can change when you change your strategy*: If a business is changing frequently, then leverage lateral ad hoc teams to change work processes quickly. The agility to change internally needs to be greater than the extent of the changes in the external environment.

- *Develop the strategy and structure with the assumption that you can access the leadership capacity you require*: Stay focused on how to capitalize on the new environment. Avoid limiting your future strategic response by your current deficiencies in leadership capacity.

Case Study: Action 3

Let's look at how the engineering firm implemented Action 3 to determine their strategic response.

> The leaders had determined that changes in the external environment were presenting opportunities for growth. They could expand their business to the private sector and secure large multinational transportation projects. The next action was to explore their strategic response to the new environment. In their deliberations, they considered the various aspects of their future strategic response:
>
> - **Vertical Structure**: They realized the organizational structure needed to change to support the strategy. The current regional structure needed to be supported by global centers of expertise in critical functions such as civil engineering and regulatory affairs. They would also need more effective business alignment of the finance, HR and information technology services to support the global business. All those enabling functions would have to work together to support the organization's expansion.
>
> - **Lateral Teams**: They recognized they needed to create global teams around the different types of projects, such as highways and roads, ports and canals, and railways. Through these teams, they would share learning and improve their techniques to increase the speed and effectiveness of future projects.
>
> - **Sourcing Relationships**: The change in structure had implications for how they would source work. With functions such as civil engineering now centralized in the corporate office, they had the opportunity to outsource lower-level functions such as computer-assisted design. Similarly, the organization was able to use a global firm to outsource its IT helpdesk function to ensure 24/7 service everywhere in the world.

Now, let's consider the next action organizations must take to determine their future leadership requirements.

Action 4: Articulate Your Future Leadership Capacity Requirements

With an understanding of the future external environment and your strategic response, it is now time to determine the leadership capacity requirements needed for future success. This is accomplished by arriving at an understanding of how enhancing holistic leadership will help you deliver the strategic response to the external environment. More specifically, you will have to identify the holistic leadership elements and capabilities that will be particularly important for the new strategic response.[4]

To address these issues, we will use the following 30-Cell Grid of Holistic Leadership (see Figure 9.7 on the following page).

Here is how we suggest you identify your specific leadership requirements on the 30-cell grid:

1. Begin with the row of the six elements of Holistic Leadership. Now read the specific definitions in those columns that reflect what you believe you will need to succeed. Circle the most critical cells.

2. Now shift your focus to the column of five capabilities of Holistic Leadership. Read the specific definitions in those rows that reflect what you will need to succeed. Circle the most critical cells.

The definitions on the 30-cell grid that you identify as most critical represent your desired future leadership capacity requirements. In Chapter 10 we will describe how to measure your current leadership capacity and determine the gap from your current state to your desired future state. The gap between the two will lead to specific recommendations for targeted investments the organization will need to build its requirements for leadership capacity.

Case Study: Action 4

Let's see how the engineering firm approached Action 4—to articulate its future leadership capacity requirements.

With a solid understanding of their future environment and the proposed strategic response, the executive team held another meeting focused on defining their future leadership capacity requirements.

The 30-Cell Grid of Holistic Leadership

	Customer Leadership	Business Strategy Leadership	Culture & Values Leadership	Organizational Leadership	Team Leadership	Personal Leadership
Sensing	Customer Sensing is the ability of the leader to solicit, understand and anticipate the needs and the values of the customer.	Strategic Sensing is the ability of the leader to explore, understand and anticipate the changes in the business environment that will impact their organization.	Culture Sensing is the ability of the leader to solicit, uncover and comprehend the culture of the organization and the impact the culture will have on the ability of the organization to achieve its goals.	Organization Sensing is the ability of the leader to identify key stakeholders throughout the organization and to understand their points of view on business issues.	Team Sensing is the ability of the leader to identify and appreciate the needs and motives of the individuals on the team.	Personal Sensing is the ability of the leader to recognize and appreciate how he is perceived by others and to understand the impact of his actions on others' perceptions.
Creating	Customer Value Proposition is the ability of the leader to build a package of solutions that meets customer needs and is appealing to the customer.	Strategy Architect is the ability of the leader to develop a business strategy that will be the most effective path to building competitive advantage.	Culture Defining is the ability of the leader to envision the type of culture that will support the achievement of the organization's goals.	Organization Design is the ability of the leader to build the appropriate structures to carry out the strategy.	Team Design is the ability of the leader to form the appropriate type of team to meet the needs of the organization.	Personal Intention is the ability of the leader to envision a personal style that she would like to project.

	Customer	Strategy	Culture	Organization	Team	Personal
Implementing	Customer Solutions is the ability of the leader to deploy products and services to optimize customer value.	Strategy Deployment is the ability of the leader to move the organization from planning to effective action.	Culture Embedding is the ability of the leader to put in place the structures and processes that will support the desired culture.	Organization Integration is the ability of the leader to build bridges across the organization by creating opportunities to communicate with people from different functions, levels and geographies.	Team Performance is the ability of the leader to motivate team members to achieve superior performance.	Personal Performance is the ability of the leader to achieve results and to accomplish the goals he sets out for himself.
Connecting	Customer Relationships is the ability of the leader to forge strong bonds with customers.	Strategic Relationships is the ability of the leader to forge relationships with people across different businesses, functions and levels of the organization.	Cultural Relationships is the ability of the leader to develop relationships with a diverse range of employees throughout the organization.	Organizational Relationships is the ability of the leader to build trust with stakeholders throughout the organization.	Team Relationships is the ability of the leader to foster trust and engage in a genuine dialogue with team members.	Personal Relationships is the ability of the leader to earn the trust of others and to develop relationships that provide both business and personal support.
Advocating	Customer Advocacy is the ability of the leader to bring the voice of the customer into the decision making of the organization.	Strategic Championing is the ability of the leader to lobby others about the importance of the strategy and to encourage them to align their actions with that strategy.	Cultural Advocacy is the ability of the leader to champion the importance of culture as a key driver of business success.	Organizational Advocacy is the ability of the leader to promote communication and co-operation throughout the organization.	Team Advocacy is the ability of the leader to rally support for the team from stakeholders in the organization.	Personal Advocacy is the ability of the leader to further his position by effectively promoting his value to the organization.

Figure 9.7 *The 30-Cell Grid of Holistic Leadership*

The team first reflected on the need to enhance holistic leadership. Overall, they knew they needed leaders to be more holistic—ready and able to lead the whole organization. They needed leaders to operate the company as "one firm," to drive a single brand worldwide to compete and win global contracts.

The team then used the 30-cell grid to determine specific leadership requirements. While the team believed most of the cells on the grid were important, they identified a few that were the most critical. Their rationale for the rankings was as follows:

- **Customer Leadership:** This element would be important because leaders would need to succeed in understanding customer needs and identify opportunities to sell cross-country services. Given the increasing importance of private sector customers, even the most seasoned leaders would need to focus on Customer Sensing to understand the perspective of non-government clients.

- **Business Strategy:** The executives believed that all leaders would need to demonstrate a strong understanding of the firm's new strategy and implement it across the organization. There would be a greater emphasis on global projects; driving alignment and mobilizing resources from around the globe would be more important than ever.

- **Organizational Leadership:** Leaders would need to build strong relationships internally with other leaders across country boundaries. These relationships would support the effective management of projects staffed by local and corporate resources.

- **Advocating:** Finally, the executives recognized the need for their leaders to demonstrate Organizational Advocacy. They believed that leaders across the organization would need to be able to promote communication and cooperation throughout the organization. They would also need to make decisions based on the best interest of the organization, rather than their local teams.

The executive team's analysis is reflected in the completed 30-cell grid (see Figure 9.8 on page 144).

The next action (Action 5) helps organizations validate their assessment of the leadership requirements identified in Actions 1-4.

Action 5: Validate Your Assessment of Future Leadership Requirements

Once the executives have a good understanding of their organization's current and future states, they then need to validate their work with other leaders. As one executive said, "A small decision made at a 50,000 foot altitude makes a lot of noise when it hits the ground." Executives need to check their perceptions with a sample of their leaders before they can be reasonably assured that their assessments of the future leadership requirements are correct.

We recommend that executive teams determine the leadership requirements and that they validate their assessment of these requirements with a cross section of leaders. The process is as follows:

1. Identify a small group of leaders from across the organization to participate in the validation process.
2. Bring the group together to share ideas about the current and future external environment.
3. Discuss the implications of the future external environment for the strategic response and for your organization's leadership requirements.
4. Review the completed 30-cell grid of holistic leadership and gain input into the required elements, capabilities and skills.
5. Use this meeting to begin the process of helping the leaders internalize the new leadership expectations for which they will be held accountable.

The leadership requirements for the future should be finalized only after other leaders review, modify and validate them. Once you identify the requirements, you can proceed to assess your organization's current leadership capacity (described in the next chapter).

Case Study: Action 5

Now let's see how the executive team for the engineering consulting company went about validating their assessment of their future leadership requirements:

The Executive Team's Completed 30-Cell Grid of Holistic Leadership

	Customer Leadership	Business Strategy Leadership	Culture & Values Leadership	Organizational Leadership	Team Leadership	Personal Leadership
Sensing	Customer Sensing is the ability of the leader to solicit, understand and anticipate the needs and the values of the customer.	Strategic Sensing is the ability of the leader to explore, understand and anticipate the changes in the business environment that will impact their organization.	Culture Sensing is the ability of the leader to solicit, uncover and comprehend the culture of the organization and the impact the culture will have on the ability of the organization to achieve its goals.	Organization Sensing is the ability of the leader to identify key stakeholders throughout the organization and to understand their points of view on business issues.	Team Sensing is the ability of the leader to identify and appreciate the needs and motives of the individuals on the team.	Personal Sensing is the ability of the leader to recognize and appreciate how he is perceived by others and to understand the impact of his actions on others' perceptions.
Creating	Customer Value Proposition is the ability of the leader to build a package of solutions that meets customer needs and is appealing to the customer.	Strategy Architect is the ability of the leader to develop a business strategy that will be the most effective path to building competitive advantage.	Culture Defining is the ability of the leader to envision the type of culture that will support the achievement of the organization's goals.	Organization Design is the ability of the leader to build the appropriate structures to carry out the strategy.	Team Design is the ability of the leader to form the appropriate type of team to meet the needs of the organization.	Personal Intention is the ability of the leader to envision a personal style that she would like to project.
Implementing	Customer Solutions is the ability of the leader to deploy products and services to optimize customer value.	Strategy Deployment is the ability of the leader to move the organization from planning to effective action.	Culture Embedding is the ability of the leader to put in place the structures and processes that will support the desired culture.	Organization Integration is the ability of the leader to build bridges across the organization by creating opportunities to communicate with people from different functions, levels and geographies.	Team Performance is the ability of the leader to motivate team members to achieve superior performance.	Personal Performance is the ability of the leader to achieve results and to accomplish the goals he sets out for himself.

	Customer	Strategic	Cultural	Organizational	Team Relation-	Personal
Connecting	Customer Relationships is the ability of the leader to forge strong bonds with customers.	Strategic Relationships is the ability of the leader to forge relationships with people across different businesses, functions and levels of the organization.	Cultural Relationships is the ability of the leader to develop relationships with a diverse range of employees throughout the organization.	Organizational Relationships is the ability of the leader to build trust with stakeholders throughout the organization.	Team Relationships is the ability of the leader to foster trust and engage in a genuine dialogue with team members.	Personal Relationships is the ability of the leader to earn the trust of others and to develop relationships that provide both business and personal support.
Advocating	Customer Advocacy is the ability of the leader to bring the voice of the customer into the decision making of the organization.	Strategic Championing is the ability of the leader to lobby others about the importance of the strategy and to encourage them to align their actions with that strategy.	Cultural Advocacy is the ability of the leader to champion the importance of culture as a key driver of business success.	Organizational Advocacy is the ability of the leader to promote communication and cooperation throughout the organization.	Team Advocacy is the ability of the leader to rally support for the team from stakeholders in the organization.	Personal Advocacy is the ability of the leader to further his position by effectively promoting his value to the organization.

Figure 9.8 *The Executive Team's Completed 30-Cell Grid of Holistic Leadership*

The executive team decided they would do a global "road show." Each team member made several trips to the company's various global locations. They agreed that at each location, each would meet with a cross section of leaders and begin the process to include them in validating the leadership requirements.

They created a common template for their discussions to explain the conclusions they reached in their meetings about the organization's current and future states. They also shared their thinking about the future environment and the strategic response. Finally, they solicited input on the ratings of importance of the six elements and five capabilities of holistic leadership on the 30-cell grid.

When the executives completed their road-show discussions, they were impressed by the high degree of leader engagement. This was exactly the kind of conversation they wanted to have. The leaders throughout the company were very interested in what the executives had done. They also presented their perspectives and insights to help strengthen the overall definition of the leadership required for the future. Two critical ideas emerged, which further refined the organization's understanding of their future leadership requirements.

First, the leaders who took part in the road show expressed a desire to be more involved in the actual creation of the new strategy. The holistic leadership skill of Strategy Architect, they believed, was not something that should be exercised exclusively by executives. All leaders would need to be able to provide input into the new strategy and identify market opportunities as part of the business planning process. This was particularly important to them because they felt that they were best positioned to give input about opportunities in their regions.

Second, they also believed that Personal Sensing was going to be important. They felt that during the acquisition phase, leaders were not given any formal development opportunities. Many leaders identified the importance of ensuring they were personally supported as the company continued to implement the new strategy.

Finally, they expressed interest in participating in the next step to measure the organization's current leadership capacity.

Consider the outcome of the executives' efforts to implement the five actions of Step 1:

The executives met briefly to share their experiences from the global road-show meetings and to plan Step 2 of the leadership solutions pathway. They described how the road-show meetings gave them a renewed sense of confidence in the current leadership capacity. They also knew that much more work needed to be done to put in place the future leadership requirements for success. The good news, however, was that the time they took to rigorously determine their leadership requirements was seen as valuable by the organization's leaders. They felt ready to assess the current state of their leadership capacity.

The five key actions in Step 1 provide a coherent and practical strategy for determining an organization's leadership requirements. The actions can be implemented with an executive team over a series of short meetings or in a one-day leadership strategy session.

CONCLUDING COMMENTS

Articulating your leadership capacity requirements is not a process that should be rushed or taken lightly. Organizations need to have a clear understanding of the leadership required for future success, so they can develop the pathway to get there.

Some executives attempt to shortchange the process. Some believe that this step is merely about coming up with a list of leadership competencies. Others try to rush this step by importing a generic leadership model that is external to the organization and that really does not represent what is required. In almost every situation, this executive behavior points the leadership solutions pathway in the wrong direction.

Executives need to understand their external environment, identify their strategic response and then define the leadership requirements they need to succeed. Only after they have determined their leadership requirements are they ready to proceed to Step 2 of the leadership solutions pathway and measure their leadership capacity (described in Chapter 10).

By completing Step 1, you have taken a very important first step on your leadership solutions pathway. In the words of Epictetus quoted at the beginning of the chapter, you have said to yourself what you would be. Now, you can do what you have to do.

CHAPTER TEN

Step 2: Measure the Gap

An old adage says that to truly know something one needs to measure it, and if you cannot measure it, then you can never really improve it.[1] Many organizations know the importance of measurement. They focus their attention on a host of measures used to understand and improve performance in core business capabilities such as in production and manufacturing, sales and marketing, innovation, human resources and finance. These measures give a sense of where the organization stands, where it is heading and what it needs to do to succeed.

The same is true with leadership capacity—it has emerged as a new organizational capability. As with any core business capability, it needs to be built on a foundation of measurement. Organizations need to develop ways of measuring their leadership capacity so they can know if they are successful in building what they need for their future success.

However, through our work, we find that many organizations are struggling to measure their leadership capacity. This brings us to the second step of the Leadership Solutions Pathway: Measure the Gap (see Figure 10.1 on the following page).

We begin by exploring the importance of leadership metrics and the shortcomings of some of the current approaches to measuring leadership. We then present four actions that help organizations measure their leadership capacity. We conclude by answering some of the most common questions about measuring the gap.

THE LEADERSHIP SOLUTIONS PATHWAY

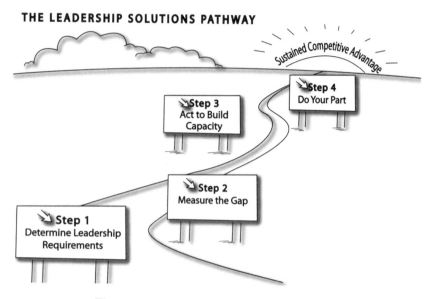

Figure 10.1 *The Leadership Solutions Pathway*

WHY MEASURE LEADERSHIP CAPACITY

Increasingly, line executives are looking for leadership capacity measures in their organizations.[2] Because leadership capacity is mission critical, executives want measures that show them where they stand. The fundamental problem is that without the right measures, organizations may not be able to fully understand the leadership capacity they have in place. Furthermore, they may make decisions about where to invest limited resources based on little or no data. This can result in spending decisions that are imprecise—not targeted to the skills that are most in need of development or to the individuals and teams that will most benefit from the investment.

Few organizations have discovered how to measure leadership capacity effectively. Some organizations have scant leadership metrics that they have collected from succession planning (e.g., percentage of "ready now" replacements), individual evaluations of leaders (e.g., 360° feedback ratings) or employee engagement surveys. Just as often, organizations admit they have no specific measures of leadership, even though they know both the executives and the board of directors will expect these measures. In fact, lack of behavioral measures of leadership capacity has been found to be the number one barrier to developing leadership capacity.[3] In this section, we identify some of the critical characteristics of an effective measure of leadership capacity.

Critical Characteristics for Effective Leadership Capacity Measures

1. Lead, not just lag, indicators.
2. All elements, not just personal and leadership.
3. Organizational, not just individual leadership capacity.

---

1. Lead, Not Just Lag, Indicators

When economists are trying to measure the strength of the economy, they don't just look at measures such as prime interest rates charged by the banks and the Consumer Price Index. These measures are lagging indicators, and as such, they don't usually change until after an important change in the economy has already occurred. Instead, economists look to the leading indicators that help predict changes that have yet to happen. For example, they look at measures such as building permits, housing starts and manufacturers' new orders. These leading indicators predict the direction of the economy while there is still time to change its course.

Many organizations are good at measuring the lag indicators of strong leadership. For example, they measure whether or not leaders have produced sustained revenue growth, managed expenses judiciously and engaged and aligned employees. We have become quite good at measuring these outcomes. Some organizations even look at direct indicators of leadership, such as the number of leadership positions filled by internal candidates.

From these lagging indicators, you get a sense of your past leadership capacity. For instance, if your organization had to fill 67 percent of its leadership positions externally, you can infer that your internal leadership capacity was poor. What you can't tell is how your current leadership capacity will impact your future performance. Are your leaders' skills stronger than they were in the past? Are leaders now paying attention to the right things to take your business forward? If you are relying on lag measures, it is impossible to know.

For example, take the case of a public sector organization that is being called on by the government to change its focus in the future. It needs to be community focused and accountable to the public. Leaders face new challenges contending with an array of external stakeholders and lobbyists. The fundamental outcomes they are expected to achieve have not changed, but shifts in the environment require the leaders to achieve these outcomes with a greater focus on building relationships and on managing stakeholder relationships. If the organization measures only the outcomes of leadership, it will have no gauge of whether current results will be sustainable in the changing environment.

Measuring your leadership capacity as a lead indicator puts you in a much better position to take action to fix weaknesses in leadership before they have wide-ranging repercussions on the business. With a clear definition of the leadership required for the future and a corresponding lead measure of the current leadership capacity, the organization can develop a targeted leadership solution to make the required improvements.

2. All Elements, Not Just Personal and Team Leadership

Measures should tap all aspects of holistic leadership. The leadership industry has done a good job of providing diagnostic tools to assess the personal or team leadership skills of individuals. Whether it is through psychometric assessments, 360° feedback or employee surveys, leaders are usually able to get good information about their strengths and weaknesses in cultivating credibility, practicing humility or building leaders.[4] But holistic leadership requires more than just good personal leadership. To be a holistic leader, one needs to demonstrate customer leadership, strategy leadership and each of the six elements of holistic leadership. Few existing measures of leadership capacity touch on these aspects of leadership.

Consider this example of the need for a measure that will identify the necessary leader capabilities as an organization shifts its structure: A highly successful functional leader is likely to demonstrate personal leadership (with strong credibility and a solid track record of results) and good team leadership (by getting the most out of a group of like-minded technical experts). Now imagine that functional leader trying to cope as her organization shifts to a customer-centered matrix structure. Suddenly, a lack of customer or organizational leadership that would not have been identified using traditional measures could threaten her success as a leader. These deficits might have been completely masked by measures that focus on traditional views of personal or team leadership.

3. Organizational, Not Just Individual, Leadership Capacity

Many organizations mistakenly view leadership as existing only within individuals and therefore use the measurement of leaders' skills as a proxy for leadership capacity. However, an organization's leadership capacity is as dependent on its practices and its culture as on the skills of individual leaders. As a result, measures of individual skills need to be complemented by an evaluation of the organization's practices and an assessment of the leadership culture. Only by examining each of the three dimensions can the organization measure its leadership capacity and diagnose specific leadership gaps.

Imagine a situation in which a board's HR committee asks the executive team to provide an assessment of the organization's leadership capacity. The executives might respond by providing detailed manager ratings, aggregate scores of employee engagement for each leader's team of employees and the succession readiness reports on the successor pool. (Having provided these measures, the organization would be significantly ahead of most.) However, without giving the board an idea of how the organization's culture and practices either support or inhibit the desired leadership behaviors, the HR committee has not given a true indication of the organization's leadership capacity. They also have reduced the board's ability to do its job in identifying and responding to what could be a significant risk to the organization's future success.

REFLECTING ON YOUR CURRENT LEADERSHIP MEASURES

Take a moment to consider the leadership measures in your organization. How are you measuring leadership capacity?

- Does the organization track only financial metrics (e.g., revenue growth, profitability)? Do you have a balanced scorecard or some other method to track forward-looking measures such as customer satisfaction or employee engagement?
- How is the performance of your leaders evaluated? Are they measured only on their outputs (e.g., productivity, margin) or are they evaluated on their ability to build teams or to develop others?

- Is the organization looking at the leadership pool overall? Do you aggregate information from 360° feedback, from psychometric assessments or from training evaluations?

When you think about the ways you are measuring leadership, ask yourself:

- Do you tend to collect lead indicators or lag indicators? Do you measure processes and/or behaviors, or do you measure outcomes?
- Which aspects of holistic leadership are included in your measurement? Do you focus on a particular element (such as team leadership) or capability (such as connecting)? Do you measure multiple cells within the 30-cell grid?
- Do you measure individual behavior, organizational practices and leadership culture?

The way you measure your leadership gap is critical to your ability to predict problems and to respond in a targeted and effective way. Your leadership measures also send a strong message about what leadership means in your organization and what types of leadership you think are important. If you are disappointed by the quality of your current leadership measures, you are in good company. The remainder of the chapter provides a step-by-step approach that will help you measure the gap.

THE FOUR ACTIONS TO MEASURE THE GAP

Once you have determined your leadership requirements for the future (Step 1, see Chapter 9), you must measure your current leadership capacity. This measurement provides important information on the current state of leadership and helps you prioritize the actions needed to build the capacity for future success. Step 2: Measure the Gap involves four actions:

- Action 1: Audit Organizational Practices
- Action 2: Conduct Survey of Leadership Culture
- Action 3: Assess Behaviors of Individual Leaders
- Action 4: Analyze Patterns of Results

In our experience, organizations are looking for a robust and proven approach to measuring leadership capacity. As a result, we have designed and developed The Leadership Gap Analysis™ (LGA). This measurement tool is the culmination of our research and development over a three-year period to develop tools that assess holistic leadership capacity. We provide the LGA in its entirety in the appendices. It is not our intention to drive all readers toward our tools, but for those who lack the inclination or the time to develop their own tools, the LGA will provide them with everything they need to begin measuring their leadership capacity.

As we discussed in Chapter 5, leadership capacity consists of three dimensions (Figure 10.2).

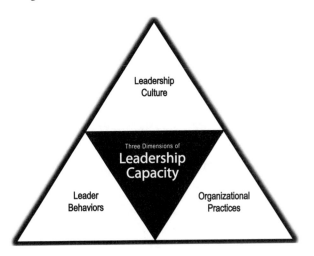

Figure 10.2 *The Three Dimensions of Leadership Capacity*

The Leadership Gap Analysis™ includes three tools to measure each of these three dimensions:

1. ***Audit of Organizational Practices:*** This tool is an audit questionnaire and scoring scheme that assesses whether the formal rules of the organization are "compliant" with building leadership capacity (see Appendix A for the Audit of Organizational Practices and the accompanying 30-Cell Grid).

2. ***Survey of Leadership Culture:*** This tool is an opinion survey that measures the expectations and norms that govern leaders within the organization (see Appendix B for the Survey of Leadership Culture and the accompanying 30-Cell Grid).

1. *Assessment of Leader Behaviors:* This tool is a feedback survey that measures the behaviors of individual leaders (see Appendix C for the Assessment of Leader Behaviors Survey and the accompanying 30-cell grid). Its results can be reported both for individuals and for the leadership pool in aggregate.

Action 1: Audit Organizational Practices

The organizational practices are the official rules by which an organization operates. They set the explicit standards for leadership. We use an audit to evaluate the extent to which the organizational practices support holistic leadership and help to build leadership capacity. This audit is similar to those that were developed in the wake of Sarbanes Oxley legislation—in that case, to assess the extent to which practices were supporting good corporate governance. Basically, the Audit of Organizational Practices assesses whether or not the organization's formal rules are compliant with building leadership capacity.

Here is how you can conduct an Audit of Organizational Practices:

The Process of Auditing Organizational Practices

1. Review the 30-cell grid for organizational practices.
2. Assemble the right people to audit organizational practices.
3. Collect information and documentation.
4. Select a method for auditing.
5. Rate the organizational practices.

---

1. Review the 30-Cell Grid for the Organizational Practices

Before embarking on an audit, become familiar with the organizational practices that are required to support the demonstration of holistic leadership. Review the 30-cell grid in Chapter 6 (Figure 6.4 or in Appendix A) and note the organizational practices that might be relevant in your organization. For example, if the main practice associated with Customer Leadership is your new product development process, then you will want to talk with the owner of this process and collect some documentation on how it works. These notes will help you identify who should participate in the audit team. They also will help you pull together a dossier of information on relevant practices.

2. Assemble the Right People to Audit Organizational Practices

Request the participation of a small group of stakeholders (6 to 10) who will provide the "expert testimony" for the audit. The participants who provide the data for the audit need to be very senior people who represent different business units and corporate functions such as marketing and HR. Because of the myriad of practices that have either a direct or an indirect impact on leadership capacity, it is likely that each participant will be able to provide only a few pieces of the puzzle. (Your notes from Action 1 will be a good source.) By including people who are experts in some of the core organizational practices, such as planning, talent management and new product development, you increase the chances of collecting valid and complete data. This corporate group should be complemented by business leaders who are in the best position to evaluate the implementation of the practices and the impact they are having on the front lines.

3. Collect Information and Documentation

To support the audit team's discussions, collect relevant information about the organizational practices. For example, to support evaluations of practices and programs within the customer leadership element, you might want to speak with someone in sales or marketing to get copies of the customer survey or with someone in customer service to get examples of customer satisfaction programs.

Although all of these data will provide useful insights into the organizational practices, time and efficiency will dictate that they be reviewed and summarized before being shared with the audit team.

4. Select a Method for Auditing

Options for conducting an audit include these:

- Collect data to support the organizational practices examples, and use the data to rate the practices without input from others (e.g., copy of the customer survey, the performance management forms, etc.).

- Conduct the audit by interviewing people separately and averaging their ratings.
- Conduct a facilitated session where people debate the organizational practices and come to consensus on an appropriate rating.
- Pre-interview participants and then conduct a group session to discuss areas with discrepancies.

The most appropriate method will depend on your particular situation. In our experience, the first option is only for extreme situations where you cannot get the participation of the appropriate stakeholders. It will be a challenge to translate program descriptions and policies into ratings because you will not have a good perspective on how well the programs have been implemented. Nonetheless, if it is your only option, conducting the audit based strictly on the data will give you a preliminary read on the size of the gap. Sharing the results will garner interest and probably allow you to conduct a more inclusive process.

If you are able to get key stakeholders involved in the audit process, you can choose between individual interviews and a group session. Ideally, the best option is to interview individuals and then bring the group together to discuss areas of disagreement. Just discussing the effectiveness of organizational practices and hearing the diverse issues from different parts of the organization can be a valuable process.

5. Rate Organizational Practices

The common approach to an audit is to use a checklist to determine if each particular program or practice meets standards or not. Evaluating the effectiveness of organizational practices that support holistic leadership is less black and white. The reason is that your audit isn't looking at a particular program or practice. Instead, the audit is examining whether the various programs or practices support the demonstration of a particular holistic leadership behavior. Moreover, our approach is to evaluate not only the existence of organizational practices but also the breadth and effectiveness of the practices. The audit tool in Appendix A provides a set of descriptions for each cell of the 30-cell grid to help evaluate the quality of the organizational practices and their impact on building leadership capacity. The Sample Audit Question in Figure 10.3 on the following page is an example of the customer sensing rating scale.

Customer Leadership			Below Average		Average		Exceptional
Sensing	1.	Describe the approach by which you try to understand the current and future needs/expectations of your external customers. Do you talk with external customers regularly? Do you collect customer data? If so, who collects it?	①	②	③	④	⑤

Figure 10.3 *Sample Audit Question and Associated Scoring*

Significantly, the scale does not force a narrowly prescribed set of practices. Instead, it provides a directional focus for the kinds of practices that could be expected in an average, below average and exceptional organization. Therefore, after you have gathered all the information and documentation for each of the Audit questions, you will need to rate the overall effectiveness of the practices for each of the cells. If you believe that your practices are weak or below average, then you will provide a rating of a 1 or a 2 on the scale. If you believe your practices are average, or if the practices are reasonably well-designed, but not well implemented, then provide a rating of a 3 on the scale. If you believe your organizational practices are exceptionally well-designed and implemented to support holistic leadership, then provide a rating of a 4 or 5 on the scale.

Challenges in Auditing Organizational Practices

Formally evaluating organizational practices can be an eye-opening exercise, revealing why certain core messages have been embraced and translated into changed behaviors and why others have never "stuck." Usually, the behaviors that are supported by organizational practices will be the ones that gain traction.

However, some situations make it harder to conduct an effective audit. These are:

- *Multiple business units:* In most organizations, a group of corporate leaders and business line leaders will be able to come to consensus on the nature and effectiveness of the organizational practices. In some cases, however, the business is so large and diverse that the group cannot come to consensus on the ratings of the organizational practices. This can mean treating each diverse group as a separate entity with its own dedicated audit of organizational practices.

  Consider a mature organization with a new start-up division. In this scenario, many of the standard organizational practices of the parent company might not yet be in place in the start-up. Alternatively, some start-ups are more nimble and dynamic than their staid and conservative parents, in which case the division might have significantly better scores on the audit. Regardless of the findings, it is important to have a relatively homogeneous organization that you are measuring, and this can require conducting the audit on one or more sub-groups within the organization.

- *Organizational practices in new organizations:* The audit is designed to reflect the expected organizational practices in growth and mature organizations. In new (start-up) organizations, the audit process may reveal a lack of supporting practices in a number of areas. However, the lack of formal practices may not negatively affect leadership in those organizations—at least in the beginning of the organization. In start-up organizations, the individual leadership behaviors and culture might be very strong and sufficient to support leadership. It is likely that formal programs just haven't been a priority. It is important, however, to gradually introduce some formal organizational practices to support leadership as the start-up organization grows. Again, it is incumbent on the organization to have a clearly defined view of the future leadership requirements in order to highlight the practices that will be the most important in the future.

Potential Pitfalls

Like all measurement initiatives, the Audit of Organizational Practices has a few potential pitfalls.

- *Chance of excluding practices:* Although assembling the right people involved in the audit will minimize the likelihood that some good practices will not be known by the audit participants, it is still possible that some will be missed.

  Solution: To reduce the chances of excluding practices, it is valuable to solicit input from many different stakeholders in advance of the audit and to confirm audit findings with those who might be able to validate the results.

- *Possibility of well-designed programs that are poorly implemented:* Many organizations have invested considerable resources in developing excellent programs and policies. These programs often represent leading practices that could drive the organization forward. Unfortunately, organizations cannot attribute too much value to a well-designed program if they are unaware of poor implementation.

  Solution: It is crucial to seek input from those with strong ties to the front-line employees. These representatives of the line will provide insight for the corporate team on how well their programs are being executed. Great programs poorly implemented are worth less in building leadership capacity than good programs implemented well.

- *Too strict a definition of organizational practices:* Some organizations can have too strict a definition of what they consider organizational practices to be. In our experience, practices that build leadership capacity can sometimes be found where you least expect them.

  Solution: The key is to focus on the organizational support you are evaluating (e.g., practices that support organizational connecting) and to be open-minded about practices that might be helpful (e.g., having a central cafeteria and subsidized meals gives employees opportunities for informal communication throughout the workday).

The Audit of Organizational Practices is an extremely valuable tool in measuring the contribution of formal programs and practices in building leadership capacity. The clear evaluation of strengths and weaknesses helps you understand where leaders are—and are not—being supported in leading holistically. The discrepancies between the views of the employees at the corporate level who have designed the programs and those in the business unit who use the programs help you understand where practices could be more effective.

Action 2: Conduct Survey of Leadership Culture

The Survey of Leadership Culture is an opinion survey that measures the expectations and norms that govern leaders within the organization.

Here is how you can conduct a Survey of Leadership Culture:

> ## The Process of Conducting a Survey of Leadership Culture
>
> 1. Tailor the survey language to your organization.
> 2. Select the survey sample.
> 3. Administer the survey.

1. Tailor the Survey Language to Your Organization

We have provided a copy of the Survey of Leadership Culture in Appendix B. This survey includes items to assess each of the 30 cells that describe a holistic leadership culture. See the Sample Questions from the Survey in Figure 10.4.

Although we have tried to provide a generic survey, you may need to modify the language in some of the questions to reflect your organization's specific situation (e.g., public sector organizations might want to replace the word "customer" with "stakeholder" or "public interest").

You will also need to customize a demographic component of the survey for your organization. Depending on the size of your sample, you might want to include more or fewer demographic questions or to subdivide the categories differently. Be sure the demographic breakdowns do not create groups of fewer than 10 respondents. Smaller groups can threaten perceptions of anonymity and reduce the quality of responses.

The leadership culture of this organization...	Strongly Disagree	Disagree	Neither Agree or Disagree	Agree	Strongly Agree
1. creates the expectation that leaders will stay informed about the current and future needs of the external customer	①	②	③	④	⑤
2. drives creativity and innovation that is focused on creating value for customers	①	②	③	④	⑤
3. reinforces the importance of getting new products and services to the market quickly	①	②	③	④	⑤

Figure 10.4 *Sample Questions from the Survey of Leadership Culture*

2. Select Survey Sample

The survey is designed to be administered to "leaders," but you can imagine that the definition of who is included in this group is as diverse as the organizations that use the tool. We would encourage organizations to sample as broad a population of leaders as is feasible, with more respondents providing a more complete picture. If you are concerned that leaders from different levels or those with direct reports will have different perspectives, include a demographic question to identify the respondents' levels and the number of their direct reports so that differences in responses can be analyzed.

3. Administer the Survey

We recommend that you randomly sample one quarter of your leaders for the first survey and that you sample equal size groups each quarter until, at the end of a year, all leaders have provided their perspectives. Multiple data points throughout the year from different stakeholder groups help you track changes without creating survey fatigue from surveying the same people over and over.

As with all surveys, it is critical that participants feel completely comfortable providing honest and candid feedback, so great effort must be taken to protect the anonymity of respondents. The survey is designed to provide an overall view of the organization's leadership capacity and should not be used to evaluate individual leaders. Organizations that use the survey for its intended purpose can assure respondents that the results will be used only to support the development of leaders.

Potential Pitfalls

Some of the pitfalls that might affect the Survey of Leadership Culture include:

- *A general sense of suspicion regarding the purpose and the outcomes of the survey might lead to biased results:* Leaders who fear the survey could be used against them might present overly positive views. In cases of low trust, the survey process often takes time to become fully effective.

  Solution: We have found that after the survey is administered two or three times and the results are shared openly, while the feedback is heard and positive actions are taken, then leaders will begin to provide more open responses.

- *Significant differences between different groups might be clouding the overall results:* In some organizations, the variation between groups is very large and pockets of high and low responses look like mediocre, almost uninteresting, scores on average.

  Solution: If this is the case, it is important to use the demographic categories to look at the results from different parts of the organization. If results are too dissimilar, it might not be useful to look at company-wide results. Instead, identify the groups with similar patterns and try to determine the root causes of the discrepancies (e.g., one business unit with particularly strong holistic role models might be rated significantly more positively).

- *Sometimes the open-ended comments provided at the end of a survey present a very different picture than do the quantitative results:* Remember, not everyone provides comments, and usually it is those who are highly motivated (either for the good or the bad) who do.

Solution: Look for areas where the qualitative and quantitative data are similar—what do those findings tell you? Also, look for areas where they diverge—can you make sense of the differences? It is always helpful to follow up puzzling results with either formal or informal discussions with focus groups of respondents. A few probing questions often lead to the answer.

Action 3: Assess Individual Leader Behaviors

The Assessment of Individual Leader Behaviors is a feedback survey that evaluates the behaviors of individual leaders. Its results can be reported both for individuals and for the leadership pool in aggregate.

Here is how you can collect Assessments of Individual Leader Behaviors:

The Process of Collecting Assessments of Leader Behaviors

1. Tailor the survey language to your organization.
2. Identify the measurement approach that best suits the needs of leaders and the organization.
3. Administer the survey and deliver individual feedback.

---

1. Tailor the Survey Language to Your Organization

We have provided a complete copy of the Assessment of Leadership Behaviors in Appendix C. See the Sample Questions from the Survey in Figure 10.5 on the following page.

As with the Survey of Leadership Culture, this generic survey should be adapted to reflect the language of your organization. Use the commonly accepted language: "customer" or "client"; "employee" or "associate"; and "company" or "organization."

The respondent demographics section also will need to be tailored to your language. For example, what do you call the leader's boss (supervisor, performance manager), peers, and their subordinates (team members, direct reports)?

Customer Leadership						
This section covers the extent to which this person drives the organization to focus on creating value for the external customer. It comprises the behaviors that create a customer-focused environment to ensure successful customer/consumer outcomes.						
	Almost Never	Rarely	Half of the time	Frequently	90% of the time	N/A
1. Demonstrates a clear understanding of what customers value	①	②	③	④	⑤	⑥
2. Anticipates the future needs of customers	①	②	③	④	⑤	⑥
3. Develops products services that provide value to customers	①	②	③	④	⑤	⑥

Figure 10.5 *Sample Questions from the Assessment of Leadership Behaviors*

2. Identify the Measurement Approach That Best Suits the Needs of Leaders and the Organization

We will consider three primary approaches to assessment in this section: self-assessment, multi-rater feedback and third-party work associate reviews.

Self-Assessment of Leadership Behaviors

Self-reflection is critical to leaders' growth and development. Often, self-assessment is the simplest way of assessing holistic leadership behaviors. At times, organizations discount self-assessment tools because they believe that leaders will not be objective in their ratings, and in order to look good, they will tend to overrate their abilities. Though this may be true, self-assessment approaches, coupled with coaching discussions with a manager or external coach, can begin a process of self-discovery and change. Self-assessment approaches are also relatively easy to do and fairly cost effective.

Multi-Rater Feedback

The use of multi-rater feedback tools has increased considerably over the past decade because they provide leaders with a broader perspective on their strengths and gaps. Multi-rater feedback approaches can include a 180° feedback (soliciting data from a leader and his or her direct manager and direct reports) or through a 360° process (assessment not just by the direct manager and direct reports, but also by peers, stakeholders and even external customers). Either way, the goal is to determine the extent the leader has moved beyond functional management to holistic leadership.

In our experience we find that the 180° approach is effective as a check-in assessment process. The data facilitates a discussion between the direct manager and the individual leader. The process is also useful when the organization does not want to invest the time and resources required for a robust process involving many raters.

The 360° assessment works well when an organization needs to significantly change its leadership culture. Soliciting data from a broad cross-section of individuals provides a leader with a more accurate picture of perceived strengths and gaps as a holistic leader. The perspective of peers is especially important for understanding the leader's strength in team leadership.

We find it works best in organizations that have an open culture where feedback is welcomed: participants know that feedback will be used solely for development purposes; and all leaders, including the executives, undergo the same process.

Third-Party Work Associate Reviews

A third-party work associate review is another strategy that can be used to measure leadership behaviors. Consider it as a qualitative multi-rater process that is completed by conducting a series of interviews with a sample of individuals. This sample might include a leader's direct manager, direct reports, peers and colleagues, customers and other stakeholders. Whereas the 360° assessment process yields numerical data, the third-party work associate review yields qualitative data that can often provide a rich story on leadership behaviors.

The third-party work associate review can be completed on its own or in conjunction with a 360° assessment process. By illuminating the overall evaluation with stories and examples from the participant, the work associate review produces extremely detailed insights into a leader's effectiveness as a holistic leader.

3. Administer the Survey and Deliver Individual Feedback

Depending on the method you choose, assessing individual leader behaviors can be a very elaborate process. If you are collecting survey data, the use of a web-based tool can ease the administrative burden. This will require that the survey website be programmed with the names of the leaders who are being evaluated, the names of the people rating them, and the relationship between the rater and the leader being evaluated. The better systems allow an employee to log on with a username and then to view all of the people they are being asked to evaluate.

Because of the sensitivity of these individual evaluations (particularly when subordinates are asked to rate their supervisors) it is important that a qualified coach deliver the feedback. This coach can review the results in detail in advance and be ready to paraphrase comments to protect the identity of the evaluator. The coach can encourage leaders to take the feedback seriously, help them interpret what the evaluators meant and ensure they are not too easy or too hard on themselves as they interpret the feedback.

Potential Pitfalls

Some of the pitfalls that might affect the Assessment of Leader Behaviors include:

- ***The leader behaviors are too high-level for some of the middle-level managers you want to assess:*** If you are including a broad sample of leaders in your assessment, you might find that certain items reflect behaviors that would not be expected of any but the most senior leaders in your organization.

  Solution: If this is the case, you can create a parallel questionnaire that better reflects the expectations of different levels of leaders. The important thing is to stick to the 30-cell grid but also to create items that reflect the role a middle-manager might play in customer sensing or organizational design. Competencies can be defined for different levels—so, too, can the cells of the 30-cell grid.

- **Leaders in corporate functions leave questions about the customer blank:** Sometimes leaders in functions such as finance, human resources, or legal (or their raters) say that the section on Customer Leadership "doesn't apply."

  Solution: This is one area where the holistic leadership model provides clear direction. The customer is the customer. That is, every leader in the organization, regardless of their function, needs to be delivering value to the external customer. If you get numerous complaints about the inapplicability of the Customer Leadership section or lots of comments translating the questions to the "internal customer" it is a very good indication that you have a leadership gap. Clarify that all leaders should be rated based on their ability to create value for the external customer, even if they do so indirectly.

- **Employees are hesitant to give candid or constructive feedback:** At times, an organization might not be ready for a rigorous assessment because the leaders fear or mistrust the process.

  Solution: You can do several things to reassure raters: reinforcing that the results are only for developmental purposes; telling them that an external consultant will be collecting and interpreting the data so that identities are protected; stipulating the number of respondents who must participate before results will be shared. The best solution to this problem is to run the program and have key leaders share the value of the constructive feedback. Employees won't truly believe the process is "safe" until they have had positive experiences.

Action 4: Analyze Patterns of Results

Once you have completed Actions 1, 2 and 3, you will have comprehensive data on your organization's leadership capacity. Now you can begin to look at patterns of results that will help you pinpoint your leadership gap.

The Process of Analyzing Patterns of Results

1. Plot the results of each of the three LGA tools on the results tracker.
2. Calculate averages for each element (columns) and capability (rows).
3. Identify priority areas for action.

---

1. Plot Results on the 3D Results Tracker

The first action is to tabulate the results from the Audit of Organizational Practices, the Survey of Leadership Culture and the Assessment of Leader Behaviors. The 3D Results Tracker (part of which is shown in Figure 10.6) brings together the three dimensions into one straightforward chart. Simply fill out the Results Tracker with the Organizational Practices scores on each cell from the audit (in the OP columns), the Leadership Culture scores from the survey (in the LC columns), and the Individual Behavior scores from the assessments (in the IB columns). In each case, the scores can range from 1 (low) to 5 (high).

	Customer			Business Strategy			Culture & Values			Organization			Team			Personal		
	OP	LC	IB	OP	LC	IB	OP	LC	IB	OP	LC	IB	OP	LC	IB	OP	LC	IB
Sensing																		
Creating																		
Implementing																		
Connecting																		
Advocating																		

Figure 10.6 *Data Entry Section of the Leadership Gap Analysis™ 3D Results Tracker*

2. Calculate Averages for Each Element and Capability

Once all the data are tabulated, you can begin to look at the patterns of results. Figure 10.7 shows the complete LGA™ 3D Results Tracker with the spots to enter the row and column averages. To compute the average for each element (column), average the 15 scores in the columns under the element. This will give you the average score for the element across

	Customer			Business Strategy			Culture & Values			Organization			Team			Personal			
	OP	LC	IB	OP	LC	IB	OP	LC	IB	OP	LC	IB	OP	LC	IB	OP	LC	IB	Capability Averages
Sensing																			= _____
Creating																			= _____
Implementing																			= _____
Connecting																			= _____
Advocating																			= _____
Element Averages	= _____			= _____			= _____			= _____			= _____			= _____			

Figure 10.7 *Leadership Gap Analysis™ 3D Results Tracker*

all five capabilities and three dimensions. Write the average in the space at the bottom of the column.

Next, compute the average for each capability (row). It is the average of the 18 cells across the row. It will give you the average score for the capability across all six elements and three dimensions. Finally, if you're interested, you can compute the overall Leadership Gap Index by averaging all 90 cells in the grid. Write this number in the bottom right-hand cell.

Now the data are organized in a way that will allow you to see patterns. Do the following:

- *Look at the Element Averages across the bottom row of the 3D Results Tracker:* Are any of the scores particularly high? If so, you are probably looking at an element that is very important in your organization. Are there any scores that are very low? Low scores reflect elements to which your organization doesn't pay much attention. Circle any low scores in the bottom row.

- *Look at the Capability Averages down the right-hand column:* Again, are there any high scores? High scores suggest that this capability is very strong in your organization. Are there low scores? If so, this might be a skill that is not well developed in your organization. Circle any worrisome scores in the right column.

- *Examine each cell in the 3D Results Tracker:* Are there any single cells that are showing lower scores? If there are low scores in one cell that is in one dimension, how do the measures of this cell in the other dimensions compare? For example, if the Team Connecting cell is poor in the Leadership Culture dimension, is it also poor in the Individual Behaviors and the Organizational Practices dimensions? Circle any cells that have particularly low scores.

3. Identify Priority Areas for Action

The data can now be used to identify priority areas for action. The greatest priorities will be a function of several things, including:

- **Magnitude of the Problem:** As you look at the cells you have circled on the Results Tracker, you need to take into consideration the magnitude of the problem and the effort required in solving it. Some cells might suggest fundamental problems in your organization (e.g., an organization design that inhibits cross-boundary communication). Others might reflect opportunities where small changes could make significant improvements (e.g., the need to share customer data more widely). Your list of priorities should include some "quick wins" and some actions that will take time and resources but will yield important improvements in leadership capacity.

- **Future Requirements:** When you completed "Step 1: Determine Your Requirements for the Future" of the Leadership Solutions Pathway (described in Chapter 9), which of the elements and capabilities did you see as the most critical to the future of your organization? If you have circled any of the cells that were central to the success of your organization in the future, these cells will need to be priorities for action. Even if you haven't circled them, if you see room for improvement in these key areas, they might still make your list of priorities.

- **Dimensions Implicated:** When you look at the cells you have circled, do the strengths and weaknesses in the three dimensions suggest priorities for action? For example, if the Business Strategy element is weak across the capabilities and the dimensions, it might not make sense to try to improve Individual Behaviors until you address any problems in the Organizational Practices dimension.

	Customer			Business Strategy			Culture & Values			Organization			Team			Personal			
	OP	LC	IB	OP	LC	IB	OP	LC	IB	OP	LC	IB	OP	LC	IB	OP	LC	IB	Capability Averages
Sensing	2.8	3.1	2.7	3.2	2.8	2.5	4.4	4.2	4.1	3.8	3.4	3.4	4.0	3.5	3.6	3.1	3.7	3.8	= 3.45
Creating	2.8	3.0	3.1	3.4	2.8	2.7	4.4	4.2	4.1	3.5	3.2	3.2	4.0	3.1	3.4	2.5	3.4	3.4	= 3.34
Implementing	2.9	3.0	3.2	3.9	4.0	3.8	4.3	4.2	4.5	3.8	3.5	3.4	4.3	3.2	3.6	3.0	3.8	3.7	= 3.67
Connecting	3.5	3.1	3.4	3.3	3.3	3.1	4.4	3.8	4.5	3.4	3.2	3.2	4.1	3.2	3.4	3.2	3.8	3.7	= 3.53
Advocating	2.6	2.8	3.2	2.8	2.9	2.9	4.1	4.0	4.1	3.5	3.6	3.5	4.2	3.3	3.5	3.1	3.3	3.2	= 3.37
Element Averages	= 3.01			= 3.16			= 4.22			= 3.44			=3.63			= 3.38			3.47

Figure 10.8 *Sample Results Tracker: Low Customer Leadership*

Sample Results

To demonstrate the thinking required to identify priority areas for action, we present below three sample Results Tracker grids.

Example #1: Low Customer Leadership

The organization represented by the data in Example #1 is not paying much attention to the customer. Results in almost all areas of Customer Leadership are weak, with particular issues in Customer Sensing and Customer Advocating. The one area that is somewhat stronger is Customer Connecting, which is likely the result of good customer relationships that nonetheless have not been translated into increased value for the customer.

The lack of Customer Leadership is likely affecting the Business Strategy Leadership, where the poor showing in Sensing and Creating suggests an organization that is inwardly focused. Organizations that excel at execution often show similar patterns, with the Customer element being weak and with the externally oriented Business Strategy cells also suffering. That interpretation is supported by the strong scores across the Implementing capability.

This organization will likely need to put a series of externally focused activities at the top of the priority list.

Example #2: Planners, Not "Doers"

	Customer			Business Strategy			Culture & Values			Organization			Team			Personal			Capability Averages
	OP	LC	IB	OP	LC	IB	OP	LC	IB	OP	LC	IB	OP	LC	IB	OP	LC	IB	
Sensing	3.8	3.9	3.8	3.9	3.7	3.7	4.4	4.2	4.1	3.8	3.4	3.4	3.2	3.1	3.3	3.1	3.7	3.8	= 3.68
Creating	4.5	4.4	4.5	4.0	4.1	3.9	4.3	4.2	4.5	3.8	3.5	3.4	3.2	3.3	3.0	3.0	3.8	3.7	= 3.84
Implementing	2.6	2.9	3.1	2.4	2.7	2.7	3.5	3.6	3.7	3.2	2.0	2.9	2.8	2.7	2.1	3.0	3.4	3.4	= 2.93
Connecting	3.3	3.0	3.2	3.2	3.1	3.1	4.2	3.8	4.3	3.3	3.2	3.1	4.0	3.7	3.9	3.7	4.2	4.3	= 3.59
Advocating	2.6	2.8	3.2	2.8	2.9	2.9	4.1	4.0	4.1	3.5	3.6	3.5	3.1	3.2	3.4	3.1	3.3	3.2	= 3.29
Element Averages	= 3.44			= 3.27			= 4.07			= 3.31			=3.20			= 3.51			3.47

Figure 10.9 *Sample Results Tracker: Poor Implementation Capability*

The organization whose data are shown in Example #2 represents another common type of organization. This is the innovative organization that is tuned in to its environment (notice the strong Sensing capability) and producing great new products and services (strong Creating capability) that shape the market. Unfortunately, this organization lacks the skills and practices to effectively bring these ideas to the market. The low Implementing scores, coupled with poor Advocating around new strategies, mean that the organization is likely to be a hotbed of ideas that are commercialized by fast followers.

The priority list for this organization will include skills and practices to help bring ideas to life and to move from planning to execution.

Example #3: Halfway to Holistic

The organization in Example #3 does not have the same pervasive challenges as those in the previous examples. Instead, it is an organization that has a few different opportunities to build leadership capacity. Take a look at the cells with weak scores.

First, notice the poor results in the Customer Sensing cells. These results are common in organizations where customer data are collected but not shared broadly in the organization. (To be sure that is the underlying issue, this organization would review the scores on the cell in the Audit to confirm that is what is happening.)

	Customer			Business Strategy			Culture & Values			Organization			Team			Personal			Capability Averages
	OP	LC	IB	OP	LC	IB	OP	LC	IB	OP	LC	IB	OP	LC	IB	OP	LC	IB	
Sensing	3.0	2.5	2.5	3.4	3.4	3.4	3.3	3.4	3.2	3.4	3.4	3.4	4.0	4.1	3.9	4.1	4.0	4.3	= 3.48
Creating	3.4	3.3	3.2	3.4	3.4	3.4	3.1	3.0	3.1	3.4	3.4	3.4	4.0	3.8	3.9	4.3	3.9	3.9	= 3.51
Implementing	3.4	3.4	3.3	4.1	4.2	4.3	3.4	3.2	3.2	3.4	3.4	3.4	4.3	3.7	3.7	4.2	4.3	3.8	= 3.71
Connecting	3.2	3.1	3.1	3.4	3.4	3.4	2.9	2.4	2.4	2.5	2.4	2.7	3.8	3.8	3.8	4.1	3.8	3.8	= 3.22
Advocating	3.2	3.1	3.0	3.4	3.4	3.4	3.4	3.4	3.4	2.4	2.5	2.2	4.2	3.9	4.1	4.1	4.1	4.1	= 3.41
Element Averages	= 3.11			= 3.56			= 3.12			= 3.02			=3.93			= 4.05			3.47

Figure 10.10 *Sample Results Tracker: Isolated Weak Cells*

Next, you'll notice that Connecting is strong in the Team and Personal elements, but much less strong in the Culture & Values and Organization elements. This is likely due to a traditional, functional bias in which relationships within a silo are very strong but the connections across organizational boundaries are not. These cells suggest that both the formal and informal connections with people in different parts of the organization are missing.

The low scores in the Organization Advocating cells further support this silo hypothesis. In contrast, Team Advocating has high scores. These scores suggest that the organization is set up to pit the interests of one group against another, rather than acting in the best interest of the organization overall.

The good news for this organization is that there are no pervasive challenges across the grid. The obvious quick win will be to share customer data with all employees. Beyond that, the priority will be to create the practices and the informal opportunities to begin to foster relationships across different parts of the organization.

MEASURING THE GAP Q&A

For many, the introduction of rigorous measurement is an exciting yet somewhat daunting task. The actions described above, along with the tools provided in the appendices should make your job somewhat easier. Below, we answer a few of the questions we are commonly asked about measuring the gap.

1. *Where Do I Start?*

There is no "right answer" for where to start. The best answer is to start wherever you can. For some, introducing the concepts of holistic leadership might require a major change management effort. Often, it is possible in these situations to find a small group of senior-level champions who will participate in the Audit. In other situations, a multi-rater feedback process is already well established, and revising the questionnaire to measure holistic leadership behaviors will not be difficult. It also is possible that a leadership offsite or other forum might create the perfect venue at which to conduct the Survey of Leadership Culture.

In our experience, once the results of one measure are shared, the enthusiasm for and investment in measurement of leadership capacity gains momentum.

2. *How Do I Get Buy-In for Measurement?*

A measurement project, just like any other initiative that requires time and money, should be based on a solid business case. If the measurement project you are trying to justify pertains to leadership capacity, then you could start by documenting the investments you are already making in leadership development. These activities cost most organizations hundreds of thousands, if not millions, of dollars annually. By demonstrating how leadership development could be better targeted on priority areas, you can estimate a significant return on investment.

3. *What If I Already Have Measures?*

Great! If you already have measures, then you likely work in an organization that values measurement. If your measures adequately capture the leadership capacity of your organization, then you can use these existing tools and move to the next step in the Leadership Solutions Pathway. If you have only parts of a complete diagnostic, then you can build on what you have. Two common examples include:

- *360° feedback:* If you already have a 360° tool, map the questions against the 30-cell grid. If there are areas that aren't currently being measured, add a few questions from the Assessment of Leadership Behaviors. Adding only the required questions is the best approach because you want to maintain as many identical questions as possible to allow for trending.

- *Employee survey:* In our experience, most employee surveys do not overlap in content with the Survey of Leadership Culture. The Survey is focused on the expectations and norms for leaders in the organization, whereas most employee surveys assess the perceptions and opinions of all employees about a variety of work-related issues. We find it is best to keep these two important initiatives separate.

4. *How Can I Establish a Leadership Capacity Metric on Our Corporate Dashboard?*

Many executives are looking for a way to keep leadership capacity front and center as a business priority in their organizations. One way to do this is to incorporate the overall grid average from the bottom right corner of the LGA 3D Results Tracker™ and use it as a metric of leadership capacity. This metric can then be incorporated into the organization's corporate dashboard of business metrics. Essentially, it acts as a Leadership Capacity Index. Tracking it on a regular basis helps ensure that the organization is paying attention to the strength of its leadership capacity.

MEASURING LEADERSHIP CAPACITY: REFLECTIONS

Some companies may see measuring leadership capacity as a time-consuming and arduous task that only delays action. These companies argue that once they have defined the leadership they require for the future, they should set straight to work on building that capacity. We would argue strongly that the investment in measurement is a very prudent one that, in the end, speeds up the process of building leadership capacity.

By focusing the organization on a short list of priorities, good measurement prevents having large amounts of time and money spent working on something that is not required. You might think there is little harm in trying to improve all aspects of holistic leadership, but with scarce resources to invest in leadership, it is important to target the areas of greatest need.

Measuring leadership capacity also allows you to identify which dimension is at the root of leadership challenges in a particular area. For example, if there is a gap in organizational leadership, the reason may be the result of poorly designed practices (such as a bottom-up planning process where different functions don't interact until the end). Alternatively, it might be the result of cultural resistance to cross-boundary relationships where an insular functional approach discourages communication with people in other departments. Finally, it is possible individual leaders don't have the skills to establish relationships with people outside their own business group. "Step 2: Measure the Gap" allows an organization to hone in on the most likely cause of the problem.

CONCLUDING COMMENTS

The investment in measuring leadership capacity creates many benefits. It helps organizations better understand the nature of their leadership capacity—both strengths and gaps. It enables organizations to focus on high-priority areas and intervene where the challenge is greatest. Finally, it provides the data to build a business case for the investment that is needed in leadership capacity.

In the next chapter of the Leadership Solutions Pathway we examine "Step Three: Act to Build Capacity," which describes how organizations can develop a targeted plan of action to build the leadership capacity they require to achieve sustainable competitive advantage.

CHAPTER ELEVEN

Step 3: Act to Build Capacity

The first two steps of the Leadership Solutions Pathway measured the gap in an organization's capacity, comparing what the organization has with what it needs. The next challenge is to develop a focused plan to build the leadership capacity in the priority areas for action.

This chapter describes the third step of the Leadership Solutions Pathway: Act to Build Capacity (Figure 11.1).

THE LEADERSHIP SOLUTIONS PATHWAY

Figure 11.1 *The Leadership Solutions Pathway*

The chapter examines the four actions that are recommended for Step 3. In describing each action, we explain why it is needed, provide specific tactics to make the action work and give examples of how that action can be applied.

THE NEED FOR THOUGHTFUL ACTIONS TO BUILD CAPACITY

Many organizations are finding that their leadership gap is reaching crisis proportions, and the prognosis is that it will continue to get worse as their workforce ages and the complexity of the work environment increases. Most organizations cannot wait patiently for a new recruiting profile to seed the organization with holistic leaders. Instead, business leaders need targeted, integrated and accelerated leadership capacity solutions. They need to pull all the levers at their disposal to prepare their internal leaders to be able to respond to current and future business challenges.

The urgency of the leadership gap often creates an impetus to jump to conclusions once Steps 1 and 2 of the Leadership Solutions Pathway are completed. The impulse to jump to implementation without a thoughtful planning process is not surprising. The pressure to address the leadership gap is severe, and the desire to resolve it quickly is great. Nevertheless, we strongly encourage executives to take thoughtful actions to build capacity.

THE FOUR ACTIONS OF STEP 3: ACT TO BUILD CAPACITY

- Action 1: Target the Priority Leadership Capacity Gap
- Action 2: Integrate the Leadership Capacity Solutions
- Action 3: Accelerate Implementation by Leveraging the Three Dimensions
- Action 4: Evolve the Solution as Conditions Change

Each action will be described in detail. We then will show how the action was used in a case example. The case example for this chapter is as follows:

The CEO of a large financial services company was faced with an interesting challenge. The organization had been very successful and had acquired other companies and had grown into new geographies. It was seen as a very good employer, and many people spent their whole careers there. But the growth and success had raised it into a new, global business environment.

Step 1: Determine Leadership Requirements of the Leadership Solutions Pathway—this had helped the leaders clarify that success on a global scale would require the following holistic leadership skills:

- **Customer Sensing**—A new level of leadership capacity centered around insights about a whole new group of customers
- **Customer Value Proposition**—The ability to identify and build a new set of solutions to meet the needs of the new group of global customers:
- **Strategic Sensing**—A more aggressive and riskier strategy
- **Strategic Architect**—A longer-term strategic perspective
- **Strategy Deployment**—The ability to take innovative ideas and implement them within the company
- **Organizational Relationships**—An increased knowledge sharing across the organization

Step 2: Measure the Gap—this revealed many challenges that the CEO had not anticipated:

- Individual behaviors were not rated positively.
- Organizational practices were viewed even more poorly, with many of the disciplined practices now beginning to choke off innovation and growth.
- The leadership culture was not supporting leaders in challenging the status quo. Leaders were being rewarded for delivering results only within their areas. As a result, little cooperation existed across different parts of the business. Worse yet, the tremendous fear of making a mistake was allowing for incremental changes and little or no truly novel thinking.

The full Leadership Gap Analysis™ results are shown in Figure 11.2 on the following page. The organization was facing challenges in several areas of the grid:

	Customer			Business Strategy			Culture & Values			Organization			Team			Personal			
	OP	LC	IB	OP	LC	IB	OP	LC	IB	OP	LC	IB	OP	LC	IB	OP	LC	IB	Capability Averages
Sensing	3.3	3.1	2.9	2.5	2.2	2.4	4.3	4.6	4.5	2.4	2.5	2.8	4.2	3.1	2.7	3.1	2.4	2.7	= 3.09
Creating	3.2	3.3	2.8	2.6	2.2	2.3	4.5	4.2	4.4	2.6	2.7	2.9	4.3	3.7	3.5	3.4	2.2	2.8	= 3.20
Implementing	3.7	3.6	3.4	3.7	3.8	4.2	4.2	4.4	4.3	2.7	3.1	2.6	4.4	3.6	3.6	3.6	2.8	2.8	= 3.58
Connecting	3.8	3.7	3.9	3.4	3.4	3.6	4.5	4.5	4.3	2.6	2.6	2.5	4.1	2.9	2.8	3.4	3.4	3.5	= 3.49
Advocating	2.9	2.7	2.7	3.1	2.9	3.2	4.3	4.6	4.3	2.5	2.7	2.7	3.8	3.6	3.5	3.5	3.8	3.6	= 3.35
Element Averages	= 3.27			= 3.03			= 4.39			= 2.65			=3.59			= 3.13			3.34

Figure 11.2 *Results Tracker for Financial Services Example*

- **Customer leadership**—These scores reflected the leaders' belief that the organization understood its current customers well but wasn't doing a good job of learning about new customers, whether they were the young technology-savvy generation who had never visited a bank branch or the potential customers in Asia-Pacific.
- **Business strategy leadership**—Scores in this element were equally poor. The emphasis on delivering business plans had created a short-term orientation with very little attention to the long-term trends that would shape the business environment.
- **Organizational leadership**—Scores reflected that the organization rewarded leaders for success within their areas and the inadvertent result was competition across areas.
- **Personal leadership**—Other areas of weakness included the individual behaviors around coaching and development. Although the organization had invested heavily in leadership development programs, individual leaders were not taking the time to have candid conversations with their direct reports. Even the senior leaders were feeling starved for feedback.

The organization's **strengths** were equally predictable:
- **Implementation capability**—Scores were extremely high in this capability. Given a task, leaders were very well supported in mobilizing the organization's resources to get the job done.
- **Culture and Values leadership**—Scores here were also very strong. The organization believed in taking care of people and

that was reflected in the behaviors, the practices and the leadership culture.

Let's look at the four actions of Step 3: Act to build capacity. After each action, we will return to the organization case example and see how that action was applied.

Action 1: Target the Priority Leadership Capacity Gap

When an organization completes Step 2: Measure the Gap, it has a list of priority areas for action. It is important not to get overwhelmed by the number and magnitude of the capacity gaps but to target specific areas that have the highest potential to meet your requirements. The priorities need to be the ones that represent the opportunity to build leadership capacity in the areas that you identified in Step 1 as the most important to your organization in the future. However, choosing the top-priority leadership capacity gaps may be difficult if many gaps appear to be equally compelling. How do you target your priorities?

When many gaps are of similar levels of importance, you need to engage in a *triage* process to target what to focus on first. We use the term "triage"[1] judiciously. "Triage" refers to the sorting out of the greater need from the lesser need. For example, in a hospital emergency environment, patients are triaged to help understand where best to use limited resources (e.g., nurses, doctors, beds, MRI machines). When you triage, you will find:[2]

- ***Some cases are critical and need attention immediately:*** In the hospital emergency room, it could be a coronary arrest in which immediate intervention with the right combination of defibrillation, epinephrine and oxygen could mean the difference between life and death. In leadership, it might be the need to focus on succession management as a strategic process to reduce the risk of being without ready-now talent for critical positions.

- ***Some cases are critical but can withstand a delayed response:*** Unfortunately, in the hospital emergency room, sometimes cases that need attention are triaged to a lower status because other cases are more critical. The delayed response does not negate the severity of the problem, but the comparative severity of more critical cases pushes it to the wait list. Those who have spent a night in a waiting room with a broken arm watching stretchers go by can attest to this phenomenon.

In leadership, for example, a problematic silo-focused research department may be a serious cause for concern, but the concern may be greater about the silo-focused sales leaders who are making decisions for personal gain rather than for the benefit of the overall business. Furthermore, the sales group is directly customer-facing, which compounds the risk associated with their behavior. Therefore, even though the research department needs attention, responding to its leadership capacity gap may be put on the wait list until the sales leadership gap is sorted out and resolved.

- *Some cases are quite minor and would not benefit tremendously from intervention:* In the emergency room, it might be a sprained ankle that shows no signs of a fracture. For a leadership capacity gap, it might be a cumbersome performance management system that, at its core, is measuring and rewarding the right kind of behaviors. It could be better, but there is probably a "patient" lurking in one of the organizational practices or leader behaviors that would benefit more from assistance.

- *Some cases are in such terrible shape that they might need to be abandoned in favor of other critical cases that have a better chance of success:* Unfortunately, in a severe crisis situation, an overwhelming number of critical cases can occur—all requiring immediate attention. The multiple competing priorities in a hospital emergency may mean that some patients who should be treated will not receive treatment. In a leadership gap crisis, some areas (either elements or capabilities) might be so dysfunctional that fixing them would be too taxing for the organization. The organization's leaders will need to decide if they can improve these areas over the long term or whether they will need to explore other business models, such as outsourcing or strategic alliances, to mitigate the risk of the gap.

Of course, one possible response is to become overwhelmed by the myriad of choices and decide to target nothing. One leader described indecision and inaction when he said, "Hope is not a strategy." Even if hope is a strategy, it is very high-risk and woefully inadequate. Without a targeted leadership response to bridge the leadership gap, the organization can anticipate some widening of the gap. The organization can reduce its risk and begin to resolve its leadership gap if it understands its leadership capacity requirements, conducts a focused diagnostic of its leadership gap and targets a leadership solution to bridge the gap.

Let's revisit the case example for this chapter to see how the financial services company used Action 1 to target its area of greatest need.

The CEO called a meeting of the executive team to review the results of the Leadership Gap Analysis™ and to determine how they would respond. It was a very uncomfortable discussion. Some in the room believed strongly in what the analysis was saying—that they didn't have what would be required to achieve their ambitious global goals. Others were resistant and unwilling to view some of the organization's strengths as liabilities for the future. The CEO challenged the group to be curious about the findings and to be open-minded about what the results were telling them.

As the conversation progressed, the VP of HR made an important point. The strategy had been to develop leaders to be more innovative and entrepreneurial. Investments were being made in training and in coaching to build leaders' skills. She commented that the investment they were making in leadership development was not likely to yield a return on investment because the practices and leadership culture inhibited innovation and entrepreneurialism. In fact, she argued, the programs were demoralizing leaders because they wanted to embrace what they were learning, but their managers were discouraging them.

She made a bold suggestion: "Let's hold off on putting more directors through the program until we take it ourselves. I think we (the executives) need to understand the main messages of the program and get an appreciation for some of the other changes that we might need to make to support them in applying what they're learning." The executives agreed, but they also did not want to stop investing in their leaders. Instead of focusing on training leaders, the executives decided they needed to reinforce the focus on coaching them.

The leadership department was providing great tools for managing performance and developing leaders; they just weren't being used. Improving the quality of coaching for leaders would be another important target area.

The conversation shifted to business strategy and customer leadership. The executive team was in agreement that strategy had been too tightly controlled at the very top of the organization. If they were going to make the jump into the global arena, more leaders would need to become externally oriented, with particular emphasis on sensing capability in both the customer and strategy elements. This would be a high priority.

Another target area emerged directly from this conversation. If they were going to increase their knowledge, understanding and insight about the customer and the competitive marketplace, they would need to support leaders in turning these insights into action. As a result, the final target area would be the capability of creating, in both the customer leadership and business strategy elements.

Predictably, someone mentioned the "moose in the room." Organizational practices were stifling innovation—most notably the business planning and financial approval processes. These processes were so rigid and tightly controlled that it would take months (if not years) to get new ideas approved. Often, on their way up the chain of command, what was truly innovative about an idea was gradually muted as the need to guarantee success and minimize risk took its toll. This was a very sensitive topic. The prudent planning and risk mitigation strategies had served the organization well as it grew. It also prevented the organization from being caught up in some of the fads that had spelled the demise of more aggressive organizations.

The debate was heated. It was clear that the planning and approval processes would need to change if they were to provide the agility needed to compete globally. But this would distract the entire organization and alter the very DNA of the organization. The final targeted action was to have a small group study this issue and propose a pilot project in one of the smaller business units. The executive team was confident they could begin to introduce positive change without risking a major organizational upheaval.

At the end of the session, the next step in the path was clear. The company would invest in understanding the customer of the future and in creating strategies for a competitive advantage. They would also shift the culture by encouraging leaders to develop their direct reports—providing the coaching and feedback that they wanted and needed. They would start to investigate how they might change some of their core processes and look for quick wins that would move things in the right direction. They would not change processes radically. Their target was set.

This case illustrates a good example of Action 1: Target the priority leadership capacity gap. The executive team was effective at choosing the priority targets and also at deciding what not to tackle. This put the organization in a good position to focus its efforts on a short list of high-priority issues.

Targeting is critical because it focuses the organization on the highest-priority areas and prevents the common failure path of trying to do too much at once. We have, however, seen mistakes made in the name of targeting. Three common mistakes include:

- *Target too big:* In some organizations that we have worked with, the response to the leadership gap and the model of holistic leadership was so positive that they wanted to run "lunch and learn" sessions for their leaders on all six elements—all at the same time. They essentially created a crash course in Holistic Leadership 101. The problem is that the leaders knew a little bit about a lot of things but not a lot about anything. It is almost impossible to build five skills or to pay attention to six different elements all at once and so quickly. Because so much of the art of leadership in today's fast-paced business environment is about managing attention and energy, it is important to be more focused as you begin to build capacity.

- *Target too small:* This mistake is the direct opposite of the first one we discussed. In this case, through a series of training courses, an organization targets specific cells of holistic leadership that it sees as critical. The problem in this case is that leaders know a lot about very discrete things but do not have the broader context of

holistic leadership. In many cases, leaders attend a series of disconnected courses or workshops to gain specific skills, but they are
left having to figure out how all the content comes together in a
meaningful manner.

- *Targeting subpopulations of leaders:* One of the most common
strategies for leadership development has been to focus on high-
potential leaders. In many organizations, these "Hi-Po's" are
invested in lavishly with executive MBA tuition, external coaches,
high-profile assignments, etc. The problem is that you need all of
your leaders, or at least most of them, to be holistic. Just targeting
the individual behavior of high potentials will not create the
change you need. We will discuss this further when we talk about
accelerating in Action 3.

Action 2: Integrate the Leadership Capacity Solutions

The Leadership Gap introduced the concept that integrated, not fragmented, leadership development is a critical success factor for organizations to
build capacity. Action 2 sets out two different aspects of integration and
provides an approach that will help you integrate your leadership solutions.[3]

When we use the term "integrated solutions," we are referring to the
integration of solutions across the 30-cell grid. Rather than thinking of
business strategy leadership as distinct from organizational leadership, an
integrated solution considers both together. Leadership solutions can be
integrated in two ways:

1. Align Solutions to an Overarching Theme

The first strategy for increasing the integration of your leadership solution
is to create one overarching theme that describes what you need to do to
close your leadership gap. This theme, which emerges from Action 1: Target
the Priority, will be the unifying force among all programs. For example,
a consumer packaged-goods company realized that its opportunity for

competitive advantage came from shifting the organization's focus from the customer (i.e., the stores that sell their products) to the consumer (the people who actually eat the products). Consumer insight became the overarching theme for all initiatives.

The theme clarifies how each of the holistic leadership elements and capabilities must work together to close the gap. For example, with the theme of "consumer insight," it is clear how the customer leadership element is central, but it is equally obvious how business strategy leadership needs to support the new focus on the consumer. Organizational leadership is also implicated; the organizational design focus on key accounts (which is a customer-centric approach) needs to give way to a design focused on the consumer.

The theme will align your efforts.

2. Ensure Solutions Are Complementary and Linked to One Another

The second strategy for integrating your leadership solution is to connect the different activities and to ensure they complement one another. Ideally, you are trying to create a collection of activities that reinforce the same messages in a variety of different ways. For example, if the theme is consumer insight, then several components come together to create the integrated solution, including:

- The hiring profile should be looking for people with consumer-facing experience, especially those who have unique perspectives on the target consumer.

- The orientation program should be providing research on the different consumer segments and on their buying habits.

- The goal-setting process should require a consumer-related objective for all leaders.

- The measurement system should include leading indicators of consumer satisfaction and brand loyalty.

- The career path for leaders should include opportunities to work on different brands and with different consumer segments.

As simple as this type of integration across different activities sounds, in our experience, it is rare. Instead, organizations drive different messages with different programs. Whereas the hiring profile might be looking for innovative new leaders who are able to work across organizational boundaries to revolutionize products and services, the reward system might be rewarding individual contribution and tried and true approaches. Once the different components of your leadership solution are working together to reinforce a consistent message, you will quickly begin to feel increased traction.

Let's consider how the case example for this chapter applied Action 2 to integrate the leadership capacity solutions.

> The executive team was united in their view of the challenges that faced them. To compete in the global financial services industry, they would need to rely on the executional excellence that had served them well, and they would need to enhance their ability to innovate.
>
> They started by developing a position statement of what they meant by innovation. Their statement was as follows: "We will turn our attention to the environments in which we operate, collecting information, gleaning insights and building solutions. We will instill in our leaders a sense of ownership to shepherd these ideas from conception through to commercialization. We will harness the skills of our diverse organization to bring the solutions the market needs."
>
> "Innovation" provided a compelling theme around which to integrate their leadership solution. Customer leadership initiatives would be focused on understanding new customer groups and emerging markets. Strategy initiatives would be directed at reaching more deeply and broadly into the organization to find ideas for new products that could change the way people manage their money. Organizational leadership initiatives would be designed to create synergies between different lines of business so that bundled products could be built to meet all the financial needs of different customer segments such as the retiring baby boomers. The overarching theme of "innovation" became the glue for the organization-wide initiatives to build leadership capacity.

The next realization was that the organization's size and scale had allowed it to create highly specialized functions that were no longer talking to one another. Even within the Human Resources function, the different groups such as Leadership Development and Compensation did not share the same viewpoints. The executive team decided to create a leadership summit for those in charge of the various key organizational practices. The summit allowed the bank to share the results of the Leadership Gap Analysis™, to share the vision of leadership capacity for the future, and to introduce the theme of innovation.

During the summit, working groups met to talk about how they could modify their programs to better fit together. A major win came when the performance management and compensation teams agreed to a new KPI (key performance indicator) around innovation and agreed on a component of the variable pay plan that would be tied to it.

Another important realization was that sending all leaders to the excellent leadership development institute built by the organization was having the unintended result of perpetuating the internal focus. To rectify this, they decided the leadership development program would include the use of an external mentor (a high-level executive outside of financial services) as well as two modules that would be delivered in different countries where the company operated. They would work hard to incorporate activities that would broaden the leaders' perspectives.

The summit was such a success that they decided to make it a biannual event. These events would give the program designers a chance to roll up their sleeves and build the programs that would increase innovation and help to close the leadership gap.

Action 3: Accelerate Implementation by Leveraging the Three Dimensions

In Part 1 of this book we introduced the three dimensions of leadership capacity (see Figure 11.3 on the following page)—individual leader behavior, organizational practices and leadership culture.

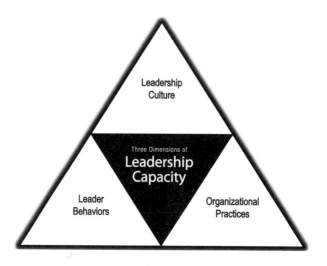

Figure 11.3 *The Three Dimensions of Leadership Capacity*

The Leadership Gap Analysis™ might identify a problem in any one of these dimensions. If that is the case, the organization can develop a targeted and integrated solution to build leadership capacity in that area.

However, the three dimensions have another very important use—to accelerate the implementation of the leadership solution. The best way is to attack the targeted leadership gap with all three dimensions. A three-pronged attack heightens the awareness of the need, sharpens the focus on the behaviors that are required, and speeds up the adherence to and power of the leadership solution.

In Chapter 3, we introduced the concept of the three dimensions of leadership capacity with an example of an organization that sent its leaders off to training, only to learn that the leadership culture and the organizational practices were preventing leaders from using their new skills. This is a very common example of a solution that is not accelerated by leveraging all dimensions.

Another example comes from the executives who believe they can create dramatic change by exercising their authority to unilaterally alter an organizational practice. For example, executives can rapidly reinforce the need for a change in behavior by restructuring their organization; changing, promoting or removing leaders; and by changing what is rewarded in an organization. They also can quickly dismantle organizational practices they believe are motivating ineffective behavior. However, the benefits of these kinds of changes are sometimes short-lived.

The introduction of a new practice does not mean that leaders have the skills to live up to the new standard. Nor does it necessarily override the expectations that have become part of the leadership culture—a standard that can be more enduring than the official practices. However, when changes in organizational practices are bolstered by changes in individual behaviors and by shifts in culture, the required changes will come much more quickly.

Here are some examples of how to leverage the three dimensions:

- *Accelerating an Individual Leadership Solution:* Overcoming a deficiency in the individual leader dimension can be accelerated by leveraging organizational practices and leadership culture. For example, the aggregate results of the Assessment of Leader Behavior might suggest that your leaders are not strong in the team leadership element. In response, you might develop a training program on team effectiveness strategies. Building the leaders' skills will slowly improve the level of team leadership, but this approach could be accelerated by leveraging an organizational practice and providing internal or external organization development experts to facilitate ongoing team sessions. Also, they could leverage the leadership culture by having the executives make an explicit statement that team effectiveness is of strategic importance throughout the organization and that they are working on the effectiveness of their own executive team.

- *Accelerating an Organizational Practices Solution:* Overcoming a deficiency in the organizational practices dimension can be accelerated by leveraging additional solutions in the individual leadership and leadership culture dimensions. For example, an organization that has inadequate succession planning practices can implement improvements in that practice. However, the leadership culture could be transformed in support of this practice if senior leaders and executives would model the way by accepting lateral transfers for people needing development opportunities for critical positions. They could also encourage individual leadership training and networking sessions on how to take control of your own career development.

- *Accelerating a Leadership Culture Solution:* Overcoming a deficiency in the leadership culture dimension can be accelerated by leveraging additional solutions in the individual leadership dimension and the organizational practices dimension. For example, an organization had a leadership culture that was very results oriented and did not reinforce the organization's values. The organization did conduct a values exercise to involve all employees in determining what the values should be. However, they needed to accelerate the adoption of the new values.

  They began by telling individual leader stories in their company newsletter about individuals who were examples of the organizational values. At the same time, they modified the organizational practice of the employee engagement survey. They included an assessment of the extent to which the respondents believed they modeled the organizational values and the extent to which they believed it was also modeled by senior leaders, their direct supervisor, and co-workers. The combination of questions was effective at highlighting the importance of values to the leaders. They also leveraged the individual leader dimension by involving leaders in defining the "dos and don'ts" of how to implement the values in their leadership responsibilities.

Let's return to the chapter case example, describing how they successfully activated all three dimensions to accelerate the implementation of their leadership solution.

The leaders at the financial services company realized they did not have the luxury of time in making the transformation to a more externally oriented and innovative organization. With consolidation happening constantly, the pressures of the global industry were great. Innovation would ensure they were the ones acquiring rather than being acquired. As a result, the executive team decided to accelerate the leadership solution by pulling all the levers at their disposal.

On the first component of the solution—increasing the external orientation—the three-pronged approach would include:
- *Building leaders' understanding and awareness of the different customer segments*
- *Striking cross-functional teams responsible for building products for a single customer group*

- *Changing the up-front piece of the strategic planning process to include a more comprehensive environmental scan.*

Interestingly, leaders commented on how they had always been discouraged from attending external events such as industry conferences. This led to an important leadership cultural intervention where leaders were encouraged to attend events and then have "lunch and learn" sessions to share the ideas they had taken away. Each small intervention was an important piece of the puzzle in accelerating the shift to greater external awareness.

On the other important component of the leadership solution—the need for leaders to become better coaches for their direct reports—the approach was also multifaceted. The biggest change was cultural. From the executives down, the perception that coaching was for poor performers had been firmly engrained. One dissenting voice on the executive team suggested they bring an executive coach in to work with the executive team. The executive coach helped them realize that coaching these days is as much for the high performers as the low. (Even Tiger Woods benefits from good coaching.)

The bank began to fund external coaching for some of its key talent. For others, a training program was rolled out that brought together coaches and their direct reports to learn about effective coaching and the responsibilities of both parties in making coaching work. The culture began to change. Conversations started to happen. Sometimes they were about how leaders could best capitalize on their strengths, which career move to make next, or how they could manage a difficult stakeholder. The culture began to embrace the importance of coaching—not only for poor performers, but for strong performers as well.

Without the luxury of time, the organization needed to use all avenues available to accelerate their leadership solution. They were selective about the use of training, but programs on emerging customers and effective coaching were high priorities. Although they had decided from the outset not to make changes in the planning or financial approval processes, they did add new components to the front end of the strategic planning process. Perhaps the most important changes they made were in the expectations of leaders. With new ways of communicating and with the executives paying attention to different things, the culture changes supported leaders in demonstrating their new skills.

It didn't take long before the leaders began to test their new skills. Instead of being discouraged by the bureaucratic process, they began to use the new practices to foster different ways of thinking. Most importantly, the bank began to celebrate small successes, most radically when they invited the leader of a failed venture to share her learnings at the company-wide leadership meeting. That was "proof in the pudding" of a shift in the culture, and it spawned more innovation. The organization began to feel the momentum as all three dimensions supported the increasing leadership capacity they required.

Action 4: Evolve the Solution as Conditions Change

One of the more challenging aspects of leadership solutions is that a solution that works today may no longer be useful tomorrow. As the business environment continues to change, it creates new strategic implications, which will in turn create changing demands of the leadership capacity required by your organization. As a result, there is a need for continuous scanning and tracking of the external environment and the internal organization to monitor ongoing requirements for leadership capacity.

Ongoing scanning and evaluation will lead to refinements to the organizational practices, individual leadership and leadership culture that are required. One option is to conduct the Leadership Gap Analysis™ on an annual basis. You can use this device to do two things:

- Track the extent to which individual leadership, organizational practices and the leadership culture are evolving as planned in the organization. Then include these annual findings in your overall balance scorecard.

- Forecast the anticipated leadership gaps that will likely emerge as environmental conditions change.

We anticipate that the challenge to continually evolve your leadership capacity needs will lead to some new business practices. These include:

- Executives will own the changes in leadership capacity and take accountability to ensure that it gets the attention that it requires.

Boards of directors will create the impetus for this change as they continue their interest in executive leadership capacity.

- Executives will demonstrate their accountability by requiring a metric of leadership capacity. The metric will be reported at least annually and tracked in the same way that an organization would track its key financial metrics.

- Leading organizations will continue to be assertive and focus on shaping the new environment rather than responding to the external environmental conditions as they change. In general, they will find that the move to the next future external environment will happen faster than anticipated. It will require ongoing agility by the organization and its leadership to respond to the rapidly changing business environment.

Let's return to the chapter case study for the final time to see how the bank evolved their solution as conditions changed.

The bank began to enjoy even greater success in their international operations. They were building better products and services and differentiating them from their competitors'. But as before, the greater the successes in the global arena, the fiercer the competition. The external environment continued to evolve.

Innovation had taken hold. The organization was recognizing opportunities more effectively and responding with unique solutions that stood out in the marketplace. But the bigger they got, the slower they got. Great ideas were surfacing, but they were coming from several layers down in the organization and not bubbling up fast enough. Aggressive regional players were moving into emerging markets and soaking up market share before the large global organization could make a decision on whether to enter. The organization's measured, deliberate approach was again creating important challenges for them.

Thus, the theme began to evolve. Although "Innovation" remained center stage, it took on a new emphasis. Not only did great products and services need to be developed, they needed to be approved and brought to the market faster. Faster responses required some new talent at the top, as well as strategic alliances with organizations that were already on the ground in emerging markets.

The organization was finally ready to tackle its approval processes, which they had known for a while were slowing down their speed to market. But the successful transformation under the theme of "Innovation" had built their confidence. They knew how to build leadership capacity. They knew that they had to be focused—that they couldn't try to change everything at once. They knew their solutions all had to make sense together and that they couldn't be seen as a series of independent activities. They knew that they had to accelerate their transformation by building skills, changing practices and shifting the leadership culture. And now they knew that evolving their leadership capacity was just part of the journey.

When organizations effectively act to build capacity, as in the case study, they are able to build leadership solutions that can give them a key source of sustainable competitive advantage. The bank now had a distinct advantage: the ability to innovate for global growth.

Here are some of the other characteristics of organizations that are effective at Step 3: Act to Build Capacity:

- At the executive table, leadership capacity often becomes an important topic at strategy discussions.

- The investment in leadership capacity is maintained during down times and low business cycles.

- They have a clear leadership story that spells out the kind of leadership the organization requires to succeed in the future.

- Many leaders become models of the leadership story and reinforce it in their words and actions.

- They also build a genuine "community of leaders" in which the leadership culture is supportive rather than sink-or-swim.

- Leaders at all levels and cross-functionally take initiative and don't wait to be told what to do. They know when to lead and when to follow.

CONCLUDING COMMENTS

The process of Step 3: Act to Build Capacity needs to be done thoughtfully. The top-priority solutions need to be targeted to avoid the tendency to fix too many things at once. Also, the solutions need to be integrated, which can be accomplished by aligning them to an overarching theme and by having them reinforce the same message with complementary approaches. Organizations should also leverage the three dimensions of leadership capacity to accelerate the process of implementing the leadership solution. Finally, the process is continuous, and executives need to engage in ongoing scanning with the intention that they can get in front of the environmental changes and begin to shape their future for competitive advantage.

The next chapter describes the part the individual leader is expected to play in the leadership solution. It will help you to see your role in building leadership capacity, whether or not your organization and its practices support you in that process.

CHAPTER TWELVE

Step 4: Do Your Part

*A midsize financial services company held an emerging leaders pro-
gram designed to bring young leaders across the company together
to learn about the company strategy, develop leadership skills and
build relationships with peers.*

*The CEO planned to close the meeting with a round of questions
and answers. During the discussion, many of the young leaders
asked about the vision and the company's strategic priorities. Others asked the CEO to recount her own leadership journey to the top
of the organization. One young leader asked a final question, "What
leadership advice would you give us based on your experiences as
a successful leader?"*

*The CEO took a moment to collect her thoughts and said, "I have
a simple message for each of you: Do your part." The room fell silent
as the young leaders pondered the advice. Then the CEO continued,
"What I have come to learn about leadership is that it is not about
leadership at the top. The company's success is not based solely on
what I do as a CEO or what our executive team does. Our success is
a function of all leaders in this company doing their part, regardless
of their roles. Do not underestimate the impact you can have in your
role. Consider where our company would be if each of you committed
to realizing your own leadership potential. And what if you worked
together to realize your collective leadership potential? Imagine the
kind of company we would build for the future." With those words,*

the session ended and the emerging leaders left with a simple yet powerful message.

All leaders today are being called upon to do their part to realize their own leadership potential and to help their organizations build leadership capacity for sustained competitive advantage.

In previous chapters we have discussed Steps 1 to 3 of the Leadership Solutions Pathway, which explain what organizations need to do to build leadership capacity. We now direct our focus to Step 4: Do Your Part (Figure 12.1).

THE LEADERSHIP SOLUTIONS PATHWAY

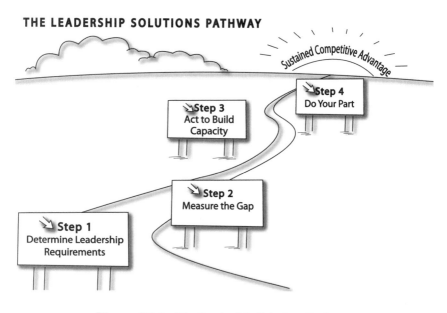

Figure 12.1 *The Leadership Solutions Pathway*

We begin this chapter by examining how individual leaders "do their part" by applying the first three steps of the Leadership Solutions Pathway to build their own leadership capacity. We then introduce the fourth step of the overall Leadership Solutions Pathway, which describes what is expected of individual leaders in doing their part to support their organization's efforts to build leadership capacity.

THE LEADERSHIP SOLUTIONS PATHWAY AND THE INDIVIDUAL LEADER

In this section we will review each of the following four steps as they apply to individual leaders:

- Step 1: Determine Your Leadership Requirements
- Step 2: Measure Your Gap
- Step 3: Act to Build Your Capacity
- Step 4: Do Your Part to Support Your Organization

As you review these four steps, it is important to point out that for some of you the journey will be relatively easy. For example, some leaders are fortunate in that they belong to very progressive organizations that invest considerable resources in building leadership capacity.[1] If you are one of these lucky leaders, then take full advantage of all the opportunities your organization provides. At the same time, do not become complacent. Do not relegate complete responsibility to your organization for your career or development as a leader.

On the other hand, if you are a leader in an organization that is not doing enough to build its overall leadership capacity, then take the lead to manage your own leadership career, implement the steps we will describe, and help build other leaders.

Finally, if you are leading your own company, do not assume that "doing your part" is not for you. In fact, as a leader of your own company, it is even more important that you invest time and resources to the Leadership Solutions Pathway for your organization and for yourself.

We are going to use a case example of Elena, a director of Portfolio Design and Risk Management with an international investment firm, to demonstrate how she applies Steps 1 and 2 of the Leadership Solutions Pathway to her specific situation. First, let's learn about her background:

Elena has been in her role three months. She is responsible for overseeing a research department that supports the firm's primary investment departments. Her team is responsible for research and analysis of the risk-return characteristics of investment opportunities, leading to recommendations to the firm's executive committee.

Elena always loved numbers. As a teenager, she worked part time in a regional bank and continued working within the banking industry while she was getting her undergraduate degree. She then completed her Masters of Science in Economics. She began her career as an analyst with a large investment bank and then left to complete her MBA.

After she graduated, Elena knew she wanted to return to an investment company. She landed a job as a senior economist with an international firm. After three years, she was promoted to senior advisor where she spent another three years, before being promoted into her current role.

Elena has developed a reputation as a hard worker with a keen intellect and sophisticated research skills. She prides herself on her strong quantitative research skills and facility with financial modeling and portfolio theory. In her current role, Elena is expected to work alongside her VP to drive the company's future research mandate. The position represents a wonderful opportunity because the firm is beginning to branch out and aggressively invest in emerging markets. Elena is being called upon to assist in the research to support this strategic direction.

STEP 1: DETERMINE YOUR LEADERSHIP REQUIREMENTS

In Chapter 9 we described how leadership is not static but rather dependent on the external environment in which organizations and leaders operate. Confronting the new dynamics in their external environments influences the leadership requirements needed for success. The first step of the Leadership Solutions Pathway requires that organizations take the time to explore the external environment so they can identify their future leadership capacity requirements.

This important step also holds true for individual leaders, who need to define their own leadership requirements. A leader's day-to-day external environment is ever-changing, and leaders need to reflect continually on the leadership requirements they will need. You need to take these actions:

The Process of Determining Your Leadership Requirements

1. Explore your external environment.
2. Identify your specific leadership requirements.
3. Validate your assessment of your future leadership requirements.

1. Explore Your External Environment

Be clear about the conditions in which you lead, because they have a direct impact on your leadership. Understanding your external environment will help you determine your future leadership requirements.

As we described in Chapter 9, the process of exploring the current and future dynamics of your external environment involves understanding the trends in your environment, and identifying its implications for leadership capacity requirements. Here are some essential questions that you should ask yourself:

- What are the key external trends and drivers in your business environment that have implications for your individual leadership capacity?

- What are the customer dynamics that you and your organization are currently facing? How do you see them changing over the next two to three years?

- What are the competitive dynamics in your marketplace?

- What are the current political, economic, social, technological and regulatory trends?

- What strategies are you and your organization using to respond to your current external environment? To what extent does your organization's current strategy position you for success in the future?

- To what extent do you as a leader feel equipped to handle the dynamics in your current and emerging environment?

For many leaders, the answers to these questions may be fairly straightforward. For others, you may find these questions to be somewhat daunting. If so, you have a unique opportunity to meet with other leaders in your organization to answer the questions and gain a deeper understanding of your external environment. It is important for leaders to take the time to explore the dynamics in their external environment. Do not bury your head and focus on execution. Stop from time to time, and explore the environment in which you lead.

Let's revisit the case of Elena and consider how she explored her external environment:

> *Elena was fortunate because her job already provided her with ample information and data to understand her external environment. The key issue that emerged in her analysis is that her company's external business environment is being driven by growth opportunities in Asia-Pacific markets. Her firm has had a very conservative stance on new or emerging markets because of the risk. So while there are many opportunities, they are clouded by political unrest, economic uncertainties, and regulatory and governmental policies, which tend to discourage investment.*

2. Identify Your Specific Future Leadership Capacity Requirements

Once you understand your external environment (current and future) you can then begin to identify your specific future leadership capacity requirements. We suggest you identify your specific leadership requirements using the 30-Cell Grid of Holistic Leadership (see Figure 12.2 on page 208).

Begin by locating the columns of holistic leadership. Read the specific definitions in those columns, and circle the cells that you believe you will need to succeed in the future.

Then locate the rows of holistic leadership capabilities. Read the specific definitions on those rows that reflect what you will need to succeed, and circle the most critical.

The completed 30-cell grid represents your desired future leadership capacity requirements. In Step 2, we will discuss how you can measure your current leadership capacity and determine the gap from your current state to your desired future state. The gap between the two will lead to specific recommendations for targeted actions that we will describe in Step 3, later in this chapter.

Let's see how Elena determined her future leadership requirements.

As Elena reviewed the dynamics in her business environment, she realized that several elements and capabilities would need to become part of her future leadership requirements:

- *She would need to pay special attention to **customer leadership** and **business strategy** because of the growing focus on investment opportunities in emerging and developing markets.*
- *These elements would then need to be supported by strong capabilities in **sensing** (understanding the markets), **creating** (developing new and innovative investment portfolios) and **implementing** (ensuring the organization and clients adopt the new investment portfolios).*
- *Elena also identified the need to build **organizational relationships** across the organization and to drive the **performance of her team**. Elena completed the 30-cell grid of her leadership requirements (see Figure 12.3 on page 210).*

3. Validate Your Assessment of Future Leadership Requirements

At this stage, some leaders find it helpful to validate their work by getting input from others. The perspective of others ensures that you develop an accurate picture of your future leadership requirements. Here are some suggestions:

- Meet with your manager to get input and guidance.
- Meet with a representative from Human Resources or someone responsible for leadership development within your organization.
- Meet with a trusted colleague, mentor, or coach.

In your meetings, explore the following questions:

- To what extent have I summarized our organization's current and emerging business environment? Is there anything missing?

The 30-Cell Grid of Holistic Leadership

	Customer Leadership	Business Strategy Leadership	Culture & Values Leadership	Organizational Leadership	Team Leadership	Personal Leadership
Sensing	Customer Sensing is the ability of the leader to solicit, understand and anticipate the needs and the values of the customer.	Strategic Sensing is the ability of the leader to explore, understand and anticipate the changes in the business environment that will impact their organization.	Culture Sensing is the ability of the leader to solicit, uncover and comprehend the culture of the organization and the impact the culture will have on the ability of the organization to achieve its goals.	Organization Sensing is the ability of the leader to identify key stakeholders throughout the organization and to understand their points of view on business issues.	Team Sensing is the ability of the leader to identify and appreciate the needs and motives of the individuals on the team.	Personal Sensing is the ability of the leader to recognize and appreciate how he is perceived by others and to understand the impact of his actions on others' perceptions.
Creating	Customer Value Proposition is the ability of the leader to build a package of solutions that meets customer needs and is appealing to the customer.	Strategy Architect is the ability of the leader to develop a business strategy that will be the most effective path to building competitive advantage.	Culture Defining is the ability of the leader to envision the type of culture that will support the achievement of the organization's goals.	Organization Design is the ability of the leader to build the appropriate structures to carry out the strategy.	Team Design is the ability of the leader to form the appropriate type of team to meet the needs of the organization.	Personal Intention is the ability of the leader to envision a personal style that she would like to project.
Implementing	Customer Solutions is the ability of the leader to deploy products and services to optimize customer value.	Strategy Deployment is the ability of the leader to move the organization from planning to effective action.	Culture Embedding is the ability of the leader to put in place the structures and processes that will support the desired culture.	Organization Integration is the ability of the leader to build bridges across the organization by creating opportunities to communicate with people from different functions, levels and geographies.	Team Performance is the ability of the leader to motivate team members to achieve superior performance.	Personal Performance is the ability of the leader to achieve results and to accomplish the goals he sets out for himself.

	Customer	Strategic	Cultural	Organizational	Team	Personal
Connecting	Customer Relationships is the ability of the leader to forge strong bonds with customers.	Strategic Relationships is the ability of the leader to forge relationships with people across different businesses, functions and levels of the organization.	Cultural Relationships is the ability of the leader to develop relationships with a diverse range of employees throughout the organization.	Organizational Relationships is the ability of the leader to build trust with stakeholders throughout the organization.	Team Relationships is the ability of the leader to foster trust and engage in a genuine dialogue with team members.	Personal Relationships is the ability of the leader to earn the trust of others and to develop relationships that provide both business and personal support.
Advocating	Customer Advocacy is the ability of the leader to bring the voice of the customer into the decision making of the organization.	Strategic Championing is the ability of the leader to lobby others about the importance of the strategy and to encourage them to align their actions with that strategy.	Cultural Advocacy is the ability of the leader to champion the importance of culture as a key driver of business success.	Organizational Advocacy is the ability of the leader to promote communication and co-operation throughout the organization.	Team Advocacy is the ability of the leader to rally support for the team from stakeholders in the organization.	Personal Advocacy is the ability of the leader to further his position by effectively promoting his value to the organization.

Figure 12.2 *The 30-Cell Grid of Holistic Leadership*

The 30-Cell Grid of Holistic Leadership						
	Customer Leadership	**Business Strategy Leadership**	**Culture & Values Leadership**	**Organizational Leadership**	**Team Leadership**	**Personal Leadership**
Sensing	Customer Sensing is the ability of the leader to solicit, understand and anticipate the needs and the values of the customer.	Strategic Sensing is the ability of the leader to explore, understand and anticipate the changes in the business environment that will impact their organization.	Culture Sensing is the ability of the leader to solicit, uncover and comprehend the culture of the organization and the impact the culture will have on the ability of the organization to achieve its goals.	Organization Sensing is the ability of the leader to identify key stakeholders throughout the organization and to understand their points of view on business issues.	Team Sensing is the ability of the leader to identify and appreciate the needs and motives of the individuals on the team.	Personal Sensing is the ability of the leader to recognize and appreciate how he is perceived by others and to understand the impact of his actions on others' perceptions.
Creating	Customer Value Proposition is the ability of the leader to build a package of solutions that meets customer needs and is appealing to the customer.	Strategy Architect is the ability of the leader to develop a business strategy that will be the most effective path to building competitive advantage.	Culture Defining is the ability of the leader to envision the type of culture that will support the achievement of the organization's goals.	Organization Design is the ability of the leader to build the appropriate structures to carry out the strategy.	Team Design is the ability of the leader to form the appropriate type of team to meet the needs of the organization.	Personal Intention is the ability of the leader to envision a personal style that she would like to project.
Implementing	Customer Solutions is the ability of the leader to deploy products and services to optimize customer value.	Strategy Deployment is the ability of the leader to move the organization from planning to effective action.	Culture Embedding is the ability of the leader to put in place the structures and processes that will support the desired culture.	Organization Integration is the ability of the leader to build bridges across the organization by creating opportunities to communicate with people from different functions, levels and geographies.	Team Performance is the ability of the leader to motivate team members to achieve superior performance.	Personal Performance is the ability of the leader to achieve results and to accomplish the goals he sets out for himself.

	Customer	Strategic	Cultural	Organizational	Team	Personal
Connecting	Customer Relationships is the ability of the leader to forge strong bonds with customers.	Strategic Relationships is the ability of the leader to forge relationships with people across different businesses, functions and levels of the organization.	Cultural Relationships is the ability of the leader to develop relationships with a diverse range of employees throughout the organization.	Organizational Relationships is the ability of the leader to build trust with stakeholders throughout the organization.	Team Relationships is the ability of the leader to foster trust and engage in a genuine dialogue with team members.	Personal Relationships is the ability of the leader to earn the trust of others and to develop relationships that provide both business and personal support.
Advocating	Customer Advocacy is the ability of the leader to bring the voice of the customer into the decision making of the organization.	Strategic Championing is the ability of the leader to lobby others about the importance of the strategy and to encourage them to align their actions with that strategy.	Cultural Advocacy is the ability of the leader to champion the importance of culture as a key driver of business success.	Organizational Advocacy is the ability of the leader to promote communication and co-operation throughout the organization.	Team Advocacy is the ability of the leader to rally support for the team from stakeholders in the organization.	Personal Advocacy is the ability of the leader to further his position by effectively promoting his value to the organization.

Figure 12.3 *Case Example: Elena's Future Leadership Requirements*

- Do the future leadership requirements make sense for my role?
- How could I capitalize on my strengths and reduce the impact of any of my weaknesses?

Once again, let's revisit Elena's case:

Elena met with a couple of trusted colleagues from within the company to get their feedback and opinions. Valuable feedback suggested she was putting too much emphasis on elements and capabilities that were already her strong areas. Her colleagues suggested that Elena pay more attention to the element of team leadership and to the capabilities of relating and advocating. She was told that her success would be less a function of her own hard work and specialized skills and based more on her ability to work with diverse stakeholders across the company.

By completing Step 1, leaders have a clear sense of the specific leadership requirements they will need to develop and demonstrate to succeed in their roles. In the next step, leaders must measure their gaps to identify their areas of strengths and the specific areas of focus for their leadership capacity development.

STEP 2: MEASURE YOUR GAP

Once you know your leadership requirements, it is time to get an accurate measure of your strengths and gaps as a leader. You want to be able to target your development in the areas critical to your future success as a holistic leader. This brings us to Step 2, Measure Your Gap, and it involves conducting the Assessment of Leadership Behaviors survey (see Appendix C).

The Process for Measuring Your Gap

1. Complete the Assessment of Leadership Behavior Survey.
2. Analyze overall patterns.

1. Complete the Assessment of Leadership Behavior Survey

The Assessment of Leadership Behavior (see Appendix C) is a feedback survey that evaluates the holistic leadership behaviors of individual leaders. You can conduct the survey on your own as a self-assessment, but we recommend completing the multi-rater feedback process; it provides a broader perspective.[2] More specifically, it provides valuable data regarding potential blind spots.

Figure 12.4 includes the summary grid of elements and capabilities based on Elena's survey results. Each skill in the 30-cell grid has its own metric that represents whether Elena is seen as a role model or a quality performer in that area, or is in need of development.

Elena's Results—Assessment of Leadership Behavior Survey						
	Customer Leadership	Business Strategy Leadership	Culture & Values Leadership	Organizational Leadership	Team Leadership	Personal Leadership
Sensing	3.2	3.6	2.9	3.2	3.6	2.5
Creating	3.0	3.1	2.5	3.2	3.1	3.0
Implementing	4.1	4.2	2.9	3.2	3.6	3.0
Connecting	2.9	2.2	2.5	2.9	2.9	2.2
Advocating	2.8	2.5	2.5	3.0	2.5	2.9

3.6–5   [ ]   Role Model

2.6–3.5   [ ]   Quality Performer

0–2.5   [ ]   Developmental Opportunity

Figure 12.4   *Case Example: Elena's Profile from the Assessment of Leader Behavior*

2. Analyze Overall Patterns

Reading vertically (the six elements), Elena appears to be strong in customer leadership and organizational leadership. However, she is weak in aspects of business strategy, culture and values, team leadership and personal leadership. Reading horizontally (the five capabilities), Elena's connecting and advocating capabilities also are somewhat weak. These findings actually validate some of the feedback that Elena had already received from some of her colleagues.

Already, Elena is beginning to understand that if she wants to succeed in her current role and assume more senior leadership positions in the future, she will need to build other holistic leadership skills.

Now let's examine the cells in more detail and look specifically at areas of strength and weakness.

- *Examine Areas of Strength*
  The table in Figure 12.5 presents the highest-rated behaviors provided by the respondents to Elena's survey. It displays the clear areas of strength.

Highest-Rated Behaviors from Respondents: Strengths			
Question	Elements	Capabilities	Average Rating
Translates strategic direction into clear organizational goals.	Business Strategy	Sensing	4.2
Demonstrates a clear understanding of what customers value.	Customer Leadership	Sensing	4.1
Understands the key opportunities and threats in the business environment.	Business Strategy	Sensing	3.6
Stays tuned in to the climate and motivation with the team.	Team Leadership	Implementing	3.6
Holds team accountable for their performance against objectives.	Team Leadership	Implementing	3.6

Figure 12.5 *Case Example: Highest-Rated Behaviors*

The conclusion we can draw is that Elena is perceived to be strong in business strategy, customer leadership and team leadership. What is particularly interesting is that the strengths occur only in two capabilities: sensing and implementing. As a strong researcher, Elena is probably very strong at sensing. This capability is about gathering data, staying in tune to the environment, customers, etc. She also demonstrates strength in the capability of implementing. Elena describes herself as a person with strong drive and an ethic of hard work, and she also drives her team to achieve high performance.

- *Examine Areas of Weakness*
  Elena's story becomes even more interesting as we examine her lowest-rated behaviors (see figure 12.6).

Lowest-Rated Behaviors from Respondents: Developmental Opportunities			
Question	Elements	Capabilities	Average Rating
Influences others to align actions with business strategy.	Business Strategy	Connecting	2.2
Uses personal credibility to influence others in the organization.	Personal Leadership	Connecting	2.2
Advocates on behalf of decisions that support the business strategy.	Business Strategy	Advocating	2.5
Defines the vision of the culture required to engage employees.	Culture & Values	Creating	2.5
Communicates effectively the desired culture and values.	Culture & Values	Advocating	2.5

Figure 12.6 *Case Example: Lowest-Rated Behaviors*

These low-rated behaviors represent key developmental opportunities. As we examine the table, we see that the areas of business strategy are a weakness, specifically in the capabilities of connecting and advocating. What this means is that Elena knows how to scan her environment and in turn develop a strategy. She probably can implement the strategy (her driver tendencies); however, she is quite weak at engaging and influencing others to the strategy. This will be a significant liability for Elena, because more of her success will be a function of her ability to build relationships with internal stakeholders. Not only was this a weakness for Elena but it was also a blind spot. She was not even aware of its importance. This weakness also is amplified by the fact that her personal leadership score in cultivating credibility is low. This means that though Elena may be respected for her functional expertise, she is not respected as a leader. She has not paid attention to cultivating her credibility, so people choose not to follow her.

Finally, another clear gap for Elena is the element of culture and values. This is an area that she readily admits is a weakness. ("I just don't get that fluffy culture stuff.") As a senior leader in her organization, Elena will need to pay particular attention to learning about culture and values and the part she has to play as a leader to create a compelling work environment for her department.

The feedback from Elena's Assessment of Leadership Behavior provides her with a targeted assessment of both her strengths and areas of development. She knows that she is seen as a strong technical leader. However, she will need to focus on her ability to work with others and to influence and advocate within her organization. She also will need to pay more attention to her own personal leadership. Elena's strengths were important to her success in previous roles where she needed to be a strong functional contributor. However, her success in the future will require her to be a holistic leader, able to drive her mandate through others on her team, in her department and across the entire investment firm.

In Step 2, we have discussed how you can measure your gap by completing the Assessment of Leadership Behavior survey. Regardless of the assessment tool that is used, it is important for you to gain an accurate measure of your leadership capacity. It is also important for you to approach the assessment process with a spirit of openness. Many times assessment data can reveal negative information that can be threatening. Avoid being defensive. Don't overact to the data or dismiss it; be open to the feedback and see it as a growth opportunity.

STEP 3: ACT TO BUILD YOUR CAPACITY

When individual leaders apply Steps 1 and 2 of the Leadership Solutions Pathway, they come away with a greater understanding of who they are as leaders, the dynamics of their business environment, the specific leadership requirements and the gaps they need to address to succeed. With this in place, a leader can then move to Step 3 to build leadership capacity. This process involves the following four actions:

The Process for Building Your Capacity

1. *Target* your priority leadership capacity gaps.
2. *Integrate* your leadership capacity solutions.
3. *Accelerate* your development.
4. *Evolve* as your external environment changes.

---

1. *Target* Your Priority Leadership Capacity Gaps

Leaders need to target their development in the areas and at the times when it matters most. Here are some key guidelines for doing this:

Guidelines to Target Priority Leadership Capacity Gaps

- Build capacity in the elements and capabilities.
- Complement your skill set.
- Target critical moments in the leadership lifecycle.

Build Capacity in the Elements and Capabilities

Leaders often ask us, "Do I need to excel at all six elements and five capabilities to be a holistic leader?" The answer is both yes and no. The six elements define the critical areas that all leaders need to pay attention to in order to demonstrate holistic leadership. Paying attention to the six elements helps leaders transition from a focus on the functional aspects of leadership to more holistic aspects. The same is true of the five capabilities. They represent what leaders need to do to demonstrate holistic leadership.

However, as we have also stated, your external environment shapes the specific elements and capabilities that will be most important for you to succeed. So, while the six elements and five capabilities are important for strong holistic leadership, they will be important at different times, based on the demands of your external environment.

Therefore, the first action demands that leaders focus their energies and target their own leadership solutions in the areas that matter most for success.[3]

Complement Your Skill Set

Another effective way to target your leadership gaps is by working with other strong leaders who complement your skill sets. If you are strong at customer sensing and creating but weak in customer implementing and customer connecting, find a colleague who is strong in these areas. By working together, you create stronger leadership capacity.

Target Critical Moments in the Leadership Life Cycle

Another way to target a leader's development is by focusing on critical moments in the leader's life cycle. These are times when a leader transitions to a new role, such as the first time an employee becomes a manager of people or the first time a leader becomes an executive. Each transition in role presents a significantly new set of leadership capacity requirements, with unique challenges and pressures. To succeed, new leaders need to develop new ways of thinking about their roles. These also are moments when leaders are most at risk of derailing.

Pay particular attention to your development when you are moving into these kinds of leadership roles. For example, if you are new to a supervisory or managerial role, you will need to understand that your success will be a function of how you get others to achieve results, rather than being based on your own efforts. If, on the other hand, you are leading a department or function for the first time, you will need to understand how your department fits into the entire organization. You will also be expected to strike a balance between your attention to your department (wearing your departmental hat) and leading with the best interest of the entire organization (wearing your organizational hat).

2. *Integrate* Your Leadership Capacity Solutions

Leaders tend to lead too much on their own—especially in senior leadership roles. We also find that many solutions fail to deliver sustained results because they do not integrate well into day-to-day roles. Therefore, the opportunity moving forward is to integrate solutions into leadership roles to improve learning and leading. Here are some strategies:

Strategies to Integrate Your Leadership Capacity Solutions

- Integrate learning into your leadership.
- Integrate leadership into teams.

Integrate Learning into Your Leadership

We hear countless leaders exclaim, "I'm so busy doing that I rarely have time to lead." This is the reality in many of today's organizations—roles have such an operational focus (doing), that the time available to engage in leading is compromised. Clearly, leaders are expected to deliver their operational mandates; however, they need to see their holistic leadership obligations as essential to their jobs.

Furthermore, leaders have been conditioned to believe that learning about leadership can only happen when they are sitting in a classroom or other environment that is removed from their day-to-day roles. This belief contributes to a sense of fragmented development. The real opportunity is for leaders to build learning into their day-to-day leadership roles in simple ways.

One powerful strategy is to keep a weekly journal of leadership lessons. You can take a few minutes at the end of each week and reflect on your experiences and identify new insights and lessons learned through your practice of leadership. Others find that working with a coach helps with this reflective process. Working with a group of like-minded individuals is also a good strategy. For example, in a large professional services firm, a small group of middle managers met on a quarterly basis to discuss their leadership roles and what they were learning while on the job.

Integrate Leadership into Teams

The charismatic model of leadership tends to view individual leaders as heroes. Many of us have been conditioned to believe that we need to be a "superhero." Unfortunately, this belief has downplayed the powerful role that team-based leadership can play in our development.

The reality is that all leaders lead in a context with other leaders. So instead of thinking about yourself as being disconnected from other leaders, it is important that you think of yourself as part of a team and consider building collective leadership capacity. For example, in one team the leaders built a high degree of trust. So instead of competing with one another, they succeeded collectively by collaborating with one another. This approach created a positive cycle because the more they succeeded as a collective team, the more their trust deepened and the more each individual leader was willing to challenge himself or herself to build personal capacity and increase the contribution to the team.

3. *Accelerate* Your Development

As organizations are working to close their leadership gaps, the focus is on accelerating the development of their leaders. The same is true at an individual level. You need to think about how you can accelerate your development.

Strategies to Accelerate Your Development

- Be ready to move across, not just up.
- Make bold career moves.
- Stay clear of leadership "derailers."
- Learn from the experience of other leaders.

Be Ready to Move Across, Not Just Up

For a long time, leaders have worked hard to climb the corporate ladder—usually as quickly as possible. This was the traditional definition of accelerated development: the first one up the ladder wins. However, in today's increasingly complex business world, leaders require broader perspectives. If you move up the corporate ladder too quickly, it may become a long-term liability.

We find that "climbing the corporate ladder" is no longer an apt metaphor for leaders today. Leaders need to slow down and move across as they move up. So the analogy of a "spiral staircase" is starting to become more meaningful. This means that you seek opportunities that give you breadth of leadership experiences.

You also may find that at some times in your career it will be better to stay in your current role longer. Most leaders have come to believe that true success can only come about from aggressively moving upward. Yet, in today's complex world, you may actually be able to accelerate over the longer term by choosing to move across or to stay put in your existing role.

Make Bold Career Moves

Many times leaders can accelerate their development by making bold moves in their careers. This means taking on large projects and difficult challenges. The opportunities may actually appear risky, but if you succeed, your development and positioning as a leader will accelerate. (You do need to know when you are ready to take on such a challenge.)

When you think about a bold move, it is often something that is contrary to conventional wisdom. For example, in one large utility, the head of Organizational Development had built a strong reputation within the company. He was seen as a strong internal consultant and was valued by his internal clients. Despite his success, he knew that a bold move was actually to assume a "line leadership role." An opportunity to run one of the utilities' generating plants presented itself. At first, the organization failed to take him seriously, but he was persistent and built a compelling case. The organization gave him the chance, and he succeeded in his new role. What bold move would accelerate your development? Is it a move to another department? Is it taking a sabbatical to learn an entirely new skill set?

Stay Clear of Leadership "Derailers"

In our research we have found that leaders can impede their careers by falling into the trap of a number of leadership derailers. Top "derailers" include personal arrogance, emotional incompetence, a domineering leadership style, conflict avoidance and being risk averse.[4] All can slow down, or halt, your development as a leader.

Here are some questions to help you reflect on the leadership derailers as they relate to you:

- Do you have a tendency to be overconfident or arrogant in the presence of others?

- Do you struggle to understand the emotional aspects or nuances of relationships at work?

- Would your colleagues or team members describe you as a "control freak" or "micromanager" or having a domineering leadership style?

- Does conflict make you uncomfortable? Do you resist or put off dealing with conflict situations?

- Do you fear taking risks, even if they are calculated and make good business sense?

Learn from the Experience of Other Leaders

Another important strategy for accelerating development is for leaders to learn from the experience of others. Too often leaders assume they need to figure it all out on their own. Though this approach has merit, it often takes a long time to learn valuable leadership lessons. It also slows down your development because much of the learning occurs through trial and error. A better strategy is to take advantage of the organizational learning opportunities and work with a cross-section of leaders to learn from their experiences. Their insights and ideas can be invaluable in helping you learn how to develop your leadership capacity.

Here's a simple way to begin to learn from others. The next time you encounter a new leadership challenge, don't ask yourself: How am I going to handle this? Rather, ask yourself: Who has encountered a similar challenge before? Connect with that individual. Tap into his or her experience and then form your strategy. Leverage the collective experiences of all leaders for your benefit as well as your organization's.

4. *Evolve* as Your Environment Changes

Leaders can never be complacent in their roles. Their external environments will always change, and new opportunities will always be available to exploit. This means that leaders will need to evolve and change how they lead if they are to succeed. Here are some strategies to consider.

Strategies for Evolving as Your Environment Changes

- Develop a broad perspective.
- Build a network across the organization.
- Learn from failure.
- Appreciate diversity.
- Deal with uncertainty.

Develop a Broad Perspective

Leaders will need to be able to respond to a variety of new and emerging business issues and opportunities. They will need to step beyond their technical expertise and become well versed in what is happening in all areas of their organizations.

By displaying a broad perspective on your organization, you keep yourself open to environmental changes and in a better position to evolve. Here are a few ideas that we've gained from the leaders we've worked with over the years:

- "I read different magazines from outside my functional area of expertise."

- "I develop a multiplicity of talents. I like the idea of being a utility player. It helps me have a broader perspective on business issues."

- "I step outside my normal duties and role as a leader. Each month I spend a day on the factory floor learning about the production process."

- "Each week I make a point of connecting with a colleague outside my business group to have a brief discussion about his or her business and explore how we might work together."

- "I get out of my organization every couple of months and attend industry meetings or networking groups."

- "I learn about as many areas of my organization as I can through research and interviews with colleagues."

Build a Network Across the Organization

Most leaders know that networking is a good career strategy. We find that leaders focus their networking outside their organizations. This is a good practice. However, do not lose sight of the value of building a network within your current organization. Why is this important? Quite simply, if you want to evolve your career, it helps to be known and to know colleagues from across your organization. We find that the best leaders have a deep network of relationships throughout their organizations and not just in their functional areas. As opportunities become available, leaders with good networks can reach out, get the information they need, assemble teams of leaders more quickly and position themselves for success in future career roles.

In today's organizations, it is also important to build a network across generational groups. For example, one senior leader who was in his late 50s built relationships not only with his peers but also with young leaders who were in their 20s and 30s. He found he learned a tremendous amount from them and included them as part of his network.

Learn from Failure

Failure is critical to success. Yet in many organizations the prevailing practice is for leaders to hide these experiences or "spin" them in a way that makes them appear like successes. We find if leaders say they've never been unsuccessful, this is actually a cause for concern and may prevent them from evolving as their environment changes. You will need to push and challenge yourself continually as a leader. Do what you can to mitigate the risk of failure, but if you do fail, learn from it and move on. Be open to confronting yourself when you fail, and demonstrate to others how you can rise above these failures. The Leadership Solutions Pathway isn't always filled with success. Failure is ever-present and a useful form of growth and development.

Appreciate Diversity

In our increasingly global business world, leaders will need to evolve themselves by appreciating diversity. Our workplaces are becoming more diverse. Leaders need to be open and accepting of cultural, gender and generational differences that diversity brings. It means becoming savvy at engaging and getting results with people from different cultural perspectives and across multiple age groups. Demonstrating that you are aware and tolerant of differences in styles and ways of thinking will be appreciated in the future. If you can, get international experience to help you expand your awareness of the business world and, more importantly, to gain deeper insights into different cultures and ways of leading and working.

Deal with Uncertainty

Individuals who want to be leaders in the future must show they are capable of moving ahead and evolving even when they do not have all the answers. In the past, leaders were expected to have answers, but today's problems are more complex. Not only will you need to understand the complexity of the business issues, you will also be expected to help others deal with uncertainty and move people through the process.

In our experience, we find that the biggest barrier to evolving as leaders is in overcoming resistance to change. This prevents leaders from operating at full throttle. At times, the resistance can feel like driving a car while having your foot on the accelerator and the brake pedal at the same time. What typically results is no movement, no evolution—just wasted energy. The reason is that many times leaders are so comfortable and successful with their current leadership approach that they don't accept what is required to evolve and respond to external challenges within their environment.

STEP 4: "DO YOUR PART" IN SUPPORT OF YOUR ORGANIZATION'S EFFORTS TO BUILD LEADERSHIP CAPACITY

So far in this chapter, we have discussed how leaders do their part by applying the first three steps of the Leadership Solutions Pathway to build their own leadership capacity. However, doing your part as a leader also requires a fourth step, which is to support your organization as it builds leadership capacity. Here are the core strategies for individuals to consider:

**Strategies for "Doing Your Part" to Support Your
Organization in Building Leadership Capacity**

1. Take part in leadership capacity projects.
2. Be a change facilitator, rather than inhibitor.
3. Leverage organizational practices to build capacity.
4. Build a holistic leadership culture within your department or team.

Let's consider each of these four strategies.

1. Take Part in Leadership Capacity Projects

As organizations implement the Leadership Solutions Pathway, leaders
will have numerous opportunities to play a role. For example, volunteer
yourself or members of your team for leadership capacity projects. A leader
in a manufacturing company volunteered to participate on a corporate-
wide committee supporting the company's leadership development
process. The experience was invaluable for the leader because it enabled
her to make sure the process considered the actual needs and concerns of
the company's operational leaders. She also was exposed to leaders in other
parts of the company that she would not normally have encountered in her
day-to-day role. In the end, the process was a success, and the company
received an industry award for best practices in leadership development.

2. Be a Change Facilitator, Rather Than Inhibitor

Another powerful way to support your organization as it implements the
Leadership Solutions Pathway is by being a facilitator of change, rather
than an inhibitor of change.

   For example, one leader did not approve of his company's decision to
roll out an intensive assessment center program for leaders. He did not
allow any leaders in his department to take part and expressed opposition
to the initiative every time he had a chance. He was against the initiative
because he feared his own leaders would be taken away from their jobs
and, in turn, their productivity would drop. The organization continued
to move forward, and they made it mandatory for this leader and his team
to attend the assessment centers. In the end, the process was valuable, for
it made all the leaders stronger.

Today more than ever, organizations and their leaders need to work together. They need to facilitate change effectively and quickly and implement the steps of the Leadership Solutions Pathway. Any slowdown along the journey will only serve to widen the leadership gap. How do you know you are a change inhibitor? Here are some statements you may hear yourself making:

- "That's just not realistic here—it will never work."
- "We tried that five years ago."
- "We don't have the time to waste on this fluffy stuff."

3. Leverage Organizational Practices to Build Capacity

As we discussed in Chapter 6, many organizational practices can either inhibit or facilitate strong holistic leadership. Leaders have an important role to play in this respect, because many of them are responsible for designing and implementing many organizational practices. Here is one key question to keep in mind when examining organizational practices in your own area: How can the practices be designed, implemented or streamlined in a way that also serves to build strong leadership capacity?

Let's consider the example of one organization:

The leadership team of a large hospital was revamping the strategic planning process for their organization. They realized that this organizational practice also provided a valuable opportunity to build the holistic leadership skills of director-level and middle-level managers. Therefore, they decided they would include a pool of high-potential directors in the strategic planning process.

In addition, they included a group of high-potential middle managers to act as shadow strategic planners to work alongside the executive team during the business planning process. The outcome was highly positive. The organization enhanced its overall leadership capacity in the area of business strategy. It also had greater success in the implementation of the strategy because the leaders had already developed a deep understanding of it.

4. Build a Holistic Leadership Culture within Your Department and Team

While an organization has a leadership culture, different segments of the organization (such as departments and teams) can also develop leadership cultures.

We find this is often a missed opportunity for leaders. Many in the middle and front lines believe that leadership culture is created at the top of the organization. However, our experience is that only exceptional organizations build holistic leadership cultures by design. Most allow their cultures to emerge on their own, without direction. So leaders cannot underestimate the power they have in shaping their local organization's leadership culture by building their own sphere of influence. Consider the following example:

> *A manager of a public works department of a large state government was frustrated with the overall lack of a leadership culture. The one that existed was very operational in nature and lacked vitality and excitement. This was reflected in the organization's employee survey data, which revealed that the department's leaders were some of the most disengaged employees in the entire organization.*
>
> *Knowing he couldn't influence the entire organization on his own, he began to focus his energies with the leaders in his own area. He brought them together and began to discuss the characteristics of a holistic leadership culture. It wasn't long before the leaders acknowledged their desire to have such a leadership culture, so they committed to work together to bring one about. As they started to turn things around, other leaders in the department began to take notice. Soon, the leader began to get many calls from his colleagues wanting to know what he was doing and how they could do the same.*

CONCLUDING COMMENTS

No matter what your level of leadership or stage in your career, you will be required to help your organization build leadership capacity for competitive advantage. In this chapter we have explained the application of the Leadership Solutions Pathway to the development of individual leaders. We have provided a series of steps and actions to enable you not only to build your own leadership capacity but to actively support your organization's efforts in building strong leadership capacity. Together, the individual and the organization can become a powerful force to overcome the leadership gap and to build the leadership capacity required for individual leader and organizational success.

CHAPTER THIRTEEN

Shape Your Future

A story is told about a traveler who heard of a great master. The traveler decided to see how smart the master was, so he put him to a test. He approached the master with a tiny bird cupped in his two hands and asked the master, "Is the bird in my hands alive or dead?" The master immediately understood the trick. If he said the bird was alive, the traveler would squeeze his hands and show that the bird was dead, and if he said that it was dead, then the traveler would open his hands and let the bird fly away. After a moment of reflection, the master said, "Whether the bird is alive or dead is in your hands." And the master passed the test.

We speak frequently at conferences about the need for leadership solutions and explain what an important and compelling issue it is. Sometimes we close our presentations with the story of the "bird in the hands." Participants have told us they love this story because it makes them feel they *can* take responsibility and make things happen.

That is our hope as you finish reading this book—that you will:

- Be an active participant as the environment around you changes

- Face the complex challenges of building leadership capacity with courage and conviction

- Take ownership of what you can do and not be discouraged by the lack of leadership capacity around you

> Shaping the future is an imperative for leaders and organizations.

We will begin this chapter by revisiting the leadership capacity business risks we introduced in Chapter 1 and show how these risks are mitigated by implementing the solutions presented in this book.

LEADERSHIP SOLUTIONS: MITIGATING THE LEADERSHIP CAPACITY RISKS

In Chapter 1 we described seven major issues that contribute to the leadership gap that still persists in many organizations. If left unresolved, they pose a considerable risk, so throughout this book we have addressed these seven issues and provided a leadership solution to mitigate the risks. In this section, we will review each of the seven leadership gap issues and specifically identify the potential risk and the leadership solution.

Leadership Gap Issue 1: Over-Reliance on Traditional Views of Leadership

- *Potential Risk to the Organization:* A focus on silo management and technical expertise rather than leading the whole organization as "one entity" will result in an inadequate response to complex cross-boundary issues.

- *The Leadership Solution:* Foster a leadership culture that focuses on holistic leadership and the leadership capabilities with customer leadership at the center and ensure leaders align and engage employees and teams to the entire organization's purpose. Refer to Chapters 4, 5 and 7.

Leadership Gap Issue 2: No Shared or Well-Defined View of Leadership for the Future

- *Potential Risk to the Organization:* No clarity about the organization's direction, resulting in wasted effort and inadequate leadership capacity to meet your organization's business needs.

- *The Leadership Solution:* Define clearly the future requirements for leadership capacity. Wherever possible, shape the future environment so that you can preplan the development of leadership capacity in the forecasted direction. Refer to Chapter 9.

Leadership Gap Issue 3: A Void of Leadership Capacity Metrics

- *Potential Risk to the Organization:* Lack of precision in efforts to build capacity, resulting in wasted effort and inadequate solutions.

- *The Leadership Solution:* Use the Leadership Gap Analysis™ to measure the three dimensions with the Assessment of Leader Behavior, the Survey of Leadership Culture and the Organizational Practices Audit. The results provide precision to target your organization's leadership solutions. Refer to Chapter 10.

Leadership Gap Issue 4: Unclear Accountability for Leadership Capacity

- *Potential Risk to the Organization:* Accountability in the organization will be dispersed, and no coordinated effort will occur; alternatively, accountability will be delegated to an internal support group, and executives will not pay attention to it.

- *The Leadership Solution:* Leadership capacity needs to be managed, monitored and enhanced as a core organizational capability by the executives and, in some organizations, by the board of directors. Refer to Chapter 6.

Leadership Gap Issue 5: Fragmented Solutions That Are Not Sustained

- *Potential Risk to the Organization:* Confusion because of multiple fragmented solutions that are poorly targeted, resulting in extensive wasted time and money.

- *The Leadership Solution:* Target the solutions based on the measurements of leadership capacity in the Leadership Gap

Analysis™. The targeted solutions need to be integrated with one another and with other business activities. Then solutions need to be accelerated by leveraging all three dimensions of leadership capacity. Refer to Chapter 11.

Leadership Gap Issue 6: Flat and Lean Organizations with Fewer Intermediate Leadership Positions

- *Potential Risk to the Organization:* Inadequate development opportunities for leaders through the traditional promotional route. Leadership talent not available when needed to lead the organization. Leaders feel "permanently stretched" and cannot afford any time away from their jobs for development or to support the development of others.

- *The Leadership Solution:* The organization finds creative ways of providing integrated leadership development for leaders. Lateral moves develop leaders without moving them up, creating a "spiral staircase" rather than a "ladder" career path. Also, if the organization does not provide leadership capacity development, individual leaders need to take responsibility for their own. If the organization does provide assistance, leaders should be active learners and participants to gain from the learning experiences. Refer to Chapters 11 and 12.

Leadership Gap Issue 7: Poor Supply of Leaders

- *Potential Risk to the Organization:* Insufficient supply of leaders to lead the organization into the future. Loss of subject matter expertise, knowledge and wisdom as long-service employees leave the organization.

- *The Leadership Solution:* Focus on critical positions and develop talent—especially for those roles that need to be developed internally. Build a leadership culture and create an employment brand that attracts hidden leadership talent to the organization. Refer to Chapters 6 and 7.

THE IMPERATIVES TO LEVERAGE LEADERSHIP CAPACITY TO SHAPE THE FUTURE

We opened this book with the statement that leadership capacity is mission critical. Although leadership development may be the purview of an HR department, the critical organizational capability of leadership capacity is an executive and board accountability.

This section describes the imperative for executives, boards of directors, HR professionals and society. Each has an essential role and accountability in order to achieve the required leadership capacity that will shape the future.

Imperatives for Executives

Executives have a vital role in making sure the organization's required leadership capacity is available when it is needed. They need to do the following:

- Focus on shaping the business environment, delivering the business strategy and creating the required leadership capacity.

- Be a consistent force for the ongoing evolution of leadership capacity as conditions change.

- Sustain investment in building leadership capacity during down times and low business cycles.

- Establish leadership capacity metrics as part of their organization's dashboard of performance measures.

- Model the commitment to leadership capacity. Participate actively in the steps in the Leadership Solutions Pathway. Executive leadership commitment to building leadership capacity will have an impact on the organization's overall leadership culture. When executives take accountability for leadership capacity, other leaders in the organization will take it seriously as well.

Imperatives for Boards of Directors

In the past few years the role of boards of directors has expanded beyond ensuring the CEO's leadership capacity to a broader role of ensuring the organization's leadership capacity. Their involvement in tracking leadership capacity also is an important influence for executives to take the risk of inadequate leadership capacity seriously. Many boards of directors must do the following:

- View leadership capacity as a source of competitive advantage and an important topic at board strategy discussions.

- Understand the risks associated with insufficient leadership capacity, and make the difficult decisions and trade-offs that are required.

- Review leadership capacity metrics, and monitor current and anticipated future leadership requirements.

- Include in the CEO's performance contract the expectation that the organization's leadership capacity will meet the ongoing business requirements.

Imperatives for HR Professionals

HR has a very important role to play in building leadership capacity. HR should be the center of expertise on leadership capacity and know how it should be built and how it should be measured. The implications of leadership capacity for HR include the following:

- Guide an organization through the Leadership Solutions Pathway.

- Help leaders understand the risks associated with leadership capacity deficits. It is a critical role of HR as a true partner to the business.

- Approach leadership solutions with an emergent approach, always fine-tuning and tweaking solutions to ensure they provide value and build the desired leadership capacity.

- Leverage the focus on leadership capacity to build a strong leadership culture and to become an employer of choice.

Imperatives for Our Society

In the end, the ultimate beneficiary of the focus on creating leadership capacity will be our communities and society. When organizations and leaders do their part to build holistic leadership capacity, the society as a whole is transformed. Their holistic leadership capacity will give them a new perspective; the new lens they look through at work will equally change the way they view the world outside of work.

- Holistic leaders will apply holistic leadership to all facets of their lives within their communities and in the broader society to address social challenges.

- Holistic leaders will lead with a more systemic perspective and will be more concerned about how their actions affect their communities.

- Holistic leaders will work together to create compelling places to work. Their organizations will attract the best available talent and will ensure they are engaged in meaningful work to make their organizations and the broader society successful.

- When we have more holistic leaders at work, we will have a better chance of building vibrant communities and a healthy society.

CONCLUDING COMMENTS

Part One (Chapters 1 through 7) focused on the "Leadership" of *Leadership Solutions* and what it means to build leadership capacity. It explained the concept of leadership capacity and its three dimensions—the individual leader dimension, the organizational practices dimension and the leadership culture dimension. All of these dimensions are anchored in the holistic leadership framework and in the capabilities needed to be effective holistic leaders.

Part Two (Chapters 8 through 12) focused on the "Solutions" of *Leadership Solutions* and explained the Leadership Solutions Pathway to build leadership capacity. Leadership solutions are essential for an organization's ultimate transformation. The leadership solutions need to be based upon data, come across as one solution rather than multiple fragmented solutions, and integrate with the existing practices and culture. Leadership solutions will make the difference between an enhanced capacity and wasted effort.

This chapter's opening story is also our closing message: Listen to the master who solved the riddle when he said, "Whether the bird is alive or dead is in your hands." For the foreseeable future, forces in our environment will increase the gap. You cannot wait for someone else to close the leadership gap. But if you as a leader take the challenge seriously, you can overcome the leadership gap. We have shown you the Leadership Solutions Pathway, and following it will create sustained competitive advantage for you and your organization. Now, it is "in your hands."

Audit of Organizational Practices and Accompanying 30-Cell Grid

LEADERSHIP GAP ANALYSIS™
Questions for the Audit of Organizational Practices

The Audit of Organizational Practices enables you to evaluate the extent that organizational practices support holistic leadership and help to build leadership capacity.

Below we have provided the questions that comprise the Audit of Organizational Practices. The questions are geared to the 30-Cell Grid of Holistic Leadership: The Organizational Practices Dimension. As you review the questions, you may find the need to modify them to better suit the specific needs of your organization.

As with any audit, the goal is to undertake a systematic process for gathering evidence regarding organizational practices. Once you have completed the Audit, rate each question using the following scale:

①	②	③	④	⑤
Below Average Organizational Practice		Average Organizational Practice		Exceptional Organizational Practice

Once all questions have been rated, transfer the ratings to the LGA™ Results Tracker.

Customer Leadership			Below Average		Average		Exceptional
Sensing	1.	Describe the approach by which you try to understand the current and future needs/expectations of your external customers. Do you talk with external customers regularly? Do you collect customer data? If so, who collects it?	①	②	③	④	⑤
Creating	2.	Describe how your organization brings solutions to customers.	①	②	③	④	⑤
Implementing	3.	Describe how the needs of the customer shape your ongoing operations.	①	②	③	④	⑤
Connecting	4.	Describe how your organization strengthens its relationship with customers.	①	②	③	④	⑤
Advocating	5.	Describe how your organization advocates for your customer.	①	②	③	④	⑤

LEADERSHIP GAP ANALYSIS™
Questions for the Audit of Organizational Practices

Business Strategy			Below Average		Average		Exceptional
Sensing	6.	Describe the way your organization assesses the competitive landscape.	①	②	③	④	⑤
Creating	7.	Describe your organization's approach to strategic planning.	①	②	③	④	⑤
Implementing	8.	Describe how your organization executes its business strategy.	①	②	③	④	⑤
Connecting	9.	Describe how your organization keeps employees connected to the strategy.	①	②	③	④	⑤
Advocating	10.	Describe how your organization aligns decision making with the strategy.	①	②	③	④	⑤

Culture & Values			Below Average		Average		Exceptional
Sensing	11.	Describe your approach to understanding your organization's culture.	①	②	③	④	⑤
Creating	12.	Describe how your organization manages its culture.	①	②	③	④	⑤
Implementing	13.	Describe how the organization's values are integrated into organizational practices.	①	②	③	④	⑤
Connecting	14.	Describe the way your organization facilitates the ability of employees to connect with one another to promote the desired culture.	①	②	③	④	⑤
Advocating	15.	Describe the role that culture & values play in guiding organizational decision making.	①	②	③	④	⑤

Organizational Leadership			Below Average		Average		Exceptional
Sensing	16.	Describe how your organization supports understanding across the business.	①	②	③	④	⑤
Creating	17.	Describe how your organization's structure optimizes the implementation of the strategy.	①	②	③	④	⑤
Implementing	18.	Describe the way that the different parts of your organization work together.	①	②	③	④	⑤
Connecting	19.	Describe the way your organization fosters relationships across the enterprise.	①	②	③	④	⑤
Advocating	20.	Describe the way your organization makes decisions in the best interest of the whole enterprise.	①	②	③	④	⑤

LEADERSHIP GAP ANALYSIS ™
Questions for the Audit of Organizational Practices

Team Leadership			Below Average		Average		Exceptional
Sensing	21.	Describe the way the organization determines the need for teams.	①	②	③	④	⑤
Creating	22.	Describe the way in which teams are created and established in your organization.	①	②	③	④	⑤
Implementing	23.	Describe the ways your organization drives high performance through teams.	①	②	③	④	⑤
Connecting	24.	Describe the way in which your organization fosters relationships and connections within teams.	①	②	③	④	⑤
Advocating	25.	Describe the mechanisms in your organization for teams to advocate on their own behalf.	①	②	③	④	⑤

Personal Leadership			Below Average		Average		Exceptional
Sensing	26.	Describe the way your organization provides tools and assessment to help leaders understand themselves and others.	①	②	③	④	⑤
Creating	27.	Describe how your organization supports leaders to build their own careers.	①	②	③	④	⑤
Implementing	28.	Describe how your organization supports leaders in optimizing their performance.	①	②	③	④	⑤
Connecting	29.	Describe the way your organization supports leaders in developing relationships.	①	②	③	④	⑤
Advocating	30.	Describe the way your organization enables leaders to promote their success.	①	②	③	④	⑤

The 30-Cell Grid of Holistic Leadership: The Organizational Practices Dimension

	Customer Leadership	Business Strategy Leadership	Culture & Values Leadership	Organizational Leadership	Team Leadership	Personal Leadership
Sensing	Collects information from current and potential customers and disseminates that information throughout the organization.	Formally examines the competitive landscape and makes environmental scanning a fundamental part of the strategic planning process.	Uses a variety of formal and informal tools to understand the culture and the needs and perceptions of employees.	Provides opportunities for employees to understand the perspectives and needs of others in different parts of the organization.	Provides the tools for individuals or teams to better understand one another and to acquire perspective on how to function effectively.	Provides the tools for leaders to help them reflect on and understand their own strengths and weaknesses.
Creating	Puts the customer at the center of new product and service development and builds solutions to respond to emerging customer needs.	Makes strategic planning an inclusive, ongoing process that focuses on building customer value and competitive advantage.	Articulates a desired culture and values that will support the business strategy.	Builds organizational structures that support a focus on the customer and promote dialogue across boundaries of the organization.	Uses and supports a variety of different types of teams depending on what is best suited to the situation.	Provides programs such as mentoring and coaching to help leaders develop their skills and set a career path.
Implementing	Makes ongoing changes at all customer touch points to continually bring increased value to the customer.	Effectively cascades the business strategy to all levels of the organization, creating alignment of individual activities and focus on high-value activities.	Uses a variety of levers (e.g., performance management, recruitment) to reinforce the desired culture.	Establishes shared goals and metrics and creates opportunities to communicate and move talent throughout the organization.	Clearly communicates team goals and effectively manages the performance of teams.	Provides the tools and accountability to help individuals optimize their productivity and contribution.

Connecting	Provides opportunities and forums to interact with the customer and to shape customer expectations.	Ensures employees stay in touch with key stakeholders both inside and outside the organization (e.g., industry associations).	Provides opportunities for employees to connect with one another and to promote the desired culture and values.	Creates opportunities for communication across the organization and encourages interaction with leaders at all levels.	Provides formal and informal opportunities for team members to interact and build effective working relationships.	Provides the formal and informal opportunities for leaders to build relationships that will help them to be successful.
Advocating	Empowers employees to respond to the needs of customers and to lobby on behalf of the customer in all decision making.	Uses decision-making processes to ensure resources are not allocated to activities that are not aligned to the business strategy.	Uses alignment with the desired culture and values as key criteria in decision making.	Ensures that the best interest of the whole organization is taken into account in decision making rather than letting the needs or best interest of one group take precedence.	Provides forums for teams to lobby on their own behalf to secure required resources to meet team goals.	Provides an opportunity for leaders to express their career interests and to help the leader develop in the areas that will increase their value to the organization.

Survey of Leadership Culture and Accompanying 30-Cell Grid

LEADERSHIP GAP ANALYSIS™
Survey of Leadership Culture

This survey has six main sections which correspond to the Six Elements of Holistic Leadership. Within each section is a series of short statements that describe various aspects of your organization's leadership culture. Read and rate each item carefully using the following scale:

Strongly Disagree	Disagree	Neither Agree nor Disagree	Agree	Strongly Agree
①	②	③	④	⑤

Customer Leadership

This section covers the extent to which the leadership culture creates an expectation for leaders to create value for the external customer.

The leadership culture in this organization…	Strongly Disagree	Disagree	Neither Agree nor Disagree	Agree	Strongly Agree
1. creates the expectation that leaders will stay informed about the current and future needs of the external customer.	①	②	③	④	⑤
2. drives creativity and innovation that is focused on creating value for customers.	①	②	③	④	⑤
3. reinforces the importance of bringing new products and services to the customer.	①	②	③	④	⑤
4. values strong customer relationships built on trust and loyalty.	①	②	③	④	⑤
5. encourages leaders to lobby on behalf of customers in decision making.	①	②	③	④	⑤

LEADERSHIP GAP ANALYSIS™
Survey of Leadership Culture

Business Strategy Leadership

This section covers the extent to which the leadership culture creates an expectation for leaders to focus on the business strategy of the organization.

The leadership culture in this organization...	Strongly Disagree	Disagree	Neither Agree nor Disagree	Agree	Strongly Agree
6. encourages all leaders to continually scan the external environment for opportunities and threats to the business.	①	②	③	④	⑤
7. focuses leaders efforts on building strategies that will create value for the customer.	①	②	③	④	⑤
8. creates a sense of drive and shared ownership for achieving the strategy.	①	②	③	④	⑤
9. creates the expectation that leaders will forge external relationships to strengthen the position of the organization.	①	②	③	④	⑤
10. drives focus and supports leaders in only taking on work that is aligned with the strategy.	①	②	③	④	⑤

Culture & Values Leadership

This section covers the extent to which the leadership culture creates the expectation for leaders to focus on building the ideal work environment based on a unique culture and set of core values.

The leadership culture in this organization...	Strongly Disagree	Disagree	Neither Agree nor Disagree	Agree	Strongly Agree
11. creates the expectation that leaders will seek feedback about employees' perceptions of the work environment.	①	②	③	④	⑤
12. encourages leaders to be deliberate in building a work environment that will propel the organization forward.	①	②	③	④	⑤
13. creates a drive toward building the desired culture.	①	②	③	④	⑤
14. fosters a spirit of cohesiveness across the whole organization.	①	②	③	④	⑤
15. expects that leaders will challenge decisions that are inconsistent with the organization's values.	①	②	③	④	⑤

LEADERSHIP GAP ANALYSIS™
Survey of Leadership Culture

Organizational Leadership

This section covers the extent to which the leadership culture creates the expectation for leaders to align and engage the organization to focus on delivering customer value and achieving business goals across functional boundaries.

The leadership culture in this organization...	Strongly Disagree	Disagree	Neither Agree nor Disagree	Agree	Strongly Agree
16. encourages leaders to seek the perspectives of others from across the organization.	①	②	③	④	⑤
17. creates an agility to new ways of structuring the organization to achieve business goals.	①	②	③	④	⑤
18. creates the expectation that leaders will consider the system-wide impact of decisions.	①	②	③	④	⑤
19. encourages leaders to build relationships across boundaries in the organization.	①	②	③	④	⑤
20. reinforces the importance of making decisions based on the best interest of the whole organization.	①	②	③	④	⑤

Team Leadership

This section involves the extent to which the leadership culture creates the expectation for leaders to lead teams effectively.

The leadership culture in this organization...	Strongly Disagree	Disagree	Neither Agree nor Disagree	Agree	Strongly Agree
21. creates the expectation that leaders will seek input about their team members and their perspectives.	①	②	③	④	⑤
22. creates flexibility to allow leaders to form and disband teams as required.	①	②	③	④	⑤
23. drives a sense of ownership and accountability for team performance.	①	②	③	④	⑤
24. values the relationships between members of a team.	①	②	③	④	⑤
25. encourages leaders to lobby on behalf of their teams and their employees.	①	②	③	④	⑤

LEADERSHIP GAP ANALYSIS™
Survey of Leadership Culture

Personal Leadership

This section involves the extent to which the leadership culture creates the expectation for leaders to take accountability for their own development.

The leadership culture in this organization...	Strongly Disagree	Disagree	Neither Agree nor Disagree	Agree	Strongly Agree
26. encourages leaders to be open to feedback and reflective in their roles as leaders.	①	②	③	④	⑤
27. creates an expectation that leaders will take initiative to develop their careers.	①	②	③	④	⑤
28. creates a sense of personal accountability for achieving results.	①	②	③	④	⑤
29. encourages leaders to seek support and development from one another.	①	②	③	④	⑤
30. creates the expectation that leaders will stand up for themselves and advocate on their own behalf.	①	②	③	④	⑤

The 30-Cell Grid of Holistic Leadership: The Leadership Culture Dimension

	Customer Leadership	Business Strategy Leadership	Culture & Values Leadership	Organizational Leadership	Team Leadership	Personal Leadership
Sensing	Expectation that all employees think about and talk about the customer and share what they know.	Leadership culture expects its leaders to be continually scanning their environments and identifying threats and opportunities.	Leaders proactively look for information and seek feedback about the work environment and employee perceptions.	Leaders are finding out what is happening cross-departmentally with total openness and candor.	Leaders understand the importance of team dynamics and ensure that they understand each other's perspectives —it's okay to ask.	Leaders are expected to be open to feedback and reflective in their roles as leaders.
Creating	Expectation that innovation is valued and encouraged: no matter where ideas come from.	Leaders are passionate about directing their efforts on delivering competitive advantage and customer value.	Leaders understand that culture can be a competitive advantage.	All leaders are open to the best structure to satisfy business needs, versus preserving their departments.	Leaders are flexible in forming and "unforming" as they design and implement teams— "flexibility to do the right thing".	Leaders take the initiative to develop their careers and know where they are going.
Implementing	People expect continuous culture improvement and are always looking to do things better.	Leaders have a shared sense of ownership for achieving the strategy.	Leaders naturally think about the impact and cultural implications of all business decisions and view opportunities to build it.	Leaders are automatically thinking about how the changes they make affect other parts of the organization.	Leaders take shared ownership of the team's mandate.	Leaders commit to achieving results.

Connecting	People are expected to strengthen customer relationships to drive trust and loyalty.	Leaders are expected to forge relationships across organization to work together.	Leaders have a total openness to diversity and where a person comes from has no impact on idea generation.	Leaders value relationship building and different perspectives across departments.	Leaders value the need of team members to get to know each other, and enjoy each other's company.	Leaders are open to sharing ideas and learning from each other.
Advocating	People are expected to respond to the needs of customers and to lobby on behalf of customers in decisions.	Leaders can advocate both for what to do and what not to do.	Leaders advocate for direction and for decisions that are culturally based, even if there are conflicts with business decisions.	Leaders ensure the best interests of the whole organization are taken into account in decision-making, rather than the needs of one group.	Leaders are able to defend their positions.	Leaders are able to stand up for themselves without repercussion to their careers.

Assessment of Leader Behaviors and Accompanying 30-Cell Grid

LEADERSHIP GAP ANALYSIS™
Assessment of Leader Behaviors

This Assessment of Leader Behaviors covers selected skills that are associated with the six elements and five capabilities of holistic leadership.

The survey has six main sections, each of which consists of short statements that describe various leadership behaviors and one question about your overall view of their effectiveness in that area.

Please read each item carefully, and then indicate by selecting the circle under the appropriate rating. Please evaluate how frequently this person engages in the behavior, using the following descriptions.

Almost Never	The individual almost never demonstrates this behavior.
Rarely	The individual seldom demonstrates this behavior.
Half the Time	The individual demonstrates this behavior about 50% of the time.
Frequently	The individual often demonstrates this behavior.
Consistently	The individual consistently demonstrates this behavior more than 90% of the times.
N/A	You have not had a legitimate opportunity to form an opinion about the person's behavior.

LEADERSHIP GAP ANALYSIS™
Assessment of Leader Behaviors

Customer Leadership

This section covers the extent to which this person drives the organization to focus on creating value for the external customer. It comprises the behaviors that create a customer-focused environment to ensure successful customer/consumer outcomes.

	Almost Never	Rarely	Half of the time	Frequently	Consistently	N/A
1. Demonstrates a clear understanding of what customers value	①	②	③	④	⑤	⑥
2. Anticipates the future needs of customers	①	②	③	④	⑤	⑥
3. Develops products/services that provide value to customers	①	②	③	④	⑤	⑥
4. Focuses on customer satisfaction in developing products/services	①	②	③	④	⑤	⑥
5. Prioritizes work to focus on bringing customer solutions to market	①	②	③	④	⑤	⑥
6. Ensures internal processes work to increase customer satisfaction	①	②	③	④	⑤	⑥
7. Builds trusting relationships with customers	①	②	③	④	⑤	⑥
8. Manages customer expectations effectively	①	②	③	④	⑤	⑥
9. Advocates on behalf of customers to internal stakeholders	①	②	③	④	⑤	⑥
10. Champions customer focus within the organization	①	②	③	④	⑤	⑥
11. Overall, to what extent does this person demonstrate Customer Leadership?	①	②	③	④	⑤	⑥

LEADERSHIP GAP ANALYSIS™
Assessment of Leader Behaviors

Business Strategy Leadership

This section covers the extent to which this person creates a focus on business strategy within the organization. This includes developing strategies and implementing plans that lead to strategic outcomes. It includes activities that are both structured and dynamic.

	Almost Never	Rarely	Half of the Time	Frequently	Consis-tently	N/A
12. Continuously evaluates comparative strengths and weaknesses of the organization	①	②	③	④	⑤	⑥
13. Understands the key opportunities and threats in the business environment	①	②	③	④	⑤	⑥
14. Builds strategies that create long-term competitive advantage	①	②	③	④	⑤	⑥
15. Creates business strategies that are aligned with the desired culture and values	①	②	③	④	⑤	⑥
16. Translates strategic direction into clear organizational goals	①	②	③	④	⑤	⑥
17. Adapts strategies to address changing circumstances	①	②	③	④	⑤	⑥
18. Develops relationships with key external stakeholders	①	②	③	④	⑤	⑥
19. Influences external stakeholders to create strategic benefit for the organization	①	②	③	④	⑤	⑥
20. Influences others to align actions with business strategy	①	②	③	④	⑤	⑥
21. Advocates on behalf of decisions that support the business strategy	①	②	③	④	⑤	⑥
22. Overall, to what extent does this person demonstrate Business Strategy Leadership?	①	②	③	④	⑤	⑥

LEADERSHIP GAP ANALYSIS ™
Assessment of Leader Behaviors

Culture & Values Leadership

This section covers the extent to which this person focuses on building the ideal culture and values that the organization requires to achieve business outcomes and drive customer leadership. It includes building an environment that guides behavior, distinguishes the organization and communicates its unique identity to employees, customers and stakeholders.

	Almost Never	Rarely	Half of the Time	Frequently	Consistently	N/A
23. Uses multiple approaches to stay tuned in to organizational culture	①	②	③	④	⑤	⑥
24. Demonstrates understanding of the existing organizational culture	①	②	③	④	⑤	⑥
25. Develops a vision of the culture required to engage employees	①	②	③	④	⑤	⑥
26. Defines the culture and values necessary to support the business strategy	①	②	③	④	⑤	⑥
27. Builds organizational structures that support the desired culture	①	②	③	④	⑤	⑥
28. Creates rewards/consequences that reinforce the desired culture and values	①	②	③	④	⑤	⑥
29. Builds relationships with a diverse range of internal stakeholders	①	②	③	④	⑤	⑥
30. Models the desired culture and values in interactions with others	①	②	③	④	⑤	⑥
31. Communicates effectively the desired culture and values	①	②	③	④	⑤	⑥
32. Holds others accountable for behaving in accordance with organizational values	①	②	③	④	⑤	⑥
33. Overall, to what extent does this person demonstrate Culture and Values Leadership?	①	②	③	④	⑤	⑥

LEADERSHIP GAP ANALYSIS™
Assessment of Leader Behaviors

Organizational Leadership

This section covers the extent to which this person aligns and engages the organization to focus on delivering customer value and achieving business goals across functional boundaries.

	Almost Never	Rarely	Half of the Time	Frequently	Consistently	N/A
34. Demonstrates understanding of the broad organizational context	①	②	③	④	⑤	⑥
35. Shows awareness of other perspectives beyond departmental boundaries	①	②	③	④	⑤	⑥
36. Designs organizational structures that promote alignment across the organization	①	②	③	④	⑤	⑥
37. Adapts organizational structures to support business strategies	①	②	③	④	⑤	⑥
38. Aligns departmental plans to other parts of the organization	①	②	③	④	⑤	⑥
39. Engages in joint problem solving across departmental boundaries	①	②	③	④	⑤	⑥
40. Shares information openly with other parts of the organization	①	②	③	④	⑤	⑥
41. Builds trusting relationships with a broad internal network	①	②	③	④	⑤	⑥
42. Helps team members build an organization-wide perspective	①	②	③	④	⑤	⑥
43. Promotes removal of departmental barriers that impede results	①	②	③	④	⑤	⑥
44. Overall, to what extent does this person demonstrate Organizational Leadership?	①	②	③	④	⑤	⑥

LEADERSHIP GAP ANALYSIS™
Assessment of Leader Behaviors

Team Leadership

This section involves the extent to which this person is able to lead teams effectively. It covers those elements that help a leader harness the potential of each team member in ways that create a whole that is greater than the sum of its parts. It involves those aspects that help to build and motivate productive work units.

	Almost Never	Rarely	Half of the Time	Frequently	Consis-tently	N/A
45. Demonstrates understanding of team dynamics	①	②	③	④	⑤	⑥
46. Stays tuned in to the climate and motivation within the team	①	②	③	④	⑤	⑥
47. Creates a team structure that supports the mandate of the team	①	②	③	④	⑤	⑥
48. Develops team goals that are aligned to organizational goals	①	②	③	④	⑤	⑥
49. Develops clear team problem-solving processes	①	②	③	④	⑤	⑥
50. Holds the team accountable for their performance against objectives	①	②	③	④	⑤	⑥
51. Builds effective relationships with team members	①	②	③	④	⑤	⑥
52. Adapts management style to fit the needs of team members	①	②	③	④	⑤	⑥
53. Advocates internally for the needs of the team	①	②	③	④	⑤	⑥
54. Influences stakeholders to support team goals	①	②	③	④	⑤	⑥
55. Overall, to what extent does this person demonstrate Team Leadership?	①	②	③	④	⑤	⑥

LEADERSHIP GAP ANALYSIS™
Assessment of Leader Behaviors

Personal Leadership

This section focuses on the ability of this person to lead in a fashion that shows a deliberate and conscious understanding of his/her impact as a leader. Personal leadership requires that leaders are deliberate and reflect on their approach to leadership and how they address the multiple challenges they face.

	Almost Never	Rarely	Half of the Time	Frequently	Consistently	N/A
56. Maintains awareness of his/her behavioral style	①	②	③	④	⑤	⑥
57. Solicits input to understand how he/she is perceived	①	②	③	④	⑤	⑥
58. Takes time to consider the appropriate approach for the situation	①	②	③	④	⑤	⑥
59. Responds to circumstances rather than reacts	①	②	③	④	⑤	⑥
60. Focuses on continuous development of competencies	①	②	③	④	⑤	⑥
61. Models work-life balance	①	②	③	④	⑤	⑥
62. Demonstrates integrity through his/her words and actions	①	②	③	④	⑤	⑥
63. Takes personal accountability for his/her mistakes and failures	①	②	③	④	⑤	⑥
64. Communicates clearly his/her commitment to the organization	①	②	③	④	⑤	⑥
65. Uses personal credibility to influence others in the organization	①	②	③	④	⑤	⑥
66. Overall, to what extent does this person demonstrate Personal Leadership?	①	②	③	④	⑤	⑥

	Customer Leadership	Business Strategy Leadership	Culture & Values Leadership	Organizational Leadership	Team Leadership	Personal Leadership
			The 30-Cell Grid of Holistic Leadership Behaviors: The Individual Dimension			
Sensing	Knows what is important to the customer (and what will be important in the future) and knows how the customer will react in response to different situations.	Is attuned to myriad different business drivers and knows what trends will have the most significant impacts over time.	Is in sync with the employees and has an astute awareness of the dynamics of the organization.	Appreciates the positions of others who have different perspectives because they come from different parts of the organization.	Demonstrates sensitivity to the individual and team dynamics at play and the impact that members of the team have on one another.	Is aware of the styles of others and is able to alter his/her style to suit different individuals and situations.
Creating	Develops the right products and services to ensure customer satisfaction.	Responds to the environmental context and to optimize the organizational response, given the available internal capacity.	Describes the way of doing things that will engage employees and align them with the strategic objectives of the organization.	Envisions the dynamics of the organization and chooses the right configuration to optimize business processes.	Uses different team structures for different situations and to dynamically change the structure or processes to adapt to changes in the environment.	Is deliberate in his/her actions and is self-reflective in evaluating his/her current and future impact.
Implementing	Brings new approaches to the market in a way that best meets the needs of the customer.	Cascades strategy into increasingly specific and relevant operational plans to mobilize the organization to achieve its priorities.	Knows all the levers that can be used to transform culture and uses these levers to institutionalize the desired behaviors.	Is aware of the interdependencies between groups and is able to bring groups together to work toward a common goal.	Builds clear expectations and accountability and uses feedback and coaching to enhance results.	Shows strong initiative and uses various techniques to preserve his/her energy and sustain performance.

Continued

	Customer Leadership	Business Strategy Leadership	Culture & Values Leadership	Organizational Leadership	Team Leadership	Personal Leadership
Connecting	Builds genuine dialogue with customers, earns their trust and influences their expectations.	Develops shared goals and engages people across the organization in activities that are mutually beneficial.	Models the desired culture and values in his/her interactions with others.	Earns the trust of others and benefits from a stronger network within the organization.	Earns the respect of team members and uses that position of trust to open up communication about shared expectations, and engages in candid conversations with individuals on the team.	Lives up to commitments, asks for support from others and provides support to others when needed.
Advocating	Presents the needs and values of the customer to others in the organization and convinces individuals to make decisions based on the best interest of the customer.	Ensures that strategic alignment is a key criterion for all decision making in the organization.	Effectively lobbies others to consider the cultural implications of business decisions and ensures programs and policies are aligned with the desired culture of the organization.	Encourages integrative thinking and resists decision making that neglects cross-functional issues.	Builds the credibility of the team and garners resources and support for the team's activities.	Clearly communicates his/her desires and expectations and defends his/her value to the organization from a position of credibility.

Endnotes

Chapter 1

1   David Weiss and Vince Molinaro co-authored the book *The Leadership Gap: Building Leadership Capacity for Competitive Advantage* (John Wiley & Sons, 2005). *The Leadership Gap* is our conceptual foundation, and it is referred to numerous times throughout *Leadership Solutions*.

2   Weiss, D. S., & Finn, R. (2005). "HR Metrics that Count." *Human Resource Planning.*

Chapter 2

1   Amazon.com. Search conducted at the time of printing this book.

2   This emerging list of leadership expectations has been provided by Brad Beveridge, Managing Director of Knightsbridge Executive Search. Over the past few years, the Search Practice Consultants have observed a significant shift in the kind of leaders our client organizations are seeking during searches for senior level leadership roles. The shift has been observed across industries and within both private and public sector organizations.

3   Heifetz, R. A. (1994). *Leadership Without Easy Answers*. Cambridge, Mass: The Belknap Press of Harvard Press and personal conversations.

4   Ulrich, D., and Lake, D. *Organizational Capability: Competing from the Inside Out.* John Wiley & Sons, 1990. p. 2.

5   The technical information about manufacturing capacity utilization was provided by Mr. Kenn Lendrum, Vice President, Global Manufacturing and Supply, GlaxoSmithKline Canada, October 2006.

Chapter 3

1   One large organization audited its training and development budget only to learn
    that 75 percent of the budget was being spent on travel and accommodations
    for elaborate, offsite development programs. The hard dollar costs for training
    can be very high, but they are overshadowed by the costs in investment of senior
    leaders' time to attend multi-day sessions.

Chapter 4

1   José Ortega y Gasset—Spanish philosopher and humanist.

2   *The Leadership Gap* devotes a complete chapter to each of the six elements.
    Readers are encouraged to review the content in those chapters for a more
    detailed explanation of the Holistic Leadership Framework.

3   Molinaro, V., *Holism at Work*. Unpublished Doctoral Thesis. 1997. Molinaro
    conducted one of the first qualitative research studies that explored the nature of
    holistic leadership and the experiences of leaders who consciously tried to bring
    about a more holistic approach to leadership within their organizations.

4   Weiss, D. S., & Molinaro, V. *The Leadership Gap: Building Leadership Capacity for
    Competitive Advantage*, John Wiley & Sons, 2005, p.32.

5   The shift toward starting with the external perspective is paralleled in our
    approach to SWOT analysis (Strengths, Weaknesses, Opportunities and
    Threats). Most organizations begin with a review of their strengths and
    weaknesses, but the results are largely irrelevant because they are without
    context. Having evaluated the opportunities and threats within the external
    environment first, the strengths can be viewed as the positive traits that will
    allow the organization to capitalize on the opportunities and mitigate the threats,
    whereas the weaknesses can be viewed as the shortcomings that will make it
    difficult to seize opportunities and will increase the risk to the organization posed
    by the threats in the environment.

6   Heifetz, R. A. (1994). *Leadership Without Easy Answers*. Cambridge, Mass: The
    Belknap Press of Harvard Press.

Chapter 5

1   One small caveat is that as you review your leadership competencies, you might
    find they represent a mix of elements (areas that leaders should pay attention to)
    and capabilities (skills that leaders should be good at). This can cause confusion.
    The value of the five core capabilities is that they pertain purely to skills and
    each applies across all elements of holistic leadership. This is somewhat easier to
    explain to leaders than competencies that are a mix of skills and elements. For

example, one competency model we have seen includes "customer service," which relates to a specific element, and also "communication," which is a generic skill that can be applied across multiple elements.

Chapter 6

1   In *The Leadership Gap (Wiley, 2005)* we devoted a major part of the book to four powerful organizational practices specifically designed to build strong leadership capacity. These included: Embedding Leadership in the Organization (Chapter 11), Focus on Critical Positions and Key Talent (Chapter 12), Integrated Leadership Development (Chapter 13) and Accountability for Leadership Capacity (Chapter 14). Readers are encouraged to review those chapters to gain an in-depth understanding of these organizational practices specifically designed to build leadership capacity.

2   When succession management is done correctly, it includes the focus on critical positions to reduce the risk of turnover in key positions as explained in critical success factor #2 of succession management and key talent retention from *The Leadership Gap*.

3   Chapter 5 of *The Leadership Gap* closed with several specific examples of how the business planning process can be leveraged to build leadership capacity.

4   Peppers and Rogers, *The One to One Manager*, p. 244, uses the term, "disrupting complacency," as essential to effective customer service leadership.

5   Galbraith, J., Downey, D., & Kates, A., in *Designing Dynamic Organizations* (American Management Association, 2002, p. ix) explain that "organization design is the means for creating a community of collective effort that yields more than the sum of each individual's efforts and results."

6   Robert Kaplan and David Norton. (1996). *The Balanced Scorecard*, Harvard Business School Press.

7   Robert Kaplan and David Norton. (1996). *The Balanced Scorecard*, Harvard Business School Press.

8   The balanced scorecard also can be leveraged to help achieve *The Leadership Gap* critical success factor #4 of ensuring executives take accountability for building leadership capacity.

Chapter 7

1   Edgar Schein. 1993. Organizational Culture and Leadership. In Classics of Organization Theory. Jay Shafritz and J. Steven Ott, eds. 2001. Fort Worth: Harcourt College Publishers. (p. 375).

2   Edgar Schein, one of the leading theorists on organizational culture, describes culture as the way members of a group perceive, think and feel in relation to

the challenges encountered in external adaptation and internal integration. Schein's definition is helpful in understanding the idea of organizational cultures, of which the leadership culture is one sub-category. See Edgar Schein. 1993. *Organizational Culture and Leadership. In Classics of Organization Theory.* Jay Shafritz and J. Steven Ott, eds. 2001. Fort Worth: Harcourt College Publishers. (p. 375).

Chapter 9

1 See *The Leadership Gap* pp. 6–13 for further discussion of the current and desired environmental challenges.

2 Michael Treacy and Fred Wiersema introduced these three areas of market leadership in *The Discipline of Market Leaders* (Perseus Books, 1995).

3 Refer to *The Leadership Gap* (Wiley 2005) that describes the four Cs of Customer Value and how to build enduring customer relationships (pp. 60–73).

4 The elements of holistic leadership are explained in Chapter 4.

Chapter 10

1 These words are attributed to William Thomson (Lord Kelvin), a mathematical physicist, engineer and leading scientist in the physical sciences of the nineteenth century. He did important work in the mathematical analysis of electricity and thermodynamics and did much to unify the emerging discipline of physics in its modern form. He is widely known for developing the Kelvin scale of absolute temperature measurement. Source: http://en.wikipedia.org/wiki/Lord_Kelvin.

2 David S. Weiss and Richard Finn, (2005). "HR Metrics That Count" Human Resource Planning.

3 Leading into the Future: A Global Study of Leadership 2005–2015. American Management Association/Human Resources Institute.

4 Cultivating credibility, practicing humility and building leaders, along with achieving results, acquiring perspective, leveraging conversations and exercising balance are the different components of the CAPABLE leadership model of personal leadership. For a complete review of this topic, see *The Leadership Gap*, Chapter 9.

Chapter 11

1 The triage "sorting" technique was first demonstrated in the United States District Court for the Eastern District of Pennsylvania in the case of the United States vs. Alexander Holmes. In 1841, Holmes was a sailor aboard a lifeboat of a wrecked passenger ship. They needed to "triage" the people in the lifeboat in

order to survive the dangerous waters. They decided to save the entire crew and let many passengers die. The case generated the concept of "lifeboat ethics"—how to choose who dies and who survives when resources are limited and insufficient for all. In a similar way, executives need to triage their investment of their scarce resources in building leadership capacity.

2   See *The Leadership Gap*, Chapter 11, "Integrated Leadership Development." Also, a version of these ideas appears in the *Journal of Industrial and Commercial Training* (UK) February 2006 in the article "Integrated Leadership Development" by David S. Weiss and Vince Molinaro.

Chapter 12

1   See research in: Gandossy, R. & Effron, M. (2004). *Leading the Way: Three Truths from the Top Companies for Leaders*. Wiley & Sons; Holstein, W. J. (2005). Best Companies for Leaders. *CEO Magazine.*

2   For more information on how you can complete the Assessment of Leader Behaviors Survey, please visit www.knightsbridge.ca.

3   Readers are encouraged to refer to the *The Leadership Gap*, where we devote an entire chapter to each of the six elements and provide ideas and strategies to develop each one.

4   In Chapter 9 (pp. 181–183) of *The Leadership Gap*, we explore these leadership derailers in greater detail and consider their implications for leaders.

Index

ABOUT KNIGHTSBRIDGE

Knightsbridge is Canada's fastest growing Human Capital Solutions organization. We create innovative solutions to complex human capital challenges. Our growing reputation for excellence is a testament to our success.

Knightsbridge delivers challenging new thinking and holistic strategies tailored specifically for each client. We combine our depth of expertise in each key discipline to deliver powerful and integrated solutions. We are highly skilled in implementation – we collaborate with our clients to position them to remain competitive in the marketplace and drive business results.

Whether its assessment and coaching, talent attraction, organizational and leadership development, or career management and transition, look to Knightsbridge for a strategic partner who works with you to ensure your company is always thinking moves ahead.

Knightsbridge has offices in 14 Canadian cities where our team of almost 200 consultants and associates are waiting to partner with you.

Knightsbridge
human capital solutions

Thinking moves *ahead*